AF544695

A Naturalist's Guide to the Year

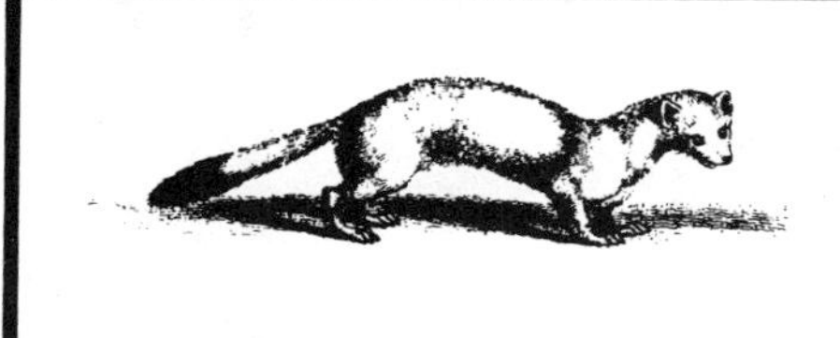

A Naturalist's Guide to the Year

HOWARD SMITH

E. P. Dutton, Inc. New York

Copyright © 1985 by Howard E. Smith, Jr.
All rights reserved. Printed in the U.S.A.

No part of this publication may be reproduced or transmitted in any form or by any means, electronic or mechanical, including photocopy, recording, or any information storage and retrieval system now known or to be invented, without permission in writing from the publisher, except by a reviewer who wishes to quote brief passages in connection with a review written for inclusion in a magazine, newspaper, or broadcast.

Published in the United States by
E. P. Dutton, Inc.,
2 Park Avenue, New York, N.Y. 10016

Library of Congress Cataloging in Publication Data

Smith, Howard Everett
A naturalist's guide to the year.
Bibliography: p.
1. Natural history—Northeastern States.
2. Seasons—
Northeastern States. I. Title.
QH104.5.N58S63 1985 574.5'42'0974 84-18697

ISBN 0-525-24297-X

Published simultaneously in Canada by
Fitzhenry & Whiteside Limited, Toronto

DESIGNED BY MARK O'CONNOR

10 9 8 7 6 5 4 3 2 1
COBE

First Edition

Grateful acknowledgment is made to the following for allowing the use of illustrations:

DOVER PUBLICATIONS, INC. *Witmer Stone,* Bird Studies at Old Cape May *(New York, 1965), vol. 2: blue jay (p. 17), cedar waxwing (p. 50), American goldfinch (p. 142), ruby-throated hummingbird (p. 146), belted kingfisher (p. 175).* Common Weeds of the United States *(U.S. Department of Agriculture, Wash-*

ington, D.C.: U.S. Government Printing Office, 1970; reprint, New York, 1971): smooth sumac (p. 51), common milkweed (p. 139), pokeweed (p. 157), common ragweed (p. 187), jimsonweed (p. 233), horseweed (p. 253), teasel (jacket). Donald J. Borror, Songs of Eastern Birds *(New York, 1970): woodcock (p. 67), killdeer (p. 91), long-billed marsh wren (p. 197).*

E. P. DUTTON, INC. *E. Laurence Palmer,* Fieldbook of Mammals *(New York, 1957): otter (p. 34), red squirrel (p. 84), muskrat (p. 99), flying squirrel (p. 183), meadow jumping mouse (p. 188), common shrew (p. 256), bobcat (p. 277), chipmunk, raccoon, red fox, and woodchuck (jacket). J. G. Wood,* Illustrated Natural History *(New York, 1923): big horned owl (jacket).*

HART PUBLISHING COMPANY, INC. *Pam Pollack, comp.,* The Animal Kingdom *(New York, 1977): great northern diver, or loon (p. 31), peregrine falcon (p. 53), sprawler (hellgrammite) (p. 57), luna moth (p. 181), white admiral butterfly (p. 203), ermine and yellow perch (jacket).*

MCGRAW-HILL BOOK COMPANY. *E. Laurence Palmer,* Fieldbook of Natural History *(New York, 1949), copyright 1949 by McGraw-Hill, Inc., renewal © 1976 by Catherine Palmer: sparrow hawk (p. 20),* bobwhite *(p. 47), spring peeper (p. 74), diving beetle (p. 101), maidenhair fern (p. 121), large duckweed and watermeal (p. 123), red maple (p. 132), cinnamon fern (132), timothy grass (p. 136), monarch butterfly (p. 141), viceroy butterfly (p. 141), fly amanita (p. 160), great spangled fritillary (p. 164),* Polistes *wasp (p. 169), orange garden spider (p. 189), wanderer butterfly (p. 203), trembling fungus (p. 229), white-lipped land snail (p. 236), black snake (p. 239), brook trout (p. 241), red-spotted newt (p. 243), snow bunting (p. 274), mud puppy (279), white pine cone (jacket). Tracy I. Storer,* General Zoology *(New York, 1943): stone fly (p. 35), springtail (p. 45), water strider (p. 77), dragonflies (p. 124), tent caterpillar (p. 134), tiger beetle and ground beetle (p. 144), katydid, field and house cricket, and tree cricket (p. 215). Joseph Maron Joseph and Sarah Lee Lippincott,* Point to the Stars, *rev. ed.* (New York, 1967), *copyright © 1967, 1963, by Joseph Maron Joseph and Sarah Lee Lippincott: world star chart (p. 36).*

G. P. PUTNAM'S SONS. *F. Schuyler Mathews,* Field Book of American Wild Flowers *(New York, 1902): great mullein (p. 23), skunk cabbage (p. 70), water lily (p. 150), Turk's-cap lily (p. 157), Indian pipe (p. 159), heath aster (p. 202).*

U.S. GOVERNMENT PRINTING OFFICE. *U.S. Department of Agriculture,* Insects: The Yearbook of Agriculture *(Washington, D.C., 1952): ladybug (jacket).*

The author wishes to express his gratitude to Dr. Andrew Spielman, Medical Entomologist, Harvard School of Public Health, for his generosity of time and spirit in making comments on the manuscript of this book.

To the memory of my mother,
in whose garden I first learned
about the world of nature

Contents

The Northeast

The Northeast is a varied place, as fascinating and beautiful as one can find anywhere on this continent. Nature in all its aspects rarely displays itself to better effect. Many more types of landscape or topographical feature than one might imagine can be found in the region. Numerous rivers meander through it, and waterfalls plunge from broken rocks. In the far northwest of the region lie lakes as large as inland seas, and throughout the area ponds, too numerous to count, dot the land. Dense forests, interspersed with pleasant fields and meadows, cover much of the region. Glaciated hills, either rounded or broken into crags, rise above gentle lowlands. Along the eastern shore, the gray Atlantic's swells break in surf. The region is truly a naturalist's paradise.

Possessed of a unique flora and fauna, the Northeast teems with life. Clouds of insects swarm over ponds. In the autumn thousands of migrating birds pass across the face of the moon. Surprisingly, in spite of the constant intrusion of cities, factories, and superhighways, huge wildlife populations thrive in our region—all there to see if we know how to look.

The seasons of the Northeast have a special significance. In no other part of the country do they follow one another with such dramatic contrasts: from a warm April day in Appalachia, where the mountains stand covered with snow while trees below bloom pink and the fragrant, delicately damp air feels fresh and soft, to a dark winter afternoon in New England, where foxes wade through dry powder snow near dark stands of white pines, searching for any signs of life. In all the world nothing comes close to the drama of red October, when colors give the hillsides bright definition. In contrast, summers at times seem tropical with green vistas that disappear into layered hazes so warm and humid. It is these seasons that we shall explore on a month-to-month basis and for which this book will serve as a guide.

THE NORTHEAST DEFINED

In terms of this book, the Northeast is defined as that region of the United States and southernmost area of Canada which lies within a particular woodland area. In general, nothing defines a region better than its woodlands, for trees are far more stable than any other living thing. Animals, which so often enter and leave regions, cannot serve as well. Most plants, other than trees, too easily spread beyond boundaries and also are often far more difficult to find. Moreover, in winter many small annual and herbaceous plants cannot be identified.

The Northeast, as defined from here on, is characterized by woodlands, which consist of the following trees: in the north, various maples, oaks, yellow birch, and pine trees; in the south, oaks, ash, basswood, and beeches. Some tree species have a range that fits almost exactly the region we are seeking to define here. They are the northern red oak (*Quercus rubra*), the eastern white pine (*Pinus strobus*), and the American basswood (*Tilia americana*). To some degree, four other trees also fit the region, namely the striped maple (*Acer pensylvanicum*), the yellow birch (*Betula alleghaniensis*), the eastern hemlock (*Tsuga canadensis*), and the black ash (*Fraxinus nigra*).

The forests consisting of these trees are similar from one end of the Northeast to the other. A summer forest in southern Ontario is remarkably like a summer forest in western North Carolina, Wisconsin, or Massachusetts. The same trees appear in all of them, as do most of the same flowers, shrubs, and animals.

Geographically, the region cannot be defined in a precise, clear-cut manner, because the woodlands made up of the trees mentioned above often merge gradually into other types of woodlands. Also, woodlands frequently intrude, like fingers, into other regions. At best, one can define the region as lying between the Atlantic Ocean and the grasslands of the Midwest. This means its western boundary includes parts of Minnesota, parts of Wisconsin, some eastern parts of Illinois, parts of western Kentucky, and parts of western Tennessee. In the north, the boundary lies more or less at the 47th parallel in Canada, from the St. Lawrence River to Lake Superior. Portions of eastern New Brunswick and western Nova Scotia are included. Along and near the Atlantic shore, the eastern edge of the region extends from northern Maine to western Virginia. The Appalachian Mountains are included, even the Smoky Mountain region, because the average temperatures in these mountains are colder than their southern location might indicate.

Land of Cities and Rural Countryside

The Northeast, oddly enough, is not nearly so urbanized as we may think it is. Even when we are out in the country, most of us rarely appreciate how rural the Northeast really is. In fact, an article written by Larry Long and Diana DeAre for the July 1983 *Scientific American,* titled "The Slowing of Urbanization in the United States," points out how rural the Northeast in reality is. As they show, New Jersey, the most urbanized state in the union, is more than 71 percent rural. More impressive is the fact that Pennsylvania is 91 percent and Vermont and West Virginia are at least 98 percent rural. Moreover, there are several state parks, such as the Adirondack Forest Preserve, or several large national parks in the region, such as the Great Smoky Mountains and Shenandoah in the United States. One can also visit the very rural Algonquin Provincial Park in Ontario, Canada.

For those who must stay in the cities, there is plenty to see in their parks. Most cities of the region have excellent parks, such as Central Park and the New York Botanical Garden in New York City; Rock Creek Park and the National Arboretum in Washington,

D.C. Such parks offer endless opportunities for seeing birds, frogs, insects, and small mammals.

The Climate of the Northeast

The Northeast can be defined not only in terms of flora and fauna but also in terms of its climate. This is a region of moderate precipitation. Between twenty and fifty inches fall on various parts of the region during the year. Each month receives just about the same amount although there is slightly more precipitation from May 1 to October 31 than from November 1 to April 30.

The Northeast is also characterized by its hot summers and cold winters. In January the normal average temperature ranges from about 20° F to 30° F and in July it is about 70° F.

It is often cloudy in the Northeast. During the period from December 1 to February 28 the region receives, on the whole, only from 20 percent to 40 percent of the sunshine it would receive if the skies remained clear from sunrise to sunset each day. No other region in all of the United States, aside from some small areas in western Oregon, northern Washington State, and northern Idaho, is more cloudy during the same period. It is no wonder that so many people complain about the dreary aspects of the Northeast in wintertime. In the summer—June through August—it fares better, but not enormously so. Much of the region receives 60 percent to 70 percent of the possible summer sunshine, but the highlands and northern regions receive only 50 percent to 60 percent. Only the northwest coast equals this poor record.

Because of high rainfall, cloud cover, and humidity, the Northeast is also an exceedingly moist region. No region in the forty-eight contiguous states surpasses it in terms of moisture aside from the Pacific Northwest and the Sierra Nevada of California. Only a few places in Canada are more moist than the parts of Canada covered here. Moisture is defined as the amount of surplus moisture a region has compared to its needs. By such a definition the region has 80 times as much moisture as it needs. In the mountains it has well over 100 times as much moisture as it needs. A region's moisture depends on rainfall, cloud cover, humidity, and latitude. The evaporation rate is important as well.

Timing the Seasons

The seasons of the Northeast are sharply defined, which makes the area an excellent place for nature lovers who wish to follow them. A region can have distinct seasons only if it has hot summers and cold winters. Heat waves with temperatures over 90° F occur in virtually all parts of the region. On the other hand, during the winter, snow will at one time or another cover all parts of the region. Very rarely do winters pass by in any given northeastern locality without a snowstorm. In places, snowfall can be heavy, especially near the Great Lakes, where blizzards occasionally dump more than two feet of snow. Temperatures of −20° F have been registered at many weather stations in the region.

Because of the excessive moisture, few regions in America or Canada can match the lush, verdant springs of the Northeast. The authoritative *Gray's Manual of Botany* lists 5,520 flowering plants and ferns that grow in the region. A large proportion of these bloom in April and May but it is important in reading this book to know that no exact dates can be given for the appearance of wild flowers or, for that matter, the migrations of birds. Because of the great north–south length of the region, about nine hundred miles, spring comes much earlier to the southern portions of the region. The first flowers bloom around the first week of April in the southernmost parts of the Northeast and around the last week of May in the northernmost parts. At higher elevations they may not bloom until the first week of June. You should keep this in mind and make compensations for your own locality.

It must also be remembered that no two years are exactly the same: an early, warm spring can hasten the blooming of flowers, whereas a late, cold spring will retard them. All that is said about blooming flowers can also be said about fall foliage. Tree colors first become established in the north—in northern Vermont and New Hampshire around October 4—and on average, about a month later in the south.

Even though the blooming of the flowers and the turning of the trees may begin early in some years and late in others, the sequence for various species never changes. For example, bloodroots always bloom before water lilies do, and they, in turn, always bloom before goldenrods. Likewise, sumacs always turn colorful in the autumn before beeches do. In a true sense, plants act as a living calendar.

The Topography of the Northeast

Vivid contrasts characterize the Northeast: ponds, great lakes, bold hills, large rivers, dashing streams, ancient lava flows, high palisades, sand dunes, rugged outcrops of granite, and gentle mountains give the Northeast some of the most varied of landscapes. This topography is the result of hundreds of millions of years of mountain building, erosion, and glacial activity. Few regions have been so geologically active.

At the surface, where one can see them, lie many of the oldest rocks on earth. In Minnesota, near Granite Falls, granite gneiss 3.8 billion years old has been found. In many parts of New England and in the Alleghenies it is not difficult at all to pick up rocks that are well over a billion years old. Most were once molten igneous rocks that welled up from deep within the earth and later cooled. The most commonly found igneous rock in the Northeast is granite. Many of the other ancient rocks were either sedimentary or igneous rocks that changed over millions of years until they metamorphosed. Although many rocks look as they did hundreds of millions of years ago, metamorphosed rocks such as lustrous phyllites (from clay) and marble (from limestone) do not look at all the way they originally did.

About 600 to 500 million years ago, during the Cambrian Period, a large trough under sea water extended over much of the Northeast. For hundreds of millions of years sediments filled it. Much later, around 250 million years ago, where the trough had once been, the Appalachians rose and folded because of powerful upheavals in the earth's crust. Their snowcapped peaks rose as high as those in today's Alps and no doubt looked just as spectacular. They were not the only high mountains to rise in the Northeast. The Green Mountains, the Taconic Range, and indeed all the mountains we see today in this region are very old. But today, after millions of years of erosion, all have been reduced to gently rolling mountains and hills.

At the end of the Paleozoic Era, one vast continent existed, which included in its landmass almost all of North and South America as well as Europe, Asia, Africa, Australia, and Antarctica. This supercontinent is called Pangaea. Following the Paleozoic Era during the Mesozoic Era, which lasted from about 230 to 65 million years ago, the continent of Pangaea broke up. North America slowly drifted away from Europe and Africa. As it did, numerous volcanic eruptions rocked the Northeast, especially along today's seacoasts. Several lava flows, such as one near Newark, New Jersey, exist from that time.

For hundreds of millions of years, rains washed rock, sands, and gravels out of mountains and hills, building up layers of rock that hardened into sedimentary rocks such as sandstones and shales. Seas invaded the region, and as they retreated they left seashells behind that turned into limestone, another sedimentary rock often filled with fossils of prehistoric animals.

In terms of today's flora and fauna, the single most important event was the coming of the Ice Ages. Time and again, over the last million years, enormous continental glaciers covered parts of the Northeast. After each advance they melted away. Forests and flowers followed the glaciers on their northward retreat, but during the glacial periods the moving ice would kill all the plants by either freezing them or crushing them.

The most recent glacier to cover the Northeast, as well as most of Canada and Greenland, reached its maximum size around 18,000 years ago. This glacier and others finally carried away the topsoil from much of the northern sections of the Northeast, leaving a rocky landscape behind. Glaciers also gouged out countless hollows in the land that later filled with water, forming the Northeast's many lakes and streams. In places major land features such as Long Island and Cape Cod were formed by sand and gravel, which were pushed ahead of glaciers in snowplow fashion.

When the last continental glacier melted and the land was ice-free again, trees and flowers once more moved north. But we might wonder where they had been when the glaciers covered so much of the Northeast. A large number of the species that we see today grew in the Great Smoky Mountains, which served as a haven for them when the last glacier covered the northern sections of the Northeast. Glaciers did not reach the Smokies, and the climate provided a cool place for the plants that would later be hardy enough to move northward. The Smokies' luxuriant forests have remained undisturbed for tens of thousands of years, and thanks to them, the Northeast today has a marvelous array of plants, from the tiniest wild flower to the greatest oak.

Not all the plants in the Northeast came from the enclave forests of the Great Smoky Mountains. Many species escaped the glaciers by living in the West and in regions northwest of the Northeast region, including such places as the Dakotas and Montana. Curiously, the continental glaciers did not enter those regions. Even more curious, there is a large section of land in Wisconsin that also escaped the glaciers. Plants and animals from Wisconsin, the Dakotas, and Montana, where the fickle glaciers did not enter, also helped reestablish the flora and fauna of the Northeast. A goodly number of plants and animals also came into the region from the South.

The next big event in the history of the Northeast was the coming of European explorers and settlers. During pre-Columbian times, the Northeast could be characterized as one large forest. It was not, however, an unbroken forest, as was believed for a very long time. We now know that native Americans had modified the region. For hunting purposes and to clear land for growing crops, they regularly set fire to undergrowth. At times large fires may have raged in the region, but frequent burning minimized such catastrophic events. Because of the fires, many clearings were formed.

Indian clearings, however, were nothing compared to those made by the European settlers. In a surprisingly short time, from the mid-1600s to roughly the early 1800s, they cut down almost all the forests. In all of the Northeast only a few virgin forests remain standing today. Remarkably, one is in New York City—the hemlock forest in the New York Botanical Garden.

The destruction of the forests had a complex and profound impact on many of the native plants and animals in the region. Many animals, such as the puma, the wolf, and the moose were greatly reduced in numbers. With the more frequent use of guns, hunting also took a great toll. Ivory-billed woodpeckers and passenger pigeons became extinct. Many bird populations dropped. Wild turkeys, wood ducks, and others came remarkably close to extinction. But, oddly enough, several animals benefited from changes the settlers made. Robins extended their range, thanks to the new tree-bordered fields and their worms. So did meadow mice in the same new fields. Barn swallows, which once nested in caves and under ledges, greatly expanded in numbers as settlers built barns.

Europeans brought to America many plants that later went native and spread rapidly in the wilds. Phlox and chickweeds originally came from Europe, while other plants came from even farther away: the velvetleaf, for example, from India. The settlers also brought in honeybees, house mice, and other animals: English sparrows, starlings, Japanese beetles, and gypsy moths. Man-made change has also caused relocation. Coyotes, which in recent decades lived exclusively west of the Appalachians, now run wild in the Northeast as well. The killing of their predators, the wolves, allows them the freedom to run wild here.

The wide variety of northeastern topography also helps account for the great variety of plants and animals in the region. Numerous unique habitats and small ecosystems have been formed because of the many different configurations of the land.

THE MAJOR HABITATS

It would be impossible, or at least unwieldy, to list all the various habitats in the Northeast. However, the region can be divided generally into four major types: woodlands; fields and meadows; wild, rocky places; and lakes, ponds, and watercourses. Although such a classification is not perfect, it can suit our needs very well. Every chapter in this book will have a section on each of the four, and I shall therefore explain them in some detail.

Woodlands

Woodlands cover much of the region. It is difficult to find a place in the whole Northeast that is more than a mile or two from a grove of trees, if not from dense forests. Trees and shrubs provide food in terms of nuts, berries, and fruits for many animals. They also provide animals with shelter, homesites, and good hiding places from predators.

It is in the woodlands that one will find maples, oaks, pines, and other splendid trees, as well as shrubs: rhododendrons, elderberries, and many others. Wild flowers abound on woodland floors, especially in the spring. One can find trilliums, jack-in-the-pulpits, bloodroots, trumpet creepers, and many others. Numerous colorful birds, such as the butterflylike warblers, various sparrows, and chickadees, inhabit the trees. Skunks, rabbits, deer, and even black bears may be seen in the woodlands. A bewildering number of insects, such as red-spotted purple butterflies, spectacular luna moths, and colorful long-horned beetles, live in woodlands. So do many spiders. Black rat snakes, garter snakes, and other snakes slither through the undergrowth. Salamanders appear on damp, decaying leaves. Fungi grow in profusion.

Fields and Meadows

Almost as common as the woodlands are fields and meadows found in areas between them. Fields and meadows lure birds and mammals with the grains and seeds they provide. Cultivated grains and seeds of countless weeds serve as a major food supply for flocks of birds and numerous rodents.

Many varieties of grasses grow in fields and meadows and move in the wind. Everywhere weeds—for example, thistles, ironweeds, goldenrods, and jewelweeds—dot the open lands, as do many bright wild flowers such as lupines, steeplebushes, sunflowers, and fireweed. All year numerous birds visit fields, sometimes in huge, wheeling flocks, among them horned larks, crows, robins, bobwhites, sparrow hawks, and pheasants. Countless butterflies dance on delicate wings over the fields. Ground beetles, ants, grasshoppers, red-and-black milkweed bugs, soldier beetles, and many other insects inhabit fields and meadows. So do such spiders as garden spiders and wolf spiders. One can also find foxes, ermines, meadow mice, shrews, and other mammals.

Wild, Rocky Places

Rocky hills, outcrops, and mountains rise in many parts of the Northeast above the surrounding lowlands. Indeed, taken as a whole, few regions in the United States are as rocky as the Northeast. Wild, rocky places form unique habitats: rugged, broken, filled with cliffs, chasms, glens, and fallen boulders. Many mammals found rarely, if ever, elsewhere in the Northeast remain hidden in such places.

Wildcats, coyotes, porcupines, ermines, and others find wild, rocky places ideal hiding places. Mosses, ferns, and lichens cover many rocky ledges and cliffs. Ruffed grouse, pine siskins, great horned owls, and wild turkeys often live there, as do the rare rattlesnakes, black rat snakes, land snails, and black widow spiders. Trees not frequently found in other areas, such as gray birches, hemlocks, and beeches, grow among rocks; so do sumacs, hobblebushes, blueberries, and trailing arbutus.

Lakes, Ponds, and Watercourses

In the tens of thousands of lakes, streams, and rivers that dot the region live a large array of animals. There are the wily brook trout, the voracious pickerel, and the common yellow perch as well as many other fish. Also living in the aquatic environment are diving beetles, giant water bugs, water spiders; many curious types of salamanders, spring peepers, bullfrogs, leopard frogs, and other frogs; snapping turtles, painted turtles, and other turtles; various insect larvae, such as hellgrammites, mayfly nymphs, and dobsonfly larvae, as well as freshwater shrimps and snails. Growing in the water are beautiful water lilies, pickerelweeds, golden clubs, and others. Across the surface of ponds skitter water striders. Many mammals—muskrats, beavers, minks, and otters, for example—stay near water. Raccoons, deer, and other mammals often appear near the shores. Ducks of all sorts land on the lakes. Common mergansers fish in the streams. Herons, redwing blackbirds, killdeers, and many other birds live in swamps and bogs. Many striking wild flowers are associated with lakes, ponds, and watercourses: the swamp rose mallows, irises, buttercups, forget-me-nots, and others. Cattails, bullrushes, tussock grasses, and many ferns grow in damp areas. Farther away from ponds, on firmer ground, grow willows, red osier dogwoods, red maples, and many other beautiful trees and shrubs. In thickets near ponds and streams we can find white-throated sparrows, kingfishers, swallows, various flycatchers, and many other birds.

WHAT TO LOOK FOR

Not a field guide, this book serves instead as a guide to seasons and habitats (also included is a selected list of books that can be used to identify plants and animals). It also attempts to describe how wild plants and animals really live and survive—how they cope with cold winters, forage for food, protect themselves from enemies, and manage from day to day. The book also answers many questions such as:

What happens in a leaf when it turns red? What colors do animals see when they look at flowers? What is known about bird migration? What is the harvest moon of September? Why is it that painted turtles and wood turtles can easily learn their way around in mazes? In short, it is my hope to reveal some of the hidden machinery of nature. As the story of the year unfolds, month by month, I hope to show you when to look, where to look, and how to look.

January

January is the time of new beginnings. One year fades and another hesitates as it commences with a profound slowness: not just for us, of course, but for the snow-covered plants and sheltered animals, too.

According to legend, the Romans named January after Janus, an enigmatic god, whose two faces looked into time past and time future. Alone, singular, and thoughtful, his purpose, whatever it was, seemed pensive. Although some of his attributes are puzzling, even lost, to historians and archaeologists, he symbolizes perfectly the quiet contemplative mood of January.

In terms of nature, January rightfully begins the new year. As a month, it marks not only the cold point of the year for us but also the low point in the living cycle of almost all plants and animals. The last flowers of December have all died, but the earliest flowers will not bloom for many weeks. And, of course, the deciduous trees stand stark against the sky.

Not that all life stops—far from it. Many birds and mammals carry on living off last season's fruits, nuts, and berries, or preying on each other. Flocks of birds keep on the move. Alert minks prowl alongside streams. Playful otters slide down snowy riverbanks. Wildcats yowl and mate. Juncos and mockingbirds flutter here and there. Mice dash through snowy tunnels. On cold moonlit nights, lonely owls hoot in distant woodlands.

WOODLANDS

Deciduous trees in January, seen silhouetted against a yellow moon, often look lifeless and stark, but at times their moods soften. If we look at a grove of trees on a late January afternoon when the sky is hazy, the trees seem to take on many unexpected tones of color. Purples, dull orange-rusts, and muted grays, for example, appear among the upper mazes of branches, while nearer the ground the silvers of gray birches and the aluminum hues of beech trunks offer a cold contrast. Nothing during the whole year can match those tremulous, fragile colors suffused by a pale winter light.

Many birds and animals find shelter from the cold winds of January among woodland trees. Few places in the winter abound with so much life. Jays, chickadees, and nuthatches stay among the trees, while mockingbirds and towhees patrol the forest edges. Foxes, rabbits and male skunks move here and there on the ground; gray squirrels chitter in branches above. Everywhere birds and mammals leave tracks in the snow.

Winter Buds

Next spring's leaves and flowers lie miniaturized in January within the flower buds; for example, there is a complete flower with all of its parts—its sepals, petals, stamens, ovary, and in some cases even its pollen. With the right equipment a scientist could find, deep within the pollen, the DNA molecules ready to program and guide the future growth of the plant. Not even the tiniest computer chips are so small, so effective, so enduring of cold, wet, and high winds. All is there just waiting to start.

Some cold, impossible January day, when you are positive that spring will never arrive, carefully open a magnolia bud lengthwise through its center. Gingerly take out its parts and explore them with a magnifying glass. You will see the future life story of the flower, its petals symmetrically and tightly held together, its stamens hardly visible, and all the rest. Nothing is missing. And so the bud calmly awaits its hour. The longer days of bright spring sunshine and the first warming breezes will trigger enzymes that will set things going. All will expand, push, and balloon out until a living flower graces the mellow, damp air of April with its perfume.

It has been said that buds are covered with furry hairs to keep them warm. On the contrary, in sustained cold weather a well-covered bud will eventually lose all of its warmth no matter how thick its hairs may be. Mammals can keep warm in their fur coats for one reason only: their bodies generate heat. Buds, of course, do not. So why the furry buds in the first place? The fur probably has some importance in protecting the buds from being eaten. Just as most animals avoid hairy caterpillars, they also avoid furry buds.

Robins

We all seem to love the myth that robins (*Turdus migratorius*) announce the coming of spring. There probably is not a single newspaper in the northern part of the country that does not have an article in March about the first robins of spring being sighted by someone. Even prestigious metropolitan papers have not been able to resist such surefire copy.

The truth about robins is quite different. Robins, those common red-breasted birds with which everyone is familiar, spend the winter in much of the Northeast, even being found in mid–New England in January. Some people may be surprised, because they know very well that robins do disappear. That's the point. They leave familiar lawns in the winter because the earthworms, which constitute a major part of the robin's food, have gone deep underground and hibernate below the frost line. Instead, robins head for dense woodlands near swampy areas, where people rarely go in the winter. There they seek wild fruits and berries, their winter food. Their winter grounds are hidden and little known.

There is one added twist to the story. Some robins do go south. Moreover, most robins will leave the Northeast during severe cold snaps. Because they can easily make long flights with their strong wings, it is nothing for robins to travel two hundred miles south in a day. After a cold snap ends, robins move back north and rejoin those who stuck it out during the cold weather. There is not one month of the year that one cannot find robins in much of the Northeast.

The only places that lack them in the dead of winter are the mountains.

Unlike many birds, robins sing all winter long. At times even in the dead of winter groups of robins can be extraordinarily noisy, making various sounds: "cuck, cuck," a rattling "shil, il, il, il, il," and other odd sounds. At dawn they greet the newly glowing sky with a clear melodic song.

Robins have adapted far better than most birds to the settlement of the continent by immigrants. In pre-Columbian times, robins dwelt in deep forests, where they survived on fruits and berries. They probably made forays to meadows for worms, but such meadows in those days were few and far between. As farmers cut down trees and plowed fields, robins found a bonanza of worms. They quickly adapted to spending the warm months of the year in mostly open country, provided that the fields were bordered by trees and thickets. Robins followed the paths of settlers who moved into the prairie states, thereby extending their range throughout much of North America.

Winter Spiders and Insects

Winter differs from the rest of the year in one notable sense: few if any insects are seen. In many ways, winter is harshest on them of any animals. Billions freeze to death. Even so, one can find some living adult insects that do survive including some that have hidden under stones, crawled up under bark, or burrowed deep into the ground. Others seek root hollows, piles of leaves, or the interiors of old haystacks or compost heaps; still others hide in or under the leaves of some plants, such as mulleins or strawberries.

By lifting loose, dead bark off a tree in a long strip, you can easily find insect dwellers. Most remain too stuporous from the cold to move, even with a good nudge. Also hidden in such places are spiders. Occasionally an observer can induce a spider to inch away with a prod. Stiffened, awkward with cold, it might move its long legs and back away in a bizarre slow-motion waltz.

Many ants escape the cold by digging down below the frost line. Others, however, make tunnels just under boulders. These intrepid workers, it seems, never stop. In all seasons they move, work, and go about their business like automatons. Hikers in January woods should have no trouble exposing their passageways by lifting up heavy rocks or boulders. Startled, the ants will scurry helplessly about; dazed by the light, they will all die unless the boulder is quickly replaced because of the chilling air.

We naturally think of the temperature on a January day as that registered on an outdoor thermometer. But household thermometers inform us only of the air temperature a few feet above ground, not underground in rotting logs, in piles of leaves, or under boulders. In fact, it can easily be fifty degrees warmer underground or under cover than in the air, especially if the wind-chill factor is taken into account.

Rotting leaves, rotting hay, and decomposing logs, for example, can be much warmer than the air, for they slowly oxidize and give off heat just as a flame does. Inside, insects and spiders absorb that heat. Outside, the winds may howl, but, cuddled down in rotting vegetation, these tiny creatures will find enough warmth to live on. Never will they feel ice crystals pierce their cell walls, robbing them of their own juices, killing them.

Flickers, woodpeckers, chickadees, and other birds hunt for insects, as well as insect eggs, in many secret hiding places.

Blue Jays

During the winter the metallic calls of blue jays (*Cyanocitta cristata*) ring out, sharpened by the cold air. They are certainly vocal, but they do not merely call or scream brassy notes. Jays often copy

Blue jay (*Cyanocitta cristata*)

the calls of hawks to a tee and mimic the mews of catbirds, as well as the songs and cries of other birds. Moreover, through a ventriloquistic trick, they throw their voices far-off or bring them near or have them move here or there. The effect might well puzzle observers, making them wonder if they hear things correctly.

Jays are known to mob sparrow hawks and red-shouldered hawks in attempts to scare them off their territory. At times they seem to us apparently to have lost all sense of reality, for they even attack sharp-shinned hawks. The hawk may fly away from its tormentors, yet at other times it brooks no nonsense and grabs a jay. Once caught, the bird fights bravely, but is doomed. Because of the dangers, jays to all appearances usually attack sharp-shinned hawks cautiously, making sure they cannot get cornered but have a path of retreat left open. Often they attack over brambles. If the hawk turns on a jay, the jay can then plunge down into the depths of the brambles below, into narrow spaces that the hawk cannot enter.

Jays often display an interest in people, especially those who walk through their woods. Out of what appears to be sheer curiosity, a blue jay will follow a person for a long way. As it does, it will try to remain out of sight, peeking furtively from behind branches or spiraling up a tree as close to the trunk as it can get. One who is followed might find his observer, but only if he acts nonchalantly and makes no threatening moves. If you know you are being followed by a blue jay, it is interesting to see how far the bird will keep at your heels.

Black Bears

Whenever we think of bears in January, we probably think of them as being curled up, hibernating, inside cozy caves. Actually, they do not hibernate in caves.

Black bears (*Ursus americanus*), which are the only bears ever seen in the Northeast, and then only in remote areas of the mountains and northern regions, select hollows or slight depressions in the ground to sleep in for the winter. They most often choose a secluded spot high up on the slope of a hill where there is heavy growth. They may curl up near a log, which serves to keep the wind from blowing directly on them. Most, however, do not even bother with that. Instead, they snuggle down into a leafy depression, toss leaves helter-skelter over themselves, and fall asleep. They seem to choose only those locations from which they can escape quickly if trouble occurs. This explains why they do not choose caves. If a hunter or other intruder were to block the entrance to the cave, the bear would be trapped.

Bears do not actually hibernate. When an animal such as a woodchuck hibernates, its body temperature, heartbeat, and breathing rate all fall dramatically. Bears merely sleep. Their temperature, heart rate, and breathing show little change at all and simulate the changes that take place during normal sleep. Because bears do not hibernate, they can rise up quickly when disturbed. At times an aroused bear can be dangerous: in a split second it is alert and ready for action. But most of the time such a bear uses all its energies to flee from an intruder.

Before going to sleep for the winter, bears stuff themselves and become quite fat. When they become overweight, their stomachs and upper intestines shrink. This reaction is advantageous to the bear, for when it sleeps, with nothing in its stomach, it will not defecate in its hollow. This becomes especially important to females when giving birth. The young will have less chance of becoming ill.

In January, while still asleep, females give birth to their cubs. Remarkably, the cubs weigh only about 6 to 8 ounces at birth, but their mothers weigh roughly 350 pounds, so a mother may weigh 900 times as much as her offspring. No other mammal in the Northeast even begins to approach this ratio. After being born in a clean hollow, newborn cubs make their way to their mother's teats and suckle while she snoozes on, completely oblivious to their existence.

FIELDS AND MEADOWS

Silent, abandoned, snowy meadows appear to be left by farmers to flocks of birds. Crows rise and wheel overhead; snow buntings dart here and there near the ground; goldfinches knock snow off tall weeds as they search for seeds; and horned larks run over snowy crusts and cry out in tinkling calls just as they flutter into the air.

Shrews hunt avidly. Mice move cautiously under the snow, hidden in their tunnels. Foxes, lurking at the edge of fields, keep on the look out for prey.

Sparrow Hawks

These small hawks (*Falco sparverius*) with swift, pointed wings make a cold January day come to life, as they either hover or fly swiftly back and forth in quest of mice. They are hunters nonpareil, and a sheer joy to watch.

The sparrow hawk, in spite of being only the size of a robin possesses all the attributes of larger falcons and in many ways surpasses them. Dramatic-looking, the male displays the most unusual and beautiful plumage of any falcon. A chestnut color covers its back, and the bird has blue-gray wings and a reddish chestnut tail. The top of its head is covered with the same reddish chestnut color. Black semicircles rise from its neck to its eyes, giving the bird the appearance of wearing a mask. Though sharp and powerful, its bill is small. The female looks very similar but has rufous wings.

Sparrow hawk (*Falco sparverius*)

Over fields, sparrow hawks often display a unique ability. They head into the wind and remain stationary over one spot by moving their wings in response to the wind, so that they neither go forward nor are pushed backward. They do this so that they can study one spot beneath them on the ground. As a bird hovers gracefully, it calls out its unique cry, "Killy, killy, killy."

Sparrow hawks, in spite of their name, do not concentrate all their efforts on sparrows. Not that they are incapable of killing them: quite the contrary. They can easily bring down a sparrow, and often do. Yet they mostly focus their attention on rodents, especially in the winter. During the warm months of the year they generally satisfy themselves with grasshoppers and at times even lowly beetles and spiders.

Few hawks ever show up in residential or downtown areas of our cities but the sparrow hawk is one of the exceptions. In the winter these hawks sojourn in such places as Brooklyn, where they do attack sparrows.

Apparently sparrows and many other birds instinctively fear hawks. Researchers have shown that a cardboard cutout in the shape of a hawk moved above newly hatched birds will produce a fearful response.

Cottontails

Cottontails (genus *Sylvilagus*), those rabbits with the white tails, are one of the few animals with which everyone is familiar. They stay active throughout the winter. One can almost always find hints of their activities, especially when snow is on the ground. Because cottontails tend to run along the same narrow paths, they tramp down the snow, making it hard-packed. Much of the time it is rather easy to find these paths, where the rabbits also leave their droppings. As the rabbits feed on buds and twigs of sapling trees and shrubs, they neatly chew them off. Their teeth cut them with an angle of about forty-five degrees. The cuts appear about two feet above the ground.

A cottontail's life is mostly spent escaping its enemies. It finds little respite. It has hardly a moment of true relaxation and certainly never the luxury of forgetting about danger. On all sides lurk animals that seek to kill it: large hawks, foxes, cats, dogs, occasionally snakes, owls, coyotes, minks, and others, as well as people with guns. One wonders how rabbits survive at all. Considering their many enemies, they should have become extinct long ago.

But, of course, they still exist, and in great numbers, too, which shows something about their splendid defenses. First and foremost is their enormous birthrate. In only one year a female can give birth to twenty young. Before the year is out, many of her offspring will in turn be giving birth to their young. The sheer numbers, which so quickly add up, go a long way toward aiding the survival of the species.

Yet reproduction alone does not count for everything. Rabbits have developed other means of survival. Young rabbits learn to stay silent and as still as statues when left alone. They are also protected because while still they produce no odor. The color of the rabbit helps it blend into its background. As long as a young rabbit stays still, its chances of being overlooked by predators are excellent.

Adult rabbits also freeze when hunters come near. Their canny instincts allow them to hide in small clearings in bushes, where dappled shade on their motionless bodies makes them almost invisible.

At other times adult rabbits run for it, darting into briers or thickets. So dependent are they on this means of escaping their enemies that most rabbits never wander far from such hiding places. Usually a rabbit will select a good, thick, next-to-impenetrable brier or part of one and become thoroughly familiar with it. It will make pathways into it, by carefully chewing away suckers and creepers, until a rabbit-width path is formed. Once that is done, the rabbit will spend much of its time grazing near the edge of the brier. On occasion a rabbit utilizes barbed-wire fences in the same way. It will purposefully lead an animal in hot pursuit right up to the barbed wire, then pop through the opening between the wires, too narrow for the predator.

All day long, rabbits check on their surroundings, mostly by listening. They hear every noise: a leaf falling, a twig gently moved, a distant footfall. Like many wild mammals, they carefully listen to nearby birds. Have the birds fallen silent because of a hawk? Do they chitter and twitter in merely a gossipy way? Do they sound an alarm note? Are they on the move away from an enemy? Birds, especially jays, serve as their eyes above ground.

Rabbits also listen for the thumping of the foot of another rabbit. These thumpings serve as signals. The sound of the thumping does not carry too well through the air, but is carried well and far by the ground. The rabbit's exquisitely sensitive ears pick up that sound. A thumping can mean danger; it can also mean that one rabbit is asking another to come to it.

Rabbits must also consider dangers while asleep, so they sleep with their powerful hind legs bent under them. If they are disturbed, their legs will automatically spring outward, launching the half-asleep rabbit into the air with forward momentum. Many a rabbit has found itself running while not yet awake. This powerful catapulting motion often saves the rabbit, for it puts it at least one bound ahead of its enemy.

Male rabbits not only have to worry about predators, they must also be prepared to fight with other males. At any time a male rabbit may be forced to defend his territory against a male intruder. Each male tries to warn off others. He will mark his territory by rubbing his chin against the bark of trees. Such rubbing leaves his scent. Moreover, it tells an intruder just how big he is: the higher the mark, the taller the rabbit.

If an intruder rabbit enters his territory, the owner will fight. The two males will bite and kick each other. A rabbit's kick can easily wound another rabbit. After the fight the winner takes over the territory, and the mauled loser must seek another place to live. By such means the best territories fall into the possession of the strongest and fittest rabbits, the weaker and least fit taking what is left.

Mullein Stalks

In January many dry, weedy stalks stand high above the fields, but few so high as those of the mullein (*Verbascum thapsus*), some of which reach a height of seven feet. During the summer the tall mullein stalks hold numerous yellow flowers. By wintertime the flowers, of course, are long gone. But the thick soft leaves often remain at the base of the plant. These leaves feel as though they were covered with a soft fur. In fact, the name *mullein* is derived from the Latin

Great mullein
(*Verbascum thapsus*)

word *mollis,* meaning "soft." These leaves have a delicate gray-green color, and the soft hairs are white.

If you pull the leaves apart carefully, you will more than likely find insects hibernating in them. The soft, thick leaves form a winter quilting that protects them from the wind and cold.

Horned Larks

In the wintertime, anyone out in the country frequently sees horned larks (*Eremophila alpestris*) nervously winging their way in small flocks just above the snow. One has a reasonable chance of identifying these small birds by their behavior alone. Characteristically, horned larks take off from the ground. Just before taking off they move nervously, seem to hesitate, then away they go in a swift flight with wings whirring. At first they move straight from their takeoff point, but then they circle back and land on outspread wings, parachuting to their takeoff point or near it.

Horned larks rarely fly any distance. Much of the time they run on the bare ground or over the snowy crust. If they run over the bare ground or in dry grass, they can easily be seen, but if they stop, even for a brief moment, they simply disappear from sight because of their camouflaging colors. Much of the time they prefer to run rather than fly. Their running motion reminds one of scurrying mice.

True creatures of the ground, they rarely perch and are almost never seen on fences, bushes, or trees. They even sleep on the ground. At night they gather in the lee of tufts of grass, which give them protection from the wind.

Aside from viewing them through binoculars, one rarely gets a chance to examine a horned lark up close. They are elegant-looking birds, slightly larger than most sparrows, with "horns" that consist of feather tufts. A black mask covers their yellowish faces. Their breasts display a black crescent, like a heraldic badge. One very long rear toe points backward from each foot.

Horned larks alone represent the true larks in America. The other members of the family, so famous for its singing abilities, live in the Old World.

During the warm months of the year, horned larks eat insects and some seeds, but during the winter their fare is exclusively seeds. When winds cover fields with blowing snow, the hardy little birds search undaunted for seeds on grass spikes and weed stalks. No winds, no snows, no blizzards will stop them. They not only survive northeastern winters with no shelter but withstand the winters of the Dakotas with nothing more than a barbed-wire fence to shelter them from forty-below-zero winds. They survive through sheer activity and a very high metabolic rate that makes their bodies like little furnaces.

Winter Seeds

Throughout the winter, seeds lie in the ground. Lifeless-looking, they wait encased in the ice. The frozen ground can exert a pressure of thousands of pounds per square inch, but seeds can withstand it. Their hard shells and spherical shapes help them resist; ice cannot crush them, it cannot even grip them properly. They are like tiny bathyspheres in that their surfaces are actually strengthened by their spherical shape.

Although ice cannot break through their shells, indirectly warm weather can and will. When the ground thaws and the warmth of the sun seeps downward through the soil to the seeds, enzymes go to work on their hard surfaces. Chemical reactions break down the armor of the seeds from within. Eventually part of the shell weakens so that a root breaks from its prison and pushes downward into the soil. But in January there is not the slightest hint of such activities.

WILD, ROCKY PLACES

In the dead of winter, few sites in all of the Northeast become more isolated than wild, rocky places. For weeks, even months, no outsider intrudes there. It is, of course, just for this reason that wild, rocky places lure a few dedicated people who seek silent, lonely landscapes, where they can be as close to nature as possible. Many birds from the Canadian north, accustomed to wild places, stay in lonely, rocky areas. Snowy owls (*Nyctea scandiaca*) show up on occasion when food supplies in regions of northern Canada falter. Porcupines munch on bark or sleep in the forks of limbs high up in pines, and occasionally wildcats, which mate in January, scream on distant crags.

Coyotes

Only a very few decades ago, no book about the nature or wildlife of the Northeast would have included a single word about coyotes (*Canis latrans*), for none inhabited the region. It is believed that wolves kept them out of the Northeast, killing any that appeared. With no wolves to threaten them, coyotes have infiltrated, and their population now increases every year, mostly in scattered remote areas.

The problems of staying alive and increasing their numbers do not daunt the adaptable coyotes in the least. They possess a keen intelligence and understand the fine edge between caution and opportunism. For example, they approach traps and humans with extreme caution. On the other hand, they live off the land like freeloaders, finding and making use of any sort of opportunity. They can also modify their carnivorous diet to match conditions. If need be, they will even eat watermelons, of all things. A coyote can quickly determine if one is ripe before opening it. They even pull up carrots and munch on them. This ability for a carnivore to shift diets goes a long way in aiding its survival. There is always food—someplace out there—for a smart coyote.

Contrary to popular belief, coyotes do not form large packs. It is true that some may gather together once in a while to go hunting for game too large for one or two to tackle alone, but such arrangements last but a short time. Moreover, these groups consist only of coyotes related to one another.

On occasion these packs will bring down a deer. The methods they use reveal sharp intelligence, for they plan their hunt carefully in terms of the topography, wind direction, cover, snow crust (if there is one), and their attack positions. Usually when a pack hunts a deer, the pack breaks up. Some coyotes will make a wide circle and go around the deer to lie in wait, so that the remaining pack members can drive the deer toward them. In spite of well-laid plans, the coyotes do not always win. Moreover, a quick deer can wound or kill a coyote with its sharp hooves. Other things may go wrong, and the deer may escape. But coyotes know what they are up to, and many such hunts end for them with a feast of venison.

Coyote social life limits itself to the family, which centers on a female. The grouping in all ways depends on and is directed by her. The cycle of her dominance begins with the breeding season, which lasts from January to March. The older and more experienced in sex a female is, the earlier in the season she will come into heat. Once in heat, a female chooses the male with whom she wants to mate. She nuzzles him, then stands in a provocative, coital position, and lifts her tail so that the male can mate with her. Not infrequently other males nearby will watch the proceedings, but make no move to disturb the copulating pair. They make no claims whatsoever on the female. For a mammal, such complete control over the mating proceedings by a female is highly unusual.

Because coyotes are very closely related to dogs, a female coyote in heat may select a dog as her mate. During the breeding season, dogs and coyotes, which normally fight, even to the death, get along.

No one knows for sure whether or not coyotes and wolves mate to produce coyote-wolf pups. Genetically speaking, it can doubtless happen, yet no certain case is known.

Once a coyote is pregnant, she will make a den, which is quite large and may extend twenty to thirty feet underground. Usually she digs a ventilator hole up through the roof. Otherwise the den is a no-frills home for her pups-to-be, for she does not even place grass, leaves, fur, or anything else on the floor for their comfort. Though her mate takes no part in the construction of the den, he will stay with her.

Females usually locate their dens on hillsides, which may or may not be in wild, rocky places, often near willow-lined streams. Such places will not flood in a rain, for water drains away from them. The nearby stream provides drinking water, and the thick willows hide the den from view.

Once the pups arrive, they will act much like the pups of domestic dogs, playing, roughhousing, and affectionately teasing one another. Even adult coyotes engage in playful activities and have been seen tossing sticks and bones about, playing catch with them.

The male takes over the chores of feeding the pups as well as the nursing mother. He goes off and hunts. Once he catches game, usually mice, he swallows it, goes back to the den, and regurgitates the food for his mate and, if the pups are weaned, for them, too.

Once the pups are old enough to hunt, the family goes off together. The parents communicate with their offspring. According to H. T. Gier of Kansas State University, they have specific sounds for the necessities of life, such as "freeze," "go off and hide," "run away," and "dinner is ready." Gier also notes that night calls are used by coyotes to announce their positions and hunting successes to each other. Moreover, he writes that their calls also express deeper, more emotional feelings. Anyone who has spent much time carefully listening to coyote calls could not agree more.

Though coyotes as hunters depend on their acute senses, they also rely on their exceptional speed. Coyotes can evidently run about forty-five miles per hour. In the West they are the only wild animals capable of running down a jackrabbit. Like all canines the world over, they can run for long distances without tiring. This ability, more than any other, accounts for the success of the canines. Over long distances they can overtake any animal they prey upon. Felines, though very fast, lack that stamina.

They possess yet another highly developed skill: they can stalk prey better than most animals. They can, for example, stalk mice better than cats can. A coyote will move slowly up on a mouse in a strange, stiff-legged manner. When near the mouse, it pounces in one clean leap. A coyote can clear fourteen feet of ground in one leap.

Coyotes hunt within a territory, which they define and mark out by urinating on trees, posts, boulders, and, if need be, the bare ground. Territories may extend for a radius of roughly six miles from a den. Coyotes, being opportunists, may quickly give up their territory and move on to a new one, if they feel threatened or if things seem better somewhere else. Distance hardly matters to them when they move. Tagged coyotes have shown up as much as four hundred miles from where they were tagged. This shows that they traverse distances impossible for most other mammals.

Coyotes may roam about, but they are here to stay in the Northeast. Without a doubt, their numbers will continue to increase, though it is difficult to say for how long. The future of the coyote in the Northeast will be an interesting study of an adaptable survivor.

Goldthreads

In January a few small evergreen plants such as goldthreads (*Coptis groenlandica*) add color to drab landscapes. Although goldthreads grow in bogs, they also grow in shaded, rocky places where they can obtain constant moisture. They often grow along ledges and can frequently be found beside narrow, hidden intimate paths through rugged rocky terrain. Their leaves, seen all winter long, make identification easy. The plant has three very dark, shiny leaves. Another way to identify the plant is carefully to separate dirt from around the roots so that the plant is not harmed and notice that the thin roots do look just like gold threads. Goldthreads belong to the buttercup family, and bloom from May to July. The flowers have the shape of buttercups, with five petallike sepals, but unlike common buttercups, they are white.

Rattlesnake Plantains

Here is an always green plant with a most unusual as well as confusing name. Rattlesnake plantains (genus *Goodyera*) in no way are related to the plantains seen growing on lawns and grassy areas. Instead, they belong to the orchid family. When in bloom, in July and August, little white orchids cluster on their flowering spike. From a distance the plant resembles common plantains, but close up, not at all.

They most certainly are not related to rattlesnakes either. Their curious name came to us because of a superstitious belief. For centuries most herbalists believed that plants showed signs that indicated what diseases they cured. Because on their leaves' upper surfaces remarkable patterns resemble the scaly back of a snake, it was thought the plants cured snakebites. Unfortunately, it seems that they don't. These leaves, however, remain on the plants all winter. To find them, look on well-drained slopes in rocky areas near conifers.

Wild Turkeys

Wild turkeys (*Meleagris gallopavo*) stay as far from human habitation as they can. They live in much of the Northeast in broken country, such as woods with openings, fields near thickets, and rocky terrain, where they can find undergrowth and trees.

Although very closely related to domestic turkeys, a wild turkey is a completely different sort of bird. In terms of wiliness, wilderness know-how, and quickness, there is no comparison. Few birds are as difficult to see or approach as wild turkeys. Once a wild turkey realizes that a hiker has entered its territory, it and its flock run with an impressive burst of speed for the nearest undergrowth. If pressed or taken by surprise in the open—a rarity—they take off on whirring wings. Though poor fliers, they will nevertheless go a good distance away from danger before landing.

The best way to study them is to come upon a flock and scatter it. After they have left, you should hide and wait about an hour. More often than not, the flock of wild turkeys, to stay together, will circle back and reassemble at the very place from which it was scattered.

It is in the interest of a flock of wild turkeys to stay together. A flock operates as a unit and each bird serves as a sentinel for the others. Turkey flocks center on a male gobbler, who keeps his harem of hens in line. His early morning gobbling call signals his hens, who collect around him, forming the flock. Once together, near dawn, they move out into open country to forage for nuts, berries, and seeds. Their keen eyes search everywhere for enemies. Their acute hearing picks up the slightest noise. Virtually nothing escapes their attention. After foraging all day, they go up into trees and roost for the night.

When the Pilgrims landed, turkeys abounded in the Eastern woodlands. However, those large flocks slowly disappeared from the American scene, as hunters and expanding farmlands and city areas expanded to reduce them. By 1930 the large population of wild turkeys had shrunk to their lowest point; it was believed that no more than 20,000 birds existed in all of America. Efforts were made to bring them back. Naturally, some people tried to crossbreed wild turkeys with domestic turkeys and set the offspring loose in the wilds. All met their end quickly. It seemed that even a drop of domestic turkey blood severely diminished the species' woodland smarts, and oddly, this was true even though domestic turkeys were originally wild. Only true wild turkeys, uncontaminated by the genes of domestic turkeys, possessed the instincts needed to survive on their own. Fortunately, work with wild turkeys succeeded beyond all expectations. In a little over fifty years the population has risen about 1,000 percent.

LAKES, PONDS, AND WATERCOURSES

In January, frozen white ponds lie in their brown settings of shores and bog plants. Tall cattails (genus *Typha*), faded to a paper-bag beige, rustle their torn leaves in the wind. Their tops come apart in shreds, like the stuffing from a ripped cushion. Each seed-bearing tuft of fluff moves away with the wind. There is a long parade of them because the flowering head of a cattail may contain 125,000 seeds. All winter, one by one, they float to their destinies over the neighboring grass tussocks that, with their rounded tops covered with snow, look like cities of miniature igloos. In thaws, however, these tussocks have rich rusty colors streaked with orange.

Loons

Loons (genus *Gavia*) symbolize all that is wild. These solitary wanderers, with their aloof, wily ways and maniacal laughter, speak of something from primeval forest lakes and some age that has passed.

Primitive they are. In fact, biologists place them among the most primitive birds ever seen in the Northeast. They are closer to being reptiles than any others. Long ago, around the time of the dinosaurs, primitive birds began branching away from the reptile line. Several million years later, loons appeared. The loons show up in fossils from the Miocene Epoch, which occured between 23 and 6 million years ago. Perhaps when we see loons, we intuitively pick up on some strange reptilian qualities that they possess.

Because of their primitiveness, their skulls are unlike those of

Loon (*Gavia immer*)

other birds. Some of their bones, mostly in the feet, are considerably heavier than the bones in more highly evolved birds. Most birds depend almost entirely on their feathers to keep them covered and insulated, but loons have a layer of fat just under the skin, which protects them from the cold. For their body length, loons have short wings.

Loons have very undeveloped legs, set way back on their bodies, so that they hardly support the birds on land. In fact, a loon on land must make its way by sliding its breast along the ground and pushing along with its wings. Because of their awkwardness, they rarely go on land except to lay eggs, and even then their nests are close to the water.

From all of this we might guess that loons act like very helpless birds. Quite the contrary. In many ways they act swiftly and surely. Although they have trouble taking off from water, needing to run a good distance on top of it, once aloft they show their stuff. Their swift flight takes them through the air with ease. Not many birds can fly faster than loons.

On the water, though, their acrobatics must be seen to be believed. Until the advent of modern high-powered rifles, hunters recorded, time after time, that if a person standing on the shore shot at a loon out on a lake, the loon could pop down underwater faster than the bullet could reach it. Although some people dispute this, it points up the birds' extraordinary diving speed and an awesome alertness—and on this everyone agrees.

Loons show another ability unique among water birds. They can simply sink down into the water so smoothly that the watcher hardly detects a ripple around the place where they disappeared. Moreover, they sink under the surface quite rapidly. For a long time no one could figure out how they did it—it seemed impossible. When the truth was known, it became clear that it would be impossible for any other birds, ducks, for example. To sink, loons both exhale and pull their feathers closer to their bodies, squeezing out the air between them and under them. These actions raise the overall density of their body. Their bones, which are denser than those in other birds, help them sink.

Two species of loons winter over in the Northeast, the common loon (*Gavia immer*) and the red-throated loon (*Gavia stellata*). Only an expert bird-watcher can tell them apart in the winter, for the winter plumage of each closely resembles the other. The common loon has, however, a darker back than does the red-throated.

One sure way to tell if a bird is a loon is to listen to it. The call of a loon will send shivers down most people's backs. No call of the wild is so lonely, so barbaric, so insane-sounding. The word *loon* is akin to an Old Norse word, *lomr*, which is connected to our word *lament*, which in turn is connected to the Latin word *latrare*, "to bark." More unnervingly, a loon occasionally lets go with an uncontrolled sound much like wild laughter.

Otters

Very few animals, especially adults, play games or appear to have fun. Dogs and coyotes wrestle and play with each other. Bear cubs frolic. Horses appear to enjoy running. Yet convincing examples are difficult to come by. However, there is one animal noted for its playful activities: the otter (*Lutra canadensis*). Otters are large members of the weasel family that live mainly along rivers. Wherever they establish themselves, they make mud or snow slides on riverbanks. Just like children sledding, they lie on their stomachs, pull their front legs under them, and *whoooosh* they go down the slide, splashing into the water. Not only do they use such slides for hours on end for no observable purpose besides fun, but they endlessly wrestle with each other in sport, as well.

Otters are good-sized animals, reaching a length of five feet. Their fur glistens. It's the most durable fur of any animal, so all other animal furs are judged in terms of durability against theirs. Otters belong to the weasel family and consequently are closely related to minks, skunks, and wolverines. Unlike other members of the family, otters have webbed feet, which, incidentally, have furry soles.

Otters seem to have a wanderlust, for they rarely stay put. They roam here and there along watercourses. Even so, they actually do stay within their own territories, but these territories are large, often extending fifty miles in length. Day or night, an otter will patrol its territory, usually traveling along streams. No matter what the weather is, it stays on the move. No snowstorm, no subzero weather will deter an otter from its rounds.

Like all weasels, they have mastered the art of hunting. In fact, because of their intelligence, they surpass their relatives. They nearly

Otter (*Lutra canadensis*)

always find prey, under any conditions. Like wolverines, otters have strength and power beyond what the size of their bodies would indicate. An otter is more than a match for any carnivore its own size. Yet otters avoid fights. They stay hidden for the most part, especially when they travel. In spite of that, you may come upon an otter anytime, even in the most unexpected places. Many have been seen calmly walking along highways or wandering into suburban areas. It is difficult, however, to find an otter slide, which they always make in some hidden river embankment where they will not be disturbed.

In January, when rivers are partly covered with ice and ponds are frozen from shore to shore, it would seem logical that otters would not hunt in the water for fish, as they can easily hunt land animals. Not at all. Otters spend much of their winter hunting in streams, ponds, and lakes, and not even the ice stops them; otters will swim right under it. As they do, they breathe the air that lies pocketed between the ice and the surface of the water. Sometimes a person walking on ice will look down and see a dark form moving mysteriously below, under the ice, like a supernatural apparition. It is an otter.

Thanks to their long streamlined bodies and their webbed feet, otters can swim swiftly underwater. They can go long distances below the surface—at least a quarter mile. They hunt mainly for fish, occasionally eating muskrats. Interestingly, they could kill as many muskrats as they pleased, but they do not. It is likely they prefer fish. On rare occasions otters even hunt beaver. To get a beaver, they must enter a lodge, a feat presenting problems, even for the powerful otter, because an otter coming up a tunnel into a beaver lodge could be confronted in a small space by the beaver. Beavers have powerful teeth capable of cutting down trees. Teeth that can cut through solid wood can and will wound an otter and serve as splendid defenses. Rarely does an otter kill a beaver.

Stone Flies

At the slightest hint of warmth in January, stone flies (order Plecoptera) quickly respond by mating. When the temperature goes above the freezing mark, as it always does at some point in January, adult stone flies emerge from their nymphal cases. Until that point the immature nymphs live underwater in streams. In January, hundreds of newly hatched stone flies circle and zigzag into the air on their new, fragile wings. They mate. Sometimes hundreds darken the snow, while others may cover fence posts.

Stone fly (*Taeniopteryx pacifica*)

While the world lives under heaps of snow, and most nonhibernating animals just fight to stay alive, hoping for a scrap of food, the stone flies mate. Why do they do so in the midst of a cold empty world? That is just the reason. The world, after all, is empty of their enemies. By mating in January, the flies are safe. They possess what most lovers desire: a world to themselves. After mating, the females lay eggs on the banks of streams. The adults, having accomplished their task, fly a few more moments, then fall and die in the snow. Many of their bodies float away on the surface of icy brooks.

CELESTIAL EVENTS

January is a month of stars. The brightest and best constellations of the year blaze high in the sky over the cold and silent land. If you can withstand the cold, January is a good time to note the different colors of stars. When the clear air lies still and cold, they show up well. Betelgeuse, the second-brightest star in the constellation Orion, up at the shoulder, is red. Arcturus, the brightest star of the constellation Boötes, found just beyond the end of the handle of the Big Dipper, is orange. The sun is yellow, as is Capella, found in the constellation Auriga, which lies just north of Orion. The star that is unmistakably

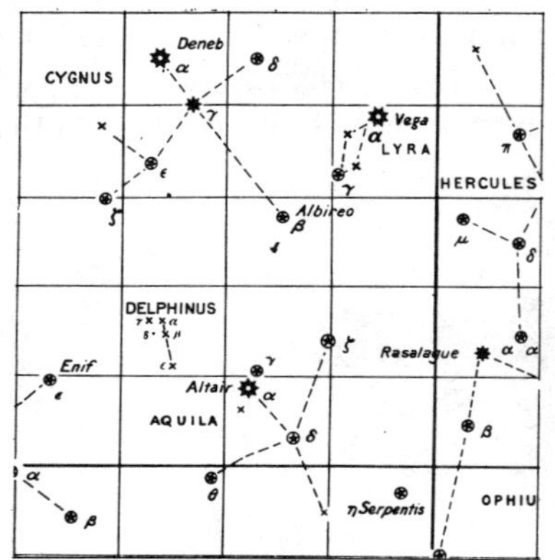

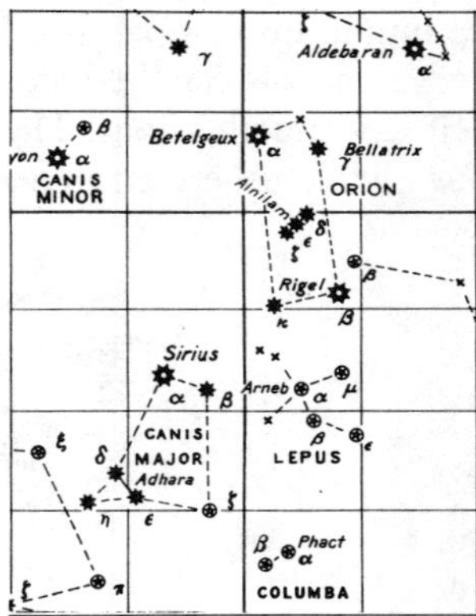

World star chart

the brightest star in the sky is Sirius, and it is white. To the northeast of it is the star Procyon, which is yellowish white. The brightest star in Orion is Rigel, and it is blue-white. Stars have different colors because they burn at different temperatures. Red stars burn at about 5,500° F; yellow at about 11,000° F; white at 20,000° F; blue-white at over 36,000° F. It takes practice to see these colors, but once you do, the sky will fill with colored jewels for you.

Nearest the Sun

As Johannes Kepler discovered in the seventeenth century, the planets orbit around the sun in ellipses. He also found out that as the planets got nearer to the sun, they moved more swiftly than when farther away from it, but he could not understand why this was so. Newton explained this phenomenon by stating that the sun's gravitational pull was greatest on a planet the closer it got to the sun. Einstein discovered that this was caused by the curvature of space, but for all practical purposes Newton's theory is used.

The earth is closest to the sun around January 2 each year, so it then travels faster in its orbit than at any other time of the year. Because of this extra speed, we in the northern hemisphere move through winter faster than we do through summer. You can find that this is true by counting up the days of winter, from the winter solstice to spring equinox, and summer, from summer solstice to autumn equinox and comparing them.

If you had the proper astronomical instruments, you could see that the sun's disk is just a tiny bit larger around January 2 than at any other time of the year because of our closeness to the sun.

In spite of our being closest to the sun in January, it is the coldest month of all, on average, in the Northeast. Days are warmer in the spring, summer, and fall because the sun is higher in the sky, concentrating more heat on each acre of the land, and also the days are longer, giving the sun more time to heat the land, sea, and atmosphere.

Venus in the Winter

Our closeness to the sun in January does, infrequently during various years, provide us with an astronomical display of great beauty. In the winter, Venus, which lies between us and the closer sun, displays its greatest brilliance. When it shines brightest, it can be fifteen times brighter than Sirius, the brightest star. But during the years its brightness varies strikingly according to its position in the sky relative to the sun and the earth.

Sometimes its light is so bright that it casts shadows on the earth. Such a scene on a blue night illuminated by silver Venus above the silhouettes of a naked tree branch is magical.

February

In February one can see few changes. The skies, however, become lighter. The days become longer, increasingly so, with increasingly earlier sunrises and later sunsets. Fading twilights linger a few minutes more. The noon sun lies higher in the sky, and by February 7 it has moved a third of the way from its December low to its June apex. Although some rare Februaries go by without a full moon (the only month in which this can happen), February, according to tradition, is the month of the snow moon, that anemic, pale full moon that illuminates the white land below. Even though deep winter grips all, signs here and there show that the season is wearing itself out. A few buds swell, mulberry bark yellows, and the bark of red osier dogwoods turns a unique rouge-red. Late in the month, pails are once more hung on the side of sugar maples to collect the sweet flowing sap.

WOODLANDS

By the second half of February the sun is really quite high in the sky—as high as it is in late October. In open woodlands the sun floods dazzling snow with light and casts sharp blue shadows that crisscross in open crochetlike patterns. On the snow one will almost surely see the tracks of birds and mammals, each with its own story to tell. Some tracks end in holes, some at the trunks of trees, some at a nibbled bush; some enter snow tunnels; and some lead to torn carcasses.

Winter Fungi

When walking in woodlands during the winter, one will come across various fungi not hidden by leaves or snow. The most common are the shelf fungi, so called because they grow like shelves from tree trunks, stumps, posts, and the like. Most often they grow on dead wood, but a few appear on living trees as well. They parasitize the wood and degrade it as they remove nutrients for their own use.

The largest common fungus, growing to a width of twenty-four inches, is the **artist's fungus** (*Ganoderma applanatum*). Concentric, brownish rings, much like tree rings, cover its upper surface. On the bottom a smooth, flat surface is indented with small, round pores. This fungus gets its name from the ease with which one can draw on the pores, which turn a sepia brown where marked with a pointed instrument. These fungi, ornamented with pictures, sometimes show up in curio stores. The artist's fungus grows with extreme slowness; a large one may be as much as fifty years old.

Maze fungi are so named because the pores on the bottom surface appear distinctly mazelike. The scientific name is *Daedalea*, after Daedalus, the mythical architect who, according to the ancient Greeks, designed the fabulous labyrinth that held the Minotaur. The fungus has a soft, corky, bouncy feeling to it. Maze fungi often measure three to eight inches in width.

Rusty-hoof fomes (*Fomes fomentarius*) resemble a horse's hoof. It has a shiny, dark, almost plasticlike upper surface. Experienced campers sometimes use it for punk—as a tinder for starting campfires. It has round pores on the bottom. If one splits a fungus in half, one can see and count the annual rings of pores. Some rusty-hoof fomes live for over thirty-five years.

One fungus that is easy to identify is **birch polyporus** (*Polyporus betulinus*), which grows only on birch trees. When fully grown, it resembles a fat half-cooked biscuit projecting from the side of a tree.

Turkey-tail fungi, also called multizoned polystictus (*Polyporus versicolor*), resemble colorful turkey tails held fanned out. Their upper surface takes on many subdued colors: yellows, dark greens, browns, grays, and dark reds, all arranged concentrically. Soft, downy hairs cover the upper surface. They are very common and are frequently found on dead oak trees, stumps, and logs, where they quickly destroy wood. These and other fungi clear woodlands of dead trees and old logs, turning them to fine dustlike particles, which enter the soil, so that future trees will have both space and nutrients.

Raccoons

In late February anyone living in the country or even in suburbia may be startled at some odd hour of the night by the most awful caterwauling, much fiercer than anything cats produce. The loud cacophony rises from the voices of male raccoons (*Procyon lotor*) who have joined in a noisy fight for a female. They go at it hammer and tongs, but rarely does one of the males get injured. Most likely one will give up and flee the scene of battle. And the female? She usually appears bored with it all, more often than not wandering off about her own business. The victorious male will follow her.

At the onset of the breeding season in late February, a female raccoon's vulva becomes red and swollen. At the same time, the male's testes enlarge and motile sperm become present. Except during the breeding season, raccoon males show no interest in the females, or any other raccoons for that matter.

Once the victorious male catches up with the female, he may or may not mate with her. Actually, it will all depend on whether or not she is ready. If not ready, she may turn viciously on the male. A raccoon male will not press himself on a hostile female. Patience is the virtue of the day. He takes his time, but nevertheless will probably move into the female's den. If he does not become pushy, she will accept such an arrangement. Time is on his side, of course. Eventually estrus will occur, and the female will definitely show a change of attitude toward him. If the weather is not too cold, mating will, at long last, take place.

If, on the other hand, a great deal of snow falls or a cold snap develops, the female will not reach estrus. Her receptivity will cease.

Later, in March, she will come back into heat, and the process will proceed to its conclusion.

The female ovulates only following sexual intercourse. In fact, coitus induces the process. Such induced ovulation is common among carnivores. From a survival standpoint, it has the advantage of greatly increasing the odds of reproductive success because the animals mate just as ovulation begins. Ovulation can be stimulated only by a rough and vigorous intercourse. To this end, male raccoons have a bone in their penis, called a *baculum.* Once the penis is within the vagina of a female, the baculum, which has a two-pronged tip, rotates ninety degrees and turns downward. It hooks into the female's pelvic bone so that she cannot escape from the male. The thrusts of the baculum may make the female cry out in pain. She often tries to bite the male, but to no avail. When the baculum is withdrawn, its tip causes a sharp pain for the female. All this pain is to one end: the ordeal itself serves as the crucial stimulus for ovulation.

One might guess that female raccoons would detest their mates, yet this does not exactly happen. Some females become attached to them in a lukewarm sort of a way. They do not cozy up, and if a male disappears for several days and comes back to the female, she greets him with a growl. But nevertheless, she stays close to him. She seems more placid than usual with her mate near her.

If a female does not have sexual intercourse, she can, to all appearances, suffer psychologically and become intractable. People who raise raccoons frequently see to it that their female raccoons mate, so that they will not suffer ill effects in the springtime. Evidently raccoons are intelligent enough to have a spectrum of moods, and mating is important to their well-being.

Evergreens

In February we really notice the evergreens, for they stand out dramatically against the snow. Though green and calm-looking in the summer, they seem defiant in the wintertime.

What allows them to keep their leaves all winter? Unlike deciduous trees, they have evolved mechanisms that allow them to withstand the winter drought. Odd as it may seem at first, the major problem for an evergreen in the winter is not the cold but the dryness of the ground. Many evergreens, such as pines and junipers, grow in desert conditions. Piñon pines and various junipers, such as the Utah juniper, grow among cacti and yuccas in the Arizona and New Mexico deserts. There is a connection between desert evergreens and the winter evergreens of the Northeast in that plants such as cacti, yuccas, and pines, which can withstand drought conditions, are designated *xerophytes* by botanists. (*Xero* means "dry" and *phyte* means "plant.") Evergreens need to be xerophytic because in the winter the ground is frozen and their roots cannot take up water. As far as the needs of the roots are concerned, the ice might as well be dry, solid rock. Because no water gets into the roots and no sap rises up the trees to the highest and farthest leaves, the leaves could easily dry out. However, they don't.

The leaves resist drying in several ways at once. Looking through a strong magnifying glass at a typical leaf of a deciduous tree, such as a maple leaf, one can see that on its underside there are numerous small holes, known as *stomata.* They allow air to enter the leaf. The air brings in needed carbon dioxide, which the leaf will use, along with water and sunlight, to manufacture its food, namely sugar. The stomata also play another important role. They allow water, as vapor, to exit from the leaves and dissipate into the surrounding atmosphere. The leaves of a medium-size elm may lose a ton of water a day through the stomata of its many leaves.

Obviously, the fewer leaves a plant has and the fewer stomata per square inch those leaves have, the less water the plant will lose. This is true for all xerophytes, including the evergreens. Moreover, the stomata are sunken in most xerophyte leaves, so that the wind cannot reach them so easily and dry them out. For added protection, tiny hairs often grow around the stomata of xerophytes. They, too, help keep down water loss.

In cold and dry weather the leaves of some evergreens, such as rhododendrons, curl up. This action shuts down the stomata, which are squeezed together, allowing for almost no water vapor loss.

But that is not the whole story. The leaves of evergreens are almost always coated with a tough, waxy waterproof layer, called the *cuticle,* which holds water and water vapors within the leaf.

When we look at evergreens, we may believe that they never lose their leaves. In fact they do: all year a few continually fall off, to be replaced by new leaves.

Maple Syrup and the Rise of Sap

The fact that native Americans used maple sap for sugar astonished European explorers, with good reason, too. It never occurred to them (or any other Europeans, Asians, or Africans, for that matter) that one could obtain sugar from a sap, most of which are very foul- or bitter-tasting. The only sweetener known to most people in the Old World was honey.

It is thought that native Americans got the idea of obtaining sugar from maple sap by noting that squirrels lick the sap that oozes from broken sugar maple branches. Once that observation was made, it was but a step toward learning how to utilize the sap. Native Americans obtained sugar very much the way it is done today, by cutting small holes in maple trees, putting in wooden funnels, catching the sap in birchbark buckets, and boiling it down. Once European settlers saw how it was done, they, too, collected sap in a similar way with metal pipes and pails and more modern equipment. Americans consumed more maple sugar than any other sweetener (for example, honey or cane sugar) until around 1875.

Maple sugar, as well as the sap of many other species of trees, begins to rise in late February, depending on how far north or south individual trees may be located. Oddly enough, a complete understanding of how sap actually rises within trees has not yet been worked out. Yet several things are known. Sap cannot rise until the ground has thawed. Until then, solid ice surrounds the roots. During and after a thaw, groundwater can move through the membranes of root hairs. These tiny hairlike roots do all of the work of obtaining water. The large roots only support a tree. Cell membranes along the outer edge of the root hair allow water to pass through them into the roots. It does so by osmosis, by which means the rather clean groundwater, containing a solution of a low concentration of minerals, passes through the semipermeable membranes of the root hair into a watery solution of higher concentrations of minerals, sugars, and other substances. As water enters the roots, it begins to rise upward into the tree. Osmotic pressure accounts for some of this rise, but as yet no one knows how sap rises in a tree to its highest and farthest branches.

The sap moves within the *xylem,* which is a tissue filled with small tubes, lying just beneath the bark of a tree. The sap flows at a rate of between one and four feet per hour. In February and early spring, sap carries stored sugar from the roots into the rest of the tree. When the leaves appear, they will produce sugar and the sap will be more watery, but it will continue to carry nutrients such as minerals upward from the roots. It is usually about six weeks after the sap starts to flow before its sugar content drops off. The sap cycle in all deciduous trees is similar.

Once leaves develop, a column of sap will have been established. As water *transpires*—that is, evaporates out of the leaves as water vapor—more sap is drawn up into them. Water molecules hang on to each other so tightly that a very long column of water in a thin tube cannot be broken. In essence, the leaves pump the sap upward.

Black-Capped Chickadees

Anyone who frequents winter parks or gardens or woodlands will see many black-capped chickadees (*Parus atricapillus*). Like daring acrobats, they walk along small branches and then—oops!—they swing down under them and, surprisingly, walk just as well upside down as they search for insect eggs that lie hidden in bark fissures. At times they also forage for pine and hemlock seeds. The worst snowstorms of February will not daunt them: they remain busy in any weather. It is thought that their ability to work branches in an upside-down manner may be an adaptation to snow. Curiously, they cannot climb up or down perpendicular tree trunks the way nuthatches can.

If you see one chickadee, you will surely see others, for they stay in flocks. Each chickadee remains in its own flock throughout the winter. It does not, for example, join a flock that might be passing by. Many birds do change from flock to flock in that way, but not chickadees.

A chickadee flock usually consists of about six to ten birds. It is a world unto itself, regimented to an extraordinary degree. A definite, strict pecking order rules within it. Curiously, the flock does not obey a single leader, but in a sense a king and queen rule the flock. As the dominant pair, they stand at the apex of the pecking order. Most of the other birds, which indisputably obey them, are juveniles, but the flock also contains other adults. How can one tell which birds are which within a flock? Ultimately, it could be difficult to unravel the whole social structure of a given flock without hours of careful observation, but it is easy to figure out which of two chickadees ranks higher. When they meet at a bird feeder or branch, the one of higher rank shoos the other away. The higher-ranking birds often scold the lower-ranking by calling "dee, dee, dee." This is a rebuke.

To operate successfully as a unit, the flock must keep together. If a foraging bird becomes separated from its companions, it must make an attempt to find them. Because chickadees often feed in dense growth, they lose sight contact and must depend on sound contact, so they call out to each other. The call they most often use for keeping in touch is "tseet, tseet." This call, going from bird to bird, lets each know where the others are located. If a bird gets lost, however, it calls "chickadee-dee." Some early naturalists, such as John Burroughs, did not understand that call. Burroughs wrote that the "chickadee" was sweet and friendly. Actually, it is about the opposite: a frightened alarm call. It is too bad, in a way, that we sometimes name birds after their worst moments.

Snow Fleas

Although almost all insect larvae or adults remain hidden away under bark or under stones, hibernating during the winter, a few do make their appearance in the dead of winter, among them the snow fleas (*Achorutes nivicolus*). Though snow fleas may at times darken the snow like dust, we often walk right by them without realizing that the "dust" is actually made up of great numbers of tiny living insects. But such is the case.

Snow fleas are not really fleas, but belong to an extremely primi-

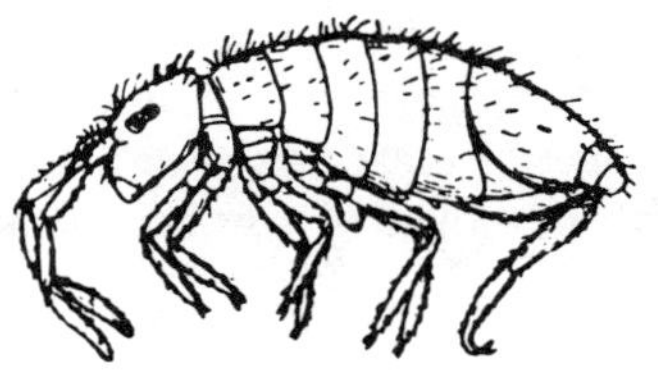

Springtail "snow flea" (*Entomobrya laguna*)

tive group of insects, the suborder Arthropleona. Unlike most insects, they lack wings or compound eyes. True fleas belong to a much more advanced order, Siphonaptera.

Snow fleas, often called springtails, barely measure one fifth of an inch in length. Under a magnifying glass one can see that they are insects. They possess six legs, which is one of the hallmarks of an insect. Although they use their legs to walk with, they are best known for their leaps. When startled they spring about. Two appendages connected to the rear parts of their bodies, called *furculae*, stay tucked up when the fleas are at rest. When they are disturbed or need to get about, the furculae are released by a hook called a *hamulus* and the spring snaps downward, catapulting the snow flea upward and forward.

Snow fleas, which usually stay in mosses, decaying leaves, bark, and anthills, react sensitively to changing weather conditions. This may be because they are so primitive that they lack breathing organs. It is believed that like many small and primitive animals, they absorb oxygen directly through the membranes of the body. To absorb oxygen, these membranes must stay moist. Because of this need, snow fleas appear only on humid days, when, of course, the temperature is above freezing.

FIELDS AND MEADOWS

Even into February, despite the fact that there are fewer seeds available, birds arrive each cold dawn to forage in the open countryside. Nervous flocks of crows, snow buntings, horned larks, and others fan out over the meadows and constantly stay on the move until night forces them to roost and sleep. At no other time do the forlorn meadows and fields become so barren, so depleted, necessitating longer flights, more searches, more frantic efforts. Hunger also gnaws at the shrunken stomachs of such carnivores as foxes and ermines, which nervously rove the edges of meadows, ever ready to make a dash into the open after a darting mouse or zigzagging rabbit.

Bobwhites

No month of the year is more difficult for the bobwhites (*Colinus virginianus*) than February and its snows. Many birds that perch in trees can, to some extent, ignore snow, but not the bobwhites. They spend their nights on the ground, and when heavy snows come, they may be buried. This in itself is not dangerous. In fact, the birds can easily escape from snow lying above them if it is dry and fluffy. The danger occurs when a cold rain falls on top of the snow and freezes, forming a hard crust over the birds or the bushes above them, creating a trap. If it does not melt within a day or so, the trapped birds will die.

Bobwhites suffer in February snowstorms in yet another way. At times the snow cover keeps them from finding gravel on the ground. It is absolutely necessary to them so that they can digest their food, for the gravel serves as their "teeth" and it grinds food, mainly seeds, in their gizzard.

During severe winters, up to 90 percent of the bobwhite population may be killed in some areas. Winter storms limit their northern range. They rarely survive north of eastern Massachusetts, southwest Maine, the southernmost areas of Ontario, and southern Minnesota.

Aside from dangerous snow conditions, bobwhites fare well during winter, for cold itself is not a problem. They have no trouble finding actual food. If the seeds of weeds or grains of wheat in harvested fields are under snow, they can, and will, eat sumac seeds and rose hips from wild roses, which remain well above the snow line of even the worst blizzards.

Bobwhites spend their nights on the ground in a tight circle, a defensive position, each bird facing outward. If a bird is startled in

Bobwhite
(*Colinus virginianus*)

the middle of the night, its near companions feel the whir of its wings. Up and away they fly. They pop into the air as though released by a powerful spring. In spite of the occasional dangers of being killed in snowstorms, this defensive position greatly helps them survive.

Newly hatched birds establish bevies. Bobwhite females lay a great number of eggs during a season. Not infrequently so many are laid that they are stacked on top of one another. When the young hatch, they stay together and will remain as a unit in the bevy as adults. This is true in spite of the apparently contradictory fact that during the mating season males often fight fiercely with any males competing with them for females.

Males take over a female's duties if she dies or is killed while brooding her eggs; he will brood the eggs and then parent the offspring when hatched, guiding them and protecting them.

The call "bobwhite," though sweet to our ears, is not voiced for its aesthetic effects; it keeps the birds together. A bird that strays from the covey can hear the others calling "bobwhite." The stray bird lets the covey know where it is by answering "bobwhite." This is not their only sound. When coveys move about, while appearing content, they often murmur to each other in low voices.

Although bobwhites frequent open country, they are masters at hiding themselves. A good thing, too, for they are one of America's most hunted birds. Their speckled coloration allows them to blend into a field of grass, and when still, they simply disappear. It is thought that the birds lack odor, for it has been noticed many times that when dogs sniff around them, they do not seem to smell them. Dogs often walk within a couple of feet of flattened birds in the open field. As long as a bird stays flat and does not move, it has little to fear. Yet bobwhites rarely hide like that in the open. More often they race into briers and thickets. At other times they depend on their powerful wings, which shoot them straight up into the air.

If you like to feed bobwhites in the winter, remember that they need some gravel, as well as grain. Small pieces of gravel or sand will do the job of helping them digest their food.

Garden Spider Egg Sacs

If you walk through a meadow in the winter and come upon a strange-looking tan-colored ball hanging from a tall weed or grass stem, it will doubtless be the egg sac of a garden spider (genus *Argiope*) or grass spider (genus *Agelenopsis*).

Inside of a peaceful-looking egg sac, a great struggle is taking place. In the autumn or early winter a female garden spider makes her egg sac, which will contain and protect her eggs. During the winter the eggs hatch, and the sac becomes filled with a large number of spiderlings. Because it is wintertime, they have no hope at all of finding either food or water on the outside. They solve this problem quite neatly by turning on one another. In a true struggle of the fittest, brothers and sisters eat their weaker siblings and suck out their juices. Thanks to their cannibalistic meals, the victors live to see spring. When the weather is warm, well-nourished winners bore a hole in the sac and leave.

If you pull an egg sac apart, you will find that there are actually two sacs, one inside the other. The outer one is made of a sticky silk that stretches easily; the inner is tougher and contains the spiderlings.

WILD, ROCKY PLACES

On a still, late winter afternoon wild, rocky places can seem as lifeless as the moon. Yet even in February, life does stir in these lonely places. Polypody ferns touch many ledges with green. Trailing arbutuses form green paths among steep slopes. Red barberries display their decorative oblong fruits. Crossbills tear cone scales apart to eat the pine seeds. And if it is warm enough in the sun, as often occurs during one or two days in February, flies may cling to south-facing cliffs and sunbathe.

Cedar Waxwings

In terms of sheer beauty, coloration, and form, cedar waxwings (*Bombycilla cedrorum*) stand apart from most birds. These small, crested birds display soft, brown, fawn, and yellow body colors that flow into each other in lovely and easy ways. Their tails are tipped with yellow ocher. On their wings lie touches of bright scarlet. They wear black masks partly outlined in white on their faces. Their crests resemble those of cardinals and titmice. Their delicate bills end in small, downward hooks.

Cedar waxwing (*Bombycilla cedrorum*)

During February as in the rest of the winter, cedar waxwings may be seen in regions south of New England flying together in roaming flocks. If you see one bird, the odds are you will see at least thirty more.

At times cedar waxwings behave in an unusual and notorious manner. They are one of the very few animals that get drunk. They do so, perhaps through no fault of their own, because they feed on fruits such as chokecherries as well as the berries of cedar trees. Fruits and berries that remain on trees and bushes awhile can ferment. Natural yeasts, which always float around in the air, land on them and turn part of their sugar into alcohol. Cedar waxwings feeding on fruits and berries with an alcohol content equal, more or less, to wine will frequently stagger about, fall to the ground, their feathers all ruffled, and act outrageously drunk. At other times they eat so much that they cannot fly. Again, they may fall to the ground, for they are too full to stay perched.

Cedar waxwings display yet another odd item of behavior. A bird in a row of cedar waxwings will take a berry in its bill and pass it to the bird next to it, which in turn will give it to the next, and so on down the line. No one knows why they do this. It is assumed that the birds that have already had enough to eat pass the food along to those that might still be hungry. Such a behavior pattern, if this is true, would have nothing whatsoever to do with politeness or kindness. It is in the interest of the birds that the flock stays healthy and together for self-protection. Consequently, it is in the interest of all that each is well fed.

The birds' crests move up and down according to their moods. When a bird is surprised or excited, it raises its creast to full height. On the other hand, when life is placid or when the bird is frightened, it keeps its crest down flat against the head.

Sumac Berries

In spite of two months of winter, with their cold weather, raw winds, and heavy snows, sumac berries (genus *Rhus*) manage to cling to sumac trees even in February. More important, the nutrients within them remain viable. They escape decomposition, oxidation and fermentation. It may seem strange at first that these edible, nutritious berries remain untouched by birds or mammals throughout the first half of winter. The reason is that they are not a favored food. They must taste awful, astringent and sour. Even the toughest fowl views them askance. Yet by February natural food supplies reach a low point, and hungry birds and mammals find themselves hard

Smooth sumac (*Rhus glabra*)

pressed to find anything at all to eat. Starvation forces them to foods they would normally overlook, so, as a last resort, they eat sumac berries of both the staghorn (*Rhus typhina*) and smooth sumac trees (*Rhus glabra*). In February many birds gather at sumac trees to eat the berries. Those most often found feeding from them are the blue jays and chickadees.

Anyone who takes strolls in wild, rocky places would do well to locate sumac trees. The staghorn sumacs will have spiky clumps of furry-looking reddish berries sticking up from their branches. The colored spikes capped with snow make a lovely winter sight. Smooth sumac trees closely resemble staghorn sumacs, but the fruits form less compact spikes. Look for sumac trees along the base of cliffs. In February check them often and see what birds might be feeding among their branches. Tracks in the snow will indicate what other birds, such as ring-necked pheasants, and mammals have also visited the sumacs.

Barberries

Scarlet berries hang in little clusters from barberry shrubs (genus *Berberis*). Being very decorative, these shrubs are often displayed in suburban gardens. One can identify them by means of their vicious-looking three-prong thorns, which grow just below the leaf buds.

During the winter many birds seek out the sour but edible berries. Indeed, some people make barberry jelly with them, with plenty of sugar added! Some of the largest birds seek out these berries; among them one can find ruffed grouse and ring-necked pheasants. Their soft bills cannot manage hard nuts and tough seedpods. During the first half of winter these birds eat buds, bark, or other berries that taste better; when these supplies diminish, usually in February, they search far and wide for meals and finally turn to the extremely sour red berries of the barberry shrubs.

Peregrine Falcons

No bird in all of America impresses so many people with such a sense of power and speed as does the peregrine falcon (*Falco peregrinus*). In Europe it is well known as a hunting falcon; it is one of

Peregrine falcon (*Falco peregrinus*)

the birds used in the sport of falconry. The sight of the speeding, elegant peregrine falcon in the sky is a stirring sight. In the winter one may sometimes see one flying near high rocky cliffs.

A peregrine falcon is usually identified by its flight, for it is by far the swiftest hawk seen in the Northeast. The adult peregrine falcon has a dark upper side and a pale underside, and a black cap to top its head. A streak of black runs down the side of its cheeks. This streak is called a moustache, but most people would liken it to sideburns. Immature birds are brown and difficult to identify. They have a brown moustache. By far the best way to identify them is by their flight.

Hawks are placed in categories according to the shape of their wings and their flight patterns, both of which vary a great deal. **Buteos** have broad wings and rounded tails; these are the soaring hawks. Their bodies lack any streamlining and tend to be wider than those of other hawks. Buteos, such as broad-winged hawks (*Buteo platypterus*), hunt by soaring high above the ground and looking downward for prey. **Harriers**, such as marsh hawks (*Circus cyaneus*), have thin, streamlined bodies and long wings with distinctly rounded tips. Their tails are also long. As they glide, the wing tips remain considerably higher than the body, in a dihedral fashion. **Accipiters**, such as sharp-shinned hawks (*Accipiter striatus*), have broad wings and long, thin tails. They beat their wings rapidly, then glide for a short distance, and repeat the process. **Falcons**, such as peregrine falcons, have large heads, long pointed wings, long tails, and streamlined bodies. The beat of their wings is powerful and rapid and they are often held in a swept-back fashion. The wings and their position resemble those of a fighter plane and aerodynamically, the air flows swiftly and easily over the wings.

Peregrine falcons are not common birds, and at one time they were threatened by insecticides. Because of efforts to control these dangerous chemicals, they have made a comeback, but not a strong one. Oddly, a few peregrines may be seen from time to time in downtown Manhattan, of all places. The birds perch on high ledges that closely resemble those of cliffs. There, high above the crowds, they do not fear human interference. Occasionally they attack city pigeons.

Their speed allows peregrine falcons to catch pigeons or other birds on the wing. They capture them by a method known as *stooping*. The falcon flies high above its intended prey, then plunges downward to land on top of it. The force of the strike can hardly be believed. Many reports state that peregrine falcons have plunged onto wooden duck decoys, mistaking them for the real thing, and have struck so hard as to knock their heads off.

At times peregrine falcons chase birds, overtake them, and grab them on the wing. They can outfly even such swift-flying birds as ducks, if they do not have a head start. A pigeon, which is a very fast bird, can give a peregrine falcon a real race. A few birds, such as hummingbirds and terns, can outmaneuver them. With some exceptions, peregrines can, and will, bring down any bird their own size or smaller.

Sometimes peregrine falcons apparently get carried away by their power and kill more birds than they need for food. They have been seen, for example, attacking flocks of sandpipers, killing one right after the other, leaving them dead and ignored in the aftermath of the slaughter. It is easy but no doubt mistaken to consider this a lust for blood or cruelty. Wild animals live in a world with no moral or philosophical restraints. Peregrine falcons probably kill because it is a reflex, thereby strengthening the bird's hunting abilities. It may be a form of practice as necessary to the falcon as exercise is to a professional athlete.

LAKES, PONDS, AND WATERCOURSES

In February, especially early in the month when the days tingle with cold, ponds are still locked in ice. But winter's cold, no matter how severe it may be, cannot lock up rivers, large, fast-moving streams, or spring-fed brooks. Their gurgling waters defy the cold and run, appearing almost as dark as ink all winter. It is near them that a person can see some of the winter sights such as water sow bugs, hellgrammites, and freshwater shrimps. Near streams, swift-flying common mergansers dart through the woods.

Common Mergansers

Common mergansers (*Mergus merganser*) are ducks that spend their lives fishing. Unlike other ducks, they have long, thin, pointed, serrated bills. When the bird catches a wiggling, struggling fish, the serrations hold it. Common mergansers fish almost exclusively in fresh water. Rarely will one spend much time near or on salt water.

Because common mergansers fish in fresh water, they need to find areas of open water. The only places likely to have open water in February are the rushing streams. In the Northeast it rarely gets cold enough to shut down the moving water in some streams. To be sure, shelves of ice may reach out over them and boulders will be glazed with thick ice, but the main currents flow on. Common mergansers brave the swiftest water, plunging into boiling foam and even into thundering waterfalls to look for fish. Their acrobatics seem impossible. Just as one seems about to be dashed to death against rocks by a waterfall, it pops up out of the racing stream with a fish in its beak.

Male common mergansers can easily be identified. They are the only ducks that have an orange bill and a green head. Females also have orange bills, but, unlike the males, they have heads of an orange-russet color.

Common mergansers spend the winter in the Northeast. They stay in forests, which are interlaced with streams. They are one of the few ducks to be seen flying about in deep woodlands, sometimes at amazing speeds of over forty miles per hour, dodging sharp tree branches, missing them by inches.

Common mergansers escape the pressures put on most ducks by hunters. First of all, their flesh is next to inedible. Those who have tasted it do not give it rave reviews—it has been compared to the taste of a wick soaked in kerosene. Also, only a few hunters have the skills needed to bring down a merganser as it zigzags through the forest. Even when the birds show themselves over ponds and lakes, they usually fly much too swiftly to make good targets.

Minks

From the price of mink coats, one would never guess that wild minks (*Mustela vison*) are not rare animals. In fact, in places where they are trapped, which today means almost everywhere, mink populations run from about 8.5 to 22 animals per square mile—not a crowd, but hardly a rarity. Because minks do not hibernate, they stay active all winter long. The odds of a person seeing one are quite good, especially near streams, lakeshores, and forest edges.

Minks do not fear people. One may walk right up and check a person out before dashing away; on the other hand, minks will never become tame. In the wilds they boldly attack prey. Minks are short-legged animals, with bodies about twenty-six inches long and tails about eight inches long. For their size they are powerful fighters and can hold their own against many animals that might try to kill them. However, wildcats, great horned owls, and coyotes eat them.

Minks do most of their hunting along watercourses. In the winter, especially, minks turn to the water for food. These expert swimmers move like shadows under the ice of streams and lakes. On lakes they breathe in air that lies between the surface of the water and the layer of ice above it. Under the ice they spend their time swimming after fish or attacking muskrats, of which over two thirds of their winter diet consists.

Minks also hunt on land, most often where forests and fields meet. They move along through the trees and peer out at the fields, searching for mice and rabbits. About one eighth of their diet is made up of mice. Although minks hunt for rabbits, they have trouble catching them.

Minks have a long mating season, beginning in February and lasting until April. During that time females come into heat about every seven to ten days. Males make no permanent attachments with the females with whom they mate, but, being exceptionally promiscuous, they go from female to female and mate with any that might be in heat.

Life of Spring-Fed Streams

Spring water pouring into streams and small brooks is considerably warmer than the water in lakes, ponds, and most places alongside streams. This is because underground water has a temperature that remains close to the yearly average temperature of the place in which it is located.

Hellgrammite (*Corydalis cornuta*)

Many small animals gather near these springs, where they escape from the intense cold of the other parts of the stream. A sharp division between a partly ice-covered stream bank and one clear of ice often indicates a spring either on the surface of the bank or underwater. Once a spring is located, an observer will probably be able to find some small animals. Small they certainly are. Actually, most are so small that they appear as tiny dots to the naked eye. But it is easy to collect them either by using a net or, simpler yet, by placing a jar in the water and letting them move into the jar with the flowing water. Later, at home, one can observe them with leisure under a magnifying glass.

One might find **freshwater shrimps**, for instance. These strange little animals are only remotely related to seagoing shrimps, but they strikingly resemble their cousins. True edible shrimps of the sea belong to the order Decapoda, whereas freshwater shrimps belong to the order Amphipoda. Even a casual observer can note the difference between the two. The back of a true shrimp of the sea is inflexible, whereas amphipods have flexible backs, because of which they can move easily in the water.

Although the little green-to-brown freshwater shrimps (*Hyalella azteca* and *Gammarus fasciatus*) are only about five eighths of an inch long, it is possible, with the aid of a magnifying glass, to see them in action. They actively swim now backward, now forward; now they dart here, now there. They propel themselves by rapidly moving legs. Look carefully at one and you will see the eyespot. Freshwater shrimps can see very well; they also have a good sense of touch. Not only can they swim remarkably well, but they can jump and climb over things underwater with their legs. They often engage in all kinds of strange and unexpected acrobatics.

Freshwater shrimps are very valuable animals in the ecology of streams, lakes, and ponds. Their importance rests on the fact that they eat vegetation and convert plant food into animal food. They also eat other animals, at times even engaging in cannibalism. In turn, they are eaten by fish. Thus they serve as a key animal in most food chains in freshwater environments.

Along with freshwater shrimps, one will probably also see **hellgrammites**. Their fierce appearance can be most startling: though small, they look dangerous. To some extent they are, for they can bite a person. When one does, it will hang on tightly. Hellgrammites grow to about three inches in length. Even though hellgrammites have six legs, they resemble segmented worms.

Hellgrammites are the larvae of dobsonflies (genus *Corydalis*). No two creatures could look more unalike. Dobsonflies have delicate long wings and long antennae and can be identified by their long, slender jaws, which cross each other. Few transformations in the insect world end with such a dramatic contrast.

Hellgrammites mostly live between stones on the bottom of brooks and streams. The best way to find one is to turn over stones to see if one is there. It might be hard to remove from the stone because it clings tightly.

Also found near springs are the **mayfly larvae** (order Ephemeroptera), often called mayfly nymphs, which are about an inch long. They can be identified because they have what appear to be two or three tails, or caudal filaments. They have six legs and medium-length antennae. There are several species of mayfly. Some of the nymphs have what appears to be fuzzy hairs that are actually gills. Others have many leaflike gills on their bodies. The nymphs often burrow into mud.

Adult mayflies can be identified by their four wings and two or three long tails. Some adult mayflies may live for only a few hours. The adults, lacking developed mouth parts, never feed. Their sole function is to mate and lay eggs.

Yellow Perch

Without a doubt, everyone who has gone fishing in the fresh waters of the Northeast knows what a yellow perch (*Perca flavescens*) looks like. It is more often than not the fish a happy, excited child holds high as his first proud catch.

Although common, yellow perch are uncommonly colorful-looking fish. They have a yellow ground color emphasized by black vertical bands on their backs. Their scales are so shiny that they glitter like polished brass. Yellow perch rarely grow large; any over fourteen inches or weighing more than about three pounds would be considered a rarity. Though much too bony for most people to bother with, they do taste good.

In many parts of the Northeast, yellow perch spawn in February or March. The process begins when male fish swim to spawning grounds located in shallow water, right at the edges of ponds. After the males have established themselves, females arrive. Someone walking along the edge of a pond might be able to catch a glimpse of them in the water, even under ice.

When they spawn, the females release eggs and at the same time the males release milt. The eggs leave the bodies of females in zigzagging bands. At first the eggs are small, but they quickly absorb water and expand. Some of these odd-looking strings of eggs may exceed eighty inches in length.

After spawning, the fish, which do not eat during their spawning season, leave the shallows and head for deeper water.

CELESTIAL EVENT

Imbolc: An Ancient First Day of Spring

We are so used to dividing the year into its seasons by means of the Gregorian calendar that we rarely if ever realize that there are other ways of doing it.

In pre-Christian Europe, the ancient Celts divided the seasons in a different manner. Their first day of spring fell between the winter solstice and the spring equinox. The halfway mark is around February 4. By tradition—at least, modern tradition, which is probably a compromise with our calendar—the first day of the Celtic spring, Imbolc, falls on February 1. The first day of the Celtic summer, Beltane, falls on May 1, halfway between the spring equinox and the summer solstice (see "May," for more about Beltane). Lammas, the first day of the Celtic autumn, falls on August 1. The first day of Celtic winter, Samhain, falls on November 1. There is a logic to the Celtic calendar because the solstices fall in the middle of summer and the middle of winter.

By February 1, at least in terms of the height of the sun and the length of the days, the Celtic winter that began with dark November is over.

March

There is a fragrance to early March—not of flowers, but of thawed mud, distant rains, green slime, and decaying leaves. These faint odors sneak up on one.

There are sounds, too: the mating calls of mourning doves, the gurgling of new-thawed brooks, the hum of the first bees, and the woodland chorus of spring peepers. The deep winter silence is no more.

Some days, one can feel the change. As the temperature rises, a winter coat feels uncomfortable. The air is softer on the cheeks. Outdoor stones do not feel like ice to the touch. A few walls, facing south into the sun, actually feel warm.

WOODLANDS

How open the sun-filled, leafless woodlands of March stand! The swollen buds of trees and shrubs, the rich smell of thawed earth, the first hints of green, which appear here and there, show conclusively that winter is over. In the woodlands one can see best that there are actually two springs to the year: one is the spring of the thaw; the other, the spring of the greening of the world. The earlier starts in February, whereas the later reaches its height in April or May. March, in a sense, straddles them, forming a unique mix, both fragile and tentative but touched with a promise all of its own.

Algae: The First Green

By March we yearn for some distinct patch of spring green. The drab, tag-end world of the dying winter demands color. Oddly, when the green arrives, we may overlook it. Even as we walk in woodlands where the green appears, it is not where we expect it to be. Moreover, it does not fulfill the myth of spring, for the earliest emerald color appears unannounced on dead trees, fallen logs, and stone walls. It is an alga, merely a scum on a surface. No doubt we might overlook it, for who would celebrate "the first scum of spring"? But there it is, extraordinarily bright—a real Kelly green. It is so highly colored because algae are plants. When the light is right, the bright green of the chlorophyll readily shines through the transparent cell walls, and there are no intervening layers of cells, such as occur in most plants, to dull that green. The alga seen on dead wood and stone walls is most likely *Protococcus*, which has the distinction of being one of the most common plants on earth.

Of Bare Trees and Flowers

As the earliest spring flowers (for example, spring beauty, early saxifrage, and purple cress) bloom on the forest floor, they need as much light and warmth as possible. Therefore it's advantageous that the deciduous trees and shrubs happen to be leafless in March and through much of April as well. If the order of things were reversed and the trees leafed first, the blooming of the flowers on the ground would be delayed for weeks. Even more likely, many of the most beautiful flowers of spring would never have come into existence in the first place if their struggling ancestors had been robbed of sunlight by leafy March trees and thereby destroyed.

Red Maples

If in March you walk in the woods, or a park, and look up to see hundreds of deep red buds against a dark blue sky, you will be sighting a red maple (*Acer rubrum*).

Once the buds open, reddish flowers drop out and hang downward like tiny bells. Thousands decorate a tree—the profligacy of nature is impressive. Why so many? Are they needed? Biologists note that nothing is ever wasted in nature. So we must assume that many are needed, for many will die—most, in fact. But as they live high above us in the icy March winds, they appear daring and brave. So slender are the long stems—the *peduncles,* as a botanist would say—that one would believe that the first gusts of wind would tear them away. Not a chance. They merely sway back and forth, giving in to each blast. Their shapes, which indicate frailness, instead show strength and the result of natural engineering.

Female maple flowers grow two paired winged seeds. If you look through a magnifying glass at a female flower—easily identified by a horn-shaped protrusion—you will see the small, partially developed seeds. Already, from the first, they deform the flower and crowd it until it is warped out of shape into a racetrack oval instead of a circle. The horn-shaped protrusion is the stigma of the flower; when male pollen falls on it, it sticks to the stigma's tiny black hairs and oozing liquid.

Male flowers, which grow on the same tree as the female, resemble them, except that long stamens hang out of the male flowers. They look like the clappers of a bell. With the aid of a magnifying glass the pollen-producing anthers, at the tips of the stamens, can easily be seen.

Hepaticas

In early March, piles of leaves and other organic matter, called *duff,* begin to thaw. Once they are released from their preserving deep freeze of winter, decay begins. The process of decay calls for oxygen. As the duff combines with oxygen it will slowly heat up. As it does, it provides enough warmth for a few early spring flowers to bloom. One is the beautiful hepatica. The round-lobed hepatica (*Hepatica americana*) and sharp-lobed hepatica (*Hepatica acutiloba*) can often be found by separating old leaves in the duff. The flowers vary in color from pale blue to white to rose. The plant is identified by its hairy stalks and by three-lobed leaves. More often than not, hepatica is the earliest spring flower to be seen.

Thanks to the death and rot of old life, new life begins. From the transformation of one generation comes another, feeding upon it, as it were. Nothing is lost; all is recycled; a new link is added to the continuing chain of life.

Birdsong

There is always that morning in March when one wakes up to the sound of birdsong, the first of the new year. The first birds to sing are not migrants up from the south but the same birds that have been around all winter long: mourning doves with their "coo-coo-coos," starlings with a variety of songs and whistles (often copied from other birds), and raucous English sparrows. For centuries people thought that birds sang to announce, in their happy way, the arrival of spring. Experiments have shown that birds have quite another reason for singing.

As birds mate, begin to build nests, and get ready to raise their young, it is important for them to mark off their territories. This will ensure the males, females, and expected young a reliable food supply. The birds must announce to other birds that they have laid claim to a given territory, and their way of doing this is to sing and also to display themselves prominently. The songs and displays warn other birds of their own species that the territory has been taken. If another bird of the same species tries to enter the territory, the owner will threaten it, hoping to force it to go away. This apparent lack of solidarity is necessary because they will compete for the food supply. Two sparrows, for example, eat the same types of seeds. If too many sparrows were in the same territory, the seeds would soon disappear. Birds need not be concerned about birds of other species nesting in their territory, if those other birds eat different sorts of foods. It is not unusual for a duck, a sparrow, and a flycatcher to nest in the same territory. There is no competition, and they can easily live together in a small area.

The reason we hear the song of the mourning dove, English sparrow, and starling before that of other birds is simple: they are hardy enough to begin mating and nest building in March, long before most birds get started. They waste no time. Before the month is over, the females will be sitting on their eggs. As these are all common birds, it is often easy to find a few that are either building nests or already in nests, sitting on their eggs.

Birds, contrary to popular belief, can and do vary their songs. Tape recordings show that individual birds will, on occasion, sing variations of their primary song. Interestingly, birds of the same species often have accents. A southern group may have a noticeably different accent from that of a northern group. Some scientists have shown that birds are directly related to certain dinosaur species. Moreover, it is believed that some dinosaurs did not become extinct at all but slowly evolved into birds. A few scientists have gone so far as to suggest that birds should be reclassified: instead of being named avians of the class Aves, they should be renamed Dinosauria. If so, it makes one wonder if those early dinosaurs sang. Did they, too, sing like birds? Were the steaming swamps of the late Jurassic, 160 million years ago, booming with dinosaur songs?

Mourning Cloak Butterflies

Colorful mourning cloak butterflies (*Nymphalis antiopa*) have eggplant-colored wings that are three inches wide and rimmed with yellow.

On warm, calm days these butterflies make their appearance. A mourning cloak will fly with lethargic wingbeats as though it had all the time in the world to do whatever it pleases. Often it flies close to the ground as it searches for food: the sweet sap that oozes from the broken twigs of sugar maples, black maples, and birch trees.

Unlike most butterflies, adult mourning cloaks hibernate in the winter, mostly under loose bark and in deep crevices. During a warm spell, even in midwinter, they often awaken and fly about.

Mourning cloaks perform an odd ritual, which is probably a mating flight. Two will spiral upward until they reach a height of about sixty feet. There, above the ground, it is likely they will mate. Then one will unexpectedly drop as if in a faint to the ground. Females lay tiny black eggs on willow and elm trees.

Chipmunks

Near woodlands and forest borders, especially where there are rocky places or old stone walls, one might hear a new spring sound, namely a "chuck, chuck, chuck," announcing that chipmunks (*Tamias striatus*) have left hibernation to scamper about.

In March the males awake from their winter hibernation, in burrows that they dug underground, slanting below boulders and rocks. The males wake up first, preceding the females by about two or three weeks or so. Hunger and the sex urge wake up the males. Just as soon as they possibly can, the males try to take care of both needs, searching the surrounding areas. Food is usually easy to obtain, but male chipmunks often encounter problems with their prospective mates.

It is risky business for a male to search for a mate, for females all too quickly fight. A male will go to the burrows of females and tentatively peer about. He must approach very cautiously; if he finds a female who has awakened from hibernation but is not yet ready for him, trouble is in the offing. If the male too boldly approaches her before she is ready, the female will give him a good thrashing. Many a battered male has come flying out of those burrows.

Sometime in March the females will have a change of heart and the chipmunks will finally mate.

When faced with danger, chipmunks call "chip, chip, chip" in rapid succession. These "chips" have been timed and found to be as many as 130 a minute. In the springtime the "chips" may or may not be used as a danger signal; they are often used then for social gatherings. Several chipmunks may gather, continually calling out their "chips." More often than not, the chipmunks are excited as they perform this social ceremony. Not infrequently birds will add their calls to the gathering, until a small section of the woods becomes quite noisy with all the excited animals taking part. A chipmunk may take a very characteristic pose during these affairs: it will stand up on its back legs on a stump or rock and clasp its forepaws to its chest, very much like an orator, while calling out.

Chipmunks stay near places where they can, if need be, make a quick escape from enemies and hide. Broken rocks or old fences offer them a hole to pop into, a rock to hide behind, or a log to dash under. Since chipmunks need to drink rather often, they also tend to stay near ponds and brooks.

Woodcocks

Let us now turn to an exceptionally wild, secretive animal, namely a bird, rarely seen—except in March. This is the woodcock (*Philohela minor*). In March it migrates north from the south and mid-Atlantic coastal regions and heads for places throughout the Northeast where it can hide from view and be as far from human habitation as possible. For sites it prefers thickets, overgrown fields,

Woodcock (*Philohela minor*)

with scattered cover, wet woods, or even the depths of swamps, if dry areas stand above the waterline.

A woodcock is slightly larger than a robin. It is a long-billed bird, brownish in color, with a tint of red-orange and black bars on its head. Its eyes are located exceptionally high up on its head. Placed so high, they look unnatural; however, they allow the bird to stay crouched in hiding and at the same time to look upward for the approach of any enemies.

If disturbed, a woodcock will fly about, then fly off at high speed in a straight line. Its wings beat so fast that they whistle.

In March the male, who usually stays so well hidden, makes his appearance. His mating ritual demands that he make a flight into the air, where he can be not only seen but heard as well. For that he must come out of hiding.

The mating ritual takes place at dawn or, more likely, at dusk. A male will suddenly shoot upward into the air as though catapulted from his hiding place. Once above the ground, he will fly in a wide circle circumscribing several acres. As he flies, he goes more and more rapidly around and around and produces an odd, nasal buzzing sound, a kind of "peent." After circling, he will begin to rise; as he does, he spirals upward, moving toward the center of the original circle. He will fly until he reaches a height of about three hundred feet—until he becomes a mere dot in the twilight sky. At the apex of the spiral he will be directly over the place where he had originally been hiding. Then he will suddenly drop. As he descends toward the ground, he sings beautiful liquid notes. He will land exactly where he took off. This whole display is called a *roding*. The word *roding* is used only to describe the woodcock ritual but for no similar ritual by any other bird. A few minutes after the first roding, the male will repeat it all in the same way. After he has gone through a roding several times, a female will come to him and they will mate.

FIELDS AND MEADOWS

Fields and meadows often betray the first signs of the thaw. The earth has heaved, cracked, and broken in countless places. Here and there melting ice has opened wounds of water in the soil. How refreshing it is to shove one's bare hands down into the cold new muck, squeeze it, lift it, and smell the rich earth. By digging about—carefully so as not to damage accidentally an endangered plant—it is easy to find new succulent bulbs and roots, such as those of wild ginger or Indian cucumber. The bulbs of wild onions are swollen with new juices. Underground, seeds have sprouted. Roots are extending downward and shoots upward toward the surface. No matter how hopeless-looking and barren the surface of the ground may appear to be, plants have responded to the thaw and are coming to life. So it is that spring starts where one might least expect it—right underfoot.

The Appearance of Earthworms

All winter long, common earthworms (*Lumbricus terrestris*) have stayed in chambers, or *hibernacula*, deep below the frost line. Dozens may coil together to conserve moisture. The ice above them, hard as rock, holds them prisoner until the spring thaw. All the ice must melt before they can tunnel to the surface. Their appearance, some cloudy day when the weather is mild, is a sure sign that the ground has thawed even to its deepest levels.

According to tradition, some tribes of native Americans called the full moon of March the worm moon. For them the major event of March was the sight of earthworms or new trailings near their tunnels. The native Americans knew that the ground would not freeze hard again; the thaw, for the season, was irreversible. The worms coming from *below* the frost line proved the point.

Spring Azures

It is a rare March that goes by without the appearance of spring azure (*Celastrina argiolus*) butterflies. These violet-blue butterflies, also called common blues, are small and energetic. Variants may have slightly different colors, but all are bright-hued and partly iridescent. Though the spring azure is dark blue in the spring, it will become paler during the summer. The difference can be so great that it is difficult to believe they are the same butterfly. The wingspan of the spring azure is about one inch, and the coloration of both the fore and hind wings is the same.

In April the females will lay short, thick green eggs in dogwood and blue cohosh flowers. In the late spring and summer sluglike caterpillars will show up on flowers. If you look carefully, you will see that these reddish-colored caterpillars are surrounded by ants, which gather around to eat the "honeydew" secreted by these caterpillars. By September three generations of spring azures will have come and gone. By then, though, we shall probably not notice, for we shall have been saturated by the colors of so many butterflies (10,000 species are found in North America). But in March it is different: in a world devoid of almost every other butterfly, we can be delighted by the sight of the spring azure's flashing blue wings.

Skunk Cabbages

Some March day, on meadows beside a noisy ice-rimmed brook, there will appear large sprouts of green. Boldly they pierce the snow and ice that may linger on the ground. These can only be skunk cabbages (*Symplocarpus foetidus*)—unique masters of survival.

It is startling to see a plant that defies all logic by daring such a feat. Why isn't it blackened and wilted? The secret is that the flowers and their stalk, or *spadix*, can generate enough heat to melt snow and ice. The heat is produced by metabolism as oxygen is consumed within the spadix and flowers. You might be surprised to know that flowers produce heat by oxidation, when it is common knowledge that leaves give off oxygen, as they manufacture food—namely, sugars—which they make from water and carbon dioxide, using the energy of sunlight. Although leaves do give off oxygen, it is also true that in some plants the flowers absorb it to generate heat. This has

Skunk cabbage (*Symplocarpus foetidus*)

been known since the eighteenth century, when the Chevalier de Lamarck, the well-known French biologist, experimented with the metabolism of flowers. Very few flowers, of course, could melt their way through snow or ice, but the spadix of the skunk cabbage is strong and large enough to do the job—indeed, it feels much like a small pineapple, firm and tough. As the spadix grows, it is protected by a hood-shaped leaflike covering. This type of covering is known as a *spathe*. All plants with both spadix and spathe, such as skunk cabbages and jack-in-the-pulpits, are related, and termed arums. They are members of the family Araceae.

The inner parts of the spathe are reddish, and the plant has a fetid odor, whence its name. Early-appearing flies, which wake from their hibernation when the temperature goes above freezing, will visit the plant. Guided to it by the smell and red color, they no doubt mistake it for a piece of meat. As they crawl over the flowers, they pollinate them with pollen they have picked up from other skunk cabbages.

WILD, ROCKY PLACES

In March, water echoes through hidden glens; springs gush and bubble. Dark water, glistening water, transparent water slides over slabs. Drips fall everywhere from cliffs and ledges. Delicate wild flowers appear against muted gray cliffs. Deep, spongy carpets of wet moss glow in a fiery green light along ledges and on top of boulders. Lichens turn scarlet, yellow, and black on cliffs. The forbidding landscape awakens and takes on a new appearance as the spring thaw touches it.

The World of Lichens

Springtime is lichen time, when they display their best and most colorful aspects. No plants surpass their rich, strong reds, yellows, and blacks. Until the invention of synthetic dyes, the Scots used lichens to dye their tartans, famous for their extraordinary colors.

Lichens, often seen on rocks, grow only in the early spring. As they do, their colors intensify. Later, when the plants cease growing, their colors noticeably fade. Their growth, in terms of increased size, is not at all dramatic—in fact, the opposite. They are among the slowest-growing of all plants: some only grow 0.04 inches each year. In the Arctic, where lichens blanket large areas of land and are often the only plants at all, they grow at even slower rates, at times only 0.0004 inches a year. Botanists who have studied these slow-growing lichens have discovered that they are extremely old: one in particular, the **yellow map lichen** (*Rhizocarpon geographicum*), some individual plants of which have been found to be hundreds of years old. Yellow map lichen can be found in the temperate zone. It is buttercup yellow and resembles tiny pieces of irregularly shaped tiles set in mosaic patterns, which also are very irregular. In temperate regions it grows faster, and the speedier growth lessens its longevity.

Lichens are unique, for they are made up of two disparate plants, algae and fungi, which aid each other. The algae, which contain chlorophyll, produce all the food for the plant. Although the fungi make no food, for they lack chlorophyll, they repay the algae by providing a support and giving the whole plant a protective cover.

Many species of lichen form fascinating ring-shaped colonies, which puzzle many hikers. The rings are formed because a colony of lichens will grow outward in all directions at an equal rate. When a colony is old, some of the original plants at the center may die, leaving a bare spot on the rock, so a ring shape occurs.

Not all lichens grow on rocks. Many thrive on decayed wood or on the ground. One lichen found near rocky areas, especially in the dirt-filled crevices of rocks, is the **British soldier lichen** (*Cladonia cristatella*). Unlike the yellow map lichen, which cling to the rocks the way fish scales cling to a fish, the British soldier has many tiny upright stalks that are tipped with brilliant red. This lichen, named for its resemblance to the red coats of British troops, is at its very best in March.

Animals of Rocky Habitats

All winter long, animals use caves and crevices as hibernation niches. Since they stay deep in rocks, they do not freeze, and they can safely wait there until spring arrives.

Usually in March there is a warm-up. Spiders deep in a crack will move. Flies will stir, stretch their wings, and fly away, no doubt headed for a skunk cabbage. Under rocks, wood lice crawl about. Salamanders ready themselves for a journey to a pond where they will lay their eggs. Deep in caves, bats may fly about.

A queen-to-be bumblebee (genus *Bombus*) may wake up deep inside a crevice. She will clean herself by pulling her feet over her wings and antennae. Once cleaned and ready for flight, she will depart. In other crevices, wasps and hornets crawl toward the light. Hikers near a rocky area may see insects dart out of these cracks, and if they lift up rocks nearby, they will see spiders, wood lice, (or pill bugs, as they are also called), and perhaps some salamanders or snakes, which are shaking off their winter sleep.

The wood lice will crawl off some damp rainy day and find decayed leaves to eat. The snakes will wait awhile. So will the spiders, which will seek the warmth of the ground until a few weeks have passed.

LAKES, PONDS, AND WATERCOURSES

On a given lake each winter ends in its own unique way. During one year the ice may thaw and re-form several times, during another year simply turn gray and thin. During the best years, odd-shaped polygons of black water appear, one after the other, across the white lake. These start where a stream, carrying newly fallen above-freezing rainwater, shoots into the lake. The slight hint of warmth in the water is enough to erode squares, trapeziums, pentagons in random patterns. Sometimes streams flood lakes. As the water rises, ice breaks. Or the end of winter may be sudden, as a gale lashes the lake, quickly breaking up the ice, grinding it, breaking and battering it to pieces and oblivion in hours.

The Spring Overturn

By early March most lakes suffer from a condition called *winterkill,* caused by a lack of oxygen in the lake.

Winterkill comes about for two reasons. First, a lid of ice on top of a lake prevents the wind from stirring the water, and consequently no oxygen circulation takes place. When the oxygen, absorbed in the layers of water at the bottom of the lake, is depleted, it cannot be replaced by wind action.

Second, in late autumn the surface layers of the lake become cold. When they cool down to a temperature of 39.2° F (4° C), their water becomes dense and heavy and sinks to the bottom of the lake. There it will stay all winter. As the lake cools down still more, the colder, lighter water will always stay above the layer at the bottom. Even if the bottom layer cools down below 39.2° F, it will stay at the bottom as long as the water above is colder. The lightest water of all is, of course, ice, which will float on top of the lake.

Many plants, of course, grow at the bottom of a lake, where they can root themselves. When the ice forms over the lake in early winter, a great deal of light will be shut off. Many, if not all, of the plants will die and begin to rot. The process of decay calls for oxygen, and soon the bottom of the lake is partly depleted of its oxygen supply.

In March, relief will finally come to the lake. After it thaws, the surface water will warm up until it reaches a temperature of 39.2° F. Because the water at lower levels will by then be colder, the denser water in the upper layers will sink to the bottom of the lake. As it does, it will carry with it life-giving oxygen, which it has picked up from the wind. The animals—fish, frogs, insect larvae—will respond to the warmer, oxygen-rich water and resume development.

Not only will the animals benefit from the opening of ice and thaw at the surface of the lake, but so will the plants. With the ice gone, light will penetrate to the depths of the lake and the plants will start growing.

This process, whereby the oxygen-rich waters sink to the bottom, and the stagnant waters at the bottom rise to the top to be oxygenated, is called the spring *overturn*. There is an autumn overturn too. The spring overturn is, of course, the most important event during the whole year for a lake and its inhabitants.

It's fortunate for us, by the way, that ice floats. If it sank or formed on the bottom of the cold dark oceans and slowly built up to the surface, there would be no life on earth as we know it. Hundreds of millions or perhaps billions of years ago the oceans, even those in the tropics, would have been filled to the surface with ice. Life, which started in the oceans, would probably never have had a chance to get started, and our planet would, no doubt, be if not a lifeless one, at least an alien-looking one.

The Spring Peepers

It is in early March that "peeps" can be heard coming in the twilight from damp swamps, deep woodlands, and bulrushes: the unmistakable sound of the frogs *Hyla crucifer*, or spring peepers. They have emerged from a winter's hibernation under the mud at

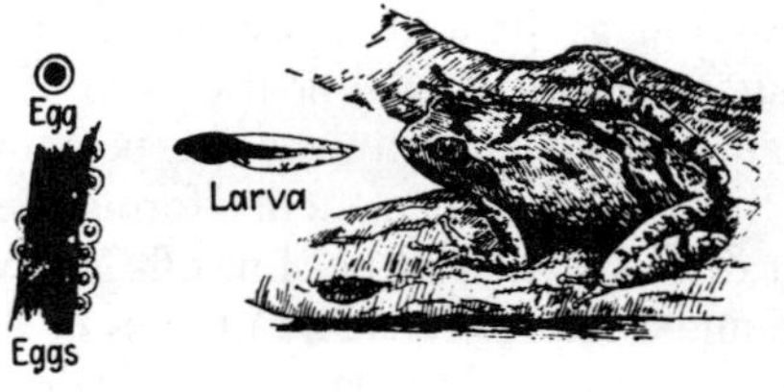

Spring peeper (*Hyla crucifer*)

the bottom of ponds. With their call, the males are urging the females to mate. These tiny green frogs, with a crude black crosslike mark on their backs, are announcing their arrival, as well as their spring urge. The call, a distinct "pee-eep," can be heard for half a mile or more—a mile if the wind is right.

Of course amphibians—and frogs are the most common of all—were the the first animals to settle on the land that rose above the surrounding seas. Some 400 million years ago, the spring peepers' amphibian ancestors, the stegocephalians, clumsily dragged their half-fishlike bodies out of the seas to become denizens of the land. Frogs date back to the Triassic Period, some 200 million years ago. Their chorus echoed in the swamps long before any dinosaurs, birds, or mammals appeared on earth. Only the buzzing of the insects predated them. Is theirs the oldest voice of all? We shall never know, but the frog's spring call is old beyond reckoning.

A spring peeper is notoriously difficult to find. In theory, you should be able to follow the sound until you are next to the frog, but with spring peepers, hunting theories break down. First of all, they are masters of concealment. They are so small—a spring peeper can sit on a postage stamp and not cover it—that they are easily overlooked, and their colors and cross-patterns make them blend into the foliage.

In early March, spring peepers stay near water, but as the weeks go by, they move farther away from it, most often climbing trees. Their toes are so sticky that spring peepers can actually climb up a vertical piece of glass. Eventually they make their way to the treetops.

A close relative is the gray tree frog (*Hyla versicolor*), which has blotches on its back. Its habits are the same as that of the peeper, but its voice is a melodious trill.

Toads

With the coming of spring, toads (family Bufonidae) dig themselves out of the ground and head for water. Like all amphibians, they must lay their eggs in water. For a toad, a trip to the nearest pond for mating is quite an adventure. That journey, even though it may be less than a mile, is a true migration; the biggest problem is to find the right direction. Experiments have shown that toads guide themselves by the sun. This may seem odd, but when one realizes that a toad is down in the grass, with no way of seeing what's ahead, one can appreciate the problem.

In the spring you may come upon a toad en route. As though governed by some great purpose, the toad will move on, filled with determination. With great effort it will make its way toward the pond, putting one clumsy foot in front of the other, waddling through grass and around logs. At one level, it is to be admired as much as a migrating bird carried aloft on streamlined wings.

Once the toads have mated and the eggs have been laid, the adults will leave the pond and go back to high ground, where they remain until the next spring arrives.

Canada Geese

In early March, a haunting sound is heard, something like a far-off barking in the air. It is not quite a barking, but neither is it a true honking. Listen and look up. There they are—the high, wobbling V of Canada geese (*Branta canadensis*) flying in an undulating formation, moving on slow wingbeats northward, "talking" all the while to one another.

It is not coincidence that they arrive just as the lakes open up. Canada geese follow the thaw. They need a place to land, to feed, and to be protected. Since waterways open up when the average temperature, for several days, reaches 35° F, the geese follow the 35° F isotherm. They begin moving with it, as it moves north, in February. By March they are in the middle Atlantic states and points west, or if the weather that year is exceptionally cold, they will wait until April. By May they will be far north on the tundra wastelands of Canada, and even crossing parts of the Arctic Ocean to nest on polar islands.

Canada geese are easily identified by their size; few birds are as large—their wingspan can be sixty-eight inches. They are the only geese that have black necks, black heads, and a white patch at the throat. Canada geese mate for life and pairs stay close to each other as much as possible.

Water Striders

In early spring, water striders (family Gerridae) slip out from under leaves and twigs at the bottom of ponds, where they have hibernated, and swim to the surface. Once there, they walk about on an invisible film of water, which appears to be such a miracle that they are sometimes called Jesus bugs. This is the same film that holds a drop of water on a faucet for a while. It is strong enough to support these lightweight insects. Helping them stay on the film are their hairy feet. If need be, for food or protection a water strider can break the surface of the film and sink into the water and can stay under for several hours. To get out again, it must climb up the branch of a water plant. Once out of the water, it must thoroughly dry off before walking across the water again.

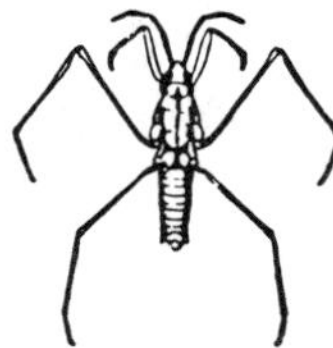

Water strider (genus *Gerris*)

Water striders have an unusual mating behavior. When males are ready to mate, they obtain small bits of wood, which will later be used as platforms for the eggs of the female. Once a male has a piece of wood, he remains next to it and signals to a female by vibrating the water surface in a particular rhythm with his foot. A female will go to the male and mate with him. Immediately afterward she will lay her eggs on the wood.

Whirligig Beetles

As anyone who has spent much time swimming will know, our eyes are poorly designed for seeing underwater, and the same holds true of most land animals.Conversely, fish cannot see very well in the air. Very few eyes work well in both environments. The real solution would be to have four eyes: two for seeing in the air and two for seeing underwater. "But, of course, no such creature exists," or so we might say.

The whirligig beetle (family Gyrinidae) is such a creature. This tiny black insect, which lives on the surface of the water of ponds, sees what is going on in the air above with the upper half of its two eyes and what is going on down below in the water with the lower half of these eyes. The two eyes are divided from each other, so that, for all practical purposes, the whirligig beetle has four eyes.

The name is well deserved, for whenever whirligig beetles move they go around and around, this way and that, on the surface of the water. A group of them looks like small, polished black beans, all in motion. Experiments have shown that no matter how close one beetle comes to another, it will not bump into it. That is saying a great deal, for groups of them make thousands of near-misses all day. But whirligig beetles avoid each other by means of a special sense organ that detects water vibrations. Just as they are about to collide, they feel the impact coming by way of water disturbances, and slip away.

Whirligig beetles spend most of their time on the surface of the water. They are hunters, always on the lookout for either insect larvae or dead insects. If threatened by an enemy, they will dive deep into the water. In addition to being good surface swimmers and divers, they are also good fliers, one of the few creatures able to move on the water's surface, in its depths, and in the air.

Redwing Blackbirds

Defiant of all March weather, redwings (*Agelaius phoeniceus*) often arrive with snow, sleet, or raw winds. Once it claims its domain, can spring be far behind? "Konk-ka-ree," it cries, a somewhat ugly sound for a beautiful moment.

The males, with bright red patches on their shiny black wings, arrive first, staking out breeding territories for their mates-to-be, who are waiting farther south for better weather.

As so often happens in the avian world, beauty is the province of the males. Beginning bird-watchers can hardly believe that the drab, large sparrow-looking (but not related) birds that appear a few weeks later can possibly be mates of those marvelous males. There is surely no American bird-watcher who has not stumbled over this identification a couple of times.

"Why is there such a difference between them?" one might ask. The drab colors will protect the female when she sits quietly on her nest, hatching the eggs. The bright colors will help the male signal to other redwings that he has claimed a nesting territory.

CELESTIAL EVENT

The Spring, or Vernal, Equinox

From the first day of our autumn to the first day of our spring, the sun is south of the equator, but on or about March 21 it crosses this "line." At this moment spring begins.

This is when the spring, or vernal, equinox takes place. *Equinox* is a Latin word meaning "equal night." It means that the length of the night equals the length of the day everywhere on earth. On all other days of the year, except the day of the autumn equinox, when the sun again crosses the equator, the days and nights are unequal in length. This is also the day when the sun rises due East and sets due West everywhere on earth.

In the Northeast we see a profound change in many plants and animals. Right after the equinox, wild flowers rapidly begin to bloom. Waves of migrating birds begin to arrive. The Northeast seems ideally suited for observation of these phenomena. Spring in the tropics brings with it few significant changes, aside from changes in rainfall. Spring comes late to the Arctic. But we in the Northeast, in the temperate zone, see a near-immediate correlation between what is happening above in the sky and here on earth.

April

If there is a recurring image in April in most of the Northeast, it is the greening of the trees. There is a time—a few days, even a few hours—in April when a haze of pale green suffuses woodlands. The light purples seen on winter branches wane, while the greens of spring take over. A delicate balance is reached wherein an unusual color, part purple, part green, and as fine as mist, is formed.

During the month of April, people who live in mountain valleys may see a curious sight. If they are so located in a valley that they have a long view both downstream and upstream, it is possible for them to watch the greening of the trees actually progress up the valley, hour by hour. The temperature difference, due to the altitude, is enough to make the difference. Moment by moment one tree, then another will turn green and hazy. The green ascends the valley, bringing April with it.

WOODLANDS

Because of the changes taking place within the woodlands, one is drawn into them. From treetops with new canopies of rustling leaves to the floor of a forest there are new signs of spring. White, many-petaled bloodroots bloom; so do the odd purple-brown flowers of wild ginger. And nothing attracts one's attention the way the new leaves of the forest do.

The Growth of Leaves

Everywhere there are leaves appearing—not only that, they come from various sizes and shapes of bud. The leaves themselves arrive in endless patterns. There are the lance-shaped willow leaves, the deeply lobed oak leaves, the mitten-shaped sassafras leaves, the triangular leaves of gray birches, and many more. One might easily wonder how all these various shapes come into being.

Until very recently, botanists thought that all leaves, whether in buds or out of buds, grew and shaped themselves only in one way, by adding cells along the edges and, especially, at the tips. However, recent evidence gathered by Donald R. Kaplan has shown that the growth of leaves is far more complicated than anyone had imagined.

As described in the July 1983 issue of *Scientific American*, Kaplan, a professor of botany at the University of California, Berkeley, and his associates used palm leaves, the largest in the plant kingdom, to see how leaves really grow. Any changes that took place within them would be magnified because of their size. As expected, the researchers found leaf growth to be marginal, with growth moving outward evenly along the edges at a steady rate. But they also found that many cells grow at different rates, especially in the interior of the leaf. This finding was unexpected. They discovered that some areas, deep within the leaf, grew in programmed spurts to form the nodules that later developed into palm fronds. Then, using philodendron leaves, Kaplan found out, to his surprise, that holes in those leaves were made because whole groups of cells in the interior of the leaf died away. In other words, some interior leaf cells were genetically programmed to die at certain times to form the holes, while other cells within the leaf thrived and multiplied; the final shape was reached by subtraction as well as addition.

It is now known that the leaves you see in the spring, with all their various patterns, were shaped by some cells growing more rapidly than others in various parts of the leaves. Researchers will continue to investigate more complicated leaves of all regions of the world to see if they are also formed by sacrificing cells during growth.

Each leaf we see is sculpted by natural forces that direct cellular growth in a most amazing way. In countless forests of trees, leaf cells grow and die, each driven and guided by coded programs inherited from an ancestor. Not one leaf seen in all of spring is arbitrary in design. Each has been shaped and molded more carefully than the most delicate man-made creation.

Black Bears

In the spring, bear cubs and their mothers are out and about. In April the cubs have reached the age where they playfully tease each other, roughhouse, wrestle, tumble, go on short exploration trips, and exuberantly carry on as mischievously as possible. At times, mothers whose nerves become frayed give the cubs a good whack. At other times, mothers dote on the cubs and watch them zealously. Mother bears can then be very dangerous, and one must be wary of them. If a mother bear thinks that someone is threatening her cubs—even if this is not true—she will attack. Males, however, attack only under the most extraordinary of circumstances.

Black bears (*Ursus americanus*) live solitary lives. In their constant search for food—and the large beasts need plenty of food—they move over wooded and remote mountainous and northern regions of the countryside in unpredictable directions. As a bear travels on foot, it walks with a peculiar rolling gait. Unlike most other four-legged mammals, which walk on their toes, bears walk on the flat soles of their feet. This gives them an awkward-appearing gait. Though the gait appears awkward, it is not, for a bear can amble on tirelessly. A bear can, and often will, cover thousands of zigzag miles in a year.

Possessing a great curiosity, bears look into everything, often exploring campsites. At times they mess things up: if they happen upon an unknown package hanging from a tree, they will attempt to get it. Young, slim bears can climb up trees to get packages, but most older bears are too fat. Things such as knapsacks lying in full view on the ground, will, however, usually not awaken a bear's curiosity. It will often leave them untouched.

Adult bears almost never have anything to do with each other, aside from their necessary June mating. During the breeding season a male will solicitously follow a female for days. He will lick her and nuzzle her. As she comes into heat she will respond to his attentions.

Sometimes the two will stand up and hug each other, each licking the other's face. After they mate, they separate. Evidently they completely ignore each other from then on. Even if they meet, they act as though they had never seen each other before.

Violets

April is a month of violets (genus *Viola*). Many species, of many colors, dot the meadows, the wild, rocky places, and the woodlands. The common violet-blue violets are among the best known of all wild flowers. For daintiness, richness of color, and full perfume, violets seem unequaled.

Oddly enough, most people who know very well what a violet looks like are unaware of the fact that the **common blue violet** (*Viola papilionacea*) actually bears two types of flowers on one plant. The first is the familiar blue flower. The second type is easily overlooked because it is much smaller and is hidden down in the leaves. This is a peculiar type of flower, which is self-fertilized by pollen from its own anthers in the bud before the flower ever opens. Botanists call it a *cleistogamous flower*. The seeds for the next year's violets are produced by it—not by the showy blue flower that catches our eyes. When the cleistogamous flower opens, it will lack petals.

Magnolias

April is best marked by magnolia blooms—those large, gaudy flowers that more than any others tell us that spring is at hand.

Magnolias (family Magnoliaceae), peculiarly, seem to change with the changing light. When the sun is at its highest, there is a blanched look to them, like a film that has been overexposed, until the details are lost. Similarly, their beauty is diminished in the light of dawn or dusk. Then their unbelievable whiteness turns ghostlike, for the whiteness is so intense that it has carrying power even through crepuscular light, and they look eerie and surrealistic. Only on a gloomy overcast day, remarkably enough, do magnolias seem like real flowers on real trees. Only then can one comfortably see the interior details of the flowers without being distracted by the intense white.

Magnolias have come down to us almost unchanged from prehistoric times. About 100 million years ago, during the Cretaceous

Period, they grew in forests where dinosaurs roamed. Magnolia flowers evolved from leaves and were among the very first flowers to do so. Other primal flowers have changed extensively, but not the magnolias. Fossils show that they have survived unchanged down to the present time, as true living fossils. It is fitting that this oldest of all flowers greets us early in the spring.

Red Squirrels

If one takes a walk through a conifer forest, looking for spring flowers, one will, sooner or later, be scolded by a red squirrel (*Tamiasciurus hudsonicus*). Of all the mammals of the northeastern forests, this is the boldest, most impudent, and most vociferous of all. Frequently a squirrel becomes so excited that it will bang its paw and wag its tail.

Red squirrel (*Tamiasciurus hudsonicus*)

Most animals of the woods survive by stealth and silence; many stay hidden much of the time—but not the red squirrel. It seems to glory in its visibility and is willing to chatter endlessly. Apparently the red squirrel survives by quickness and intelligence. Red squirrels are known to scout out their forest territory and test every escape route up trees, down branches, and, most of all, across the yawning gap between trees. If an enemy appears, the red squirrel is off and running. Up a tree it will dart, down a branch, and then with a great leap it will land on a branch that it has pretested. Because of such forethought, a squirrel can keep out of the clutches of its enemies, at least most of the time.

Although it can outwit four-legged pursuers by scampering up trees and leaping from branch to branch, the red squirrel adopts other strategies for dealing with hawks. When a hawk plunges, the squirrel will delay its escape until the last moment, just before the talons strike. Then when all appears hopeless, it will swing under the branch it is on and scamper away upside down. Realizing that it has missed, the hawk will circle around again. By then the squirrel is spiraling at high speed around the tree trunk, outdistancing the hawk, which must describe a much greater circumference. Occasionally a hawk will nab a red squirrel, but most of the time the squirrel will escape. With such skills red squirrels can enjoy the luxury of staying visible and being vociferous. Few rodents have such privileges.

It is in April or May and often again in August or September that the young red squirrels are born in nests located in holes in trees. At first they are blind and naked, but in about sixteen days a fine fur covers them. All during the summer their mother will nurse them. If she moves them from one place to another, she will carry them in her mouth in an unusual way, by the skin of their bellies. This gives the upside-down young a chance to grasp its mother by its forefeet and tail. The young make a "churring" sound if they are disturbed in their nests.

Though red squirrels prefer nests in the holes of trees for raising families, they also make two other types of nest: under tree roots or under rocks. To keep warm, they will line their nests with leaves, lichen, or found scraps of rabbit or deer fur. The nests that most strollers in a forest would first see are those that are built in the forks of tree branches. From the ground they appear to be nothing more or less than a large bundle of leaves, precariously stacked together. Actually, they are far better made than they appear. To begin with, each nest has two entrances: the primary one, which is always open, and a back exit, which is blocked with lightweight materials that suffice to keep out the wind and hide the exit. If an intruder pokes its nose in the main entrance, the squirrels inside the nest can burst through the walls of the exit and escape.

The squirrel's fluffy tail serves many useful purposes. When a red squirrel jumps from tree to tree, the tail acts much like an airplane rudder, directing the right and left motion of the red squirrel in midair. In case the animal falls, it acts as a parachute. Witnesses have seen red squirrels fall fifty feet with no sign of damage. Not that they always come out of such a fall in one piece: if things go wrong, a lesser fall may prove fatal. In the wintertime the red squirrel sits out an exceptionally cold day in its nest and the tail acts as a handy blanket.

During the year the fur and looks of a red squirrel change. During the warmer months of the year the fur is reddish on the upper parts of its body and almost white on the lower parts. When you are then trying to identify a red squirrel, it is best to look for a horizontal black band on its side; gray squirrels, which can be confused with red squirrels, do not have those bands. During the colder months of the year the fur turns grayer and the band is lost, but the red squirrel will now have prominent tufts on its ears. In distinguishing the two species, the best guide is their behavior. Red squirrels are far more nervous, and vociferous, than the more sluggish gray squirrels.

Whenever you visit the woodlands, especially those that contain conifers, such as pines, look for a red squirrel midden. This is a pile of dropped pine cones, cuttings, and other debris left from meals. A midden will be found under a tree branch where a red squirrel habitually eats its meals. Because it returns time and again to this favorite spot, the trash from its meals gathers in a pile on the ground. Many middens are so large that they could fill several bushel baskets. Once you have found a midden, you will know where you can see a red squirrel. Sooner or later it will return.

Broad-Winged Hawks

In April a sound that has not been heard since September echoes once more through the woodlands. It is a sharp "pee-weeeee" that comes not from the trees but from the sky above, for it is the call of the broad-winged hawk (*Buteo platypterus*). One of the earliest migrants of the year, it is returning to the Northeast. Slowly it circles above, moving each day farther north.

No other bird of prey is more a denizen of the deep silent forests. It is a daylight hunter that, more often than not, hunts by patiently waiting for prey. An observant visitor may note one sitting so silently on a tree branch as to appear asleep or dazed. Neither is the case. The hawk is alert as can be and is using its stillness and silence as a tactic. Most animals, including humans, can easily perceive a motion from the corner of the eye. When animals see no motion at all, they often make the mistake of believing that they are safe. The broad-winged hawk takes advantage of this error. Its prey, such as mice, insects, small snakes, or salamanders, seeing nothing move, will themselves make a move or begin to dash across the forest floor. Then it is too late. With terrific speed the broad-winged hawk launches itself and pounces on the animal.

In spite of this *modus operandi*, the broad-winged hawk spends much of its time circling high above the woodlands. In flight it is rather easy to identify. In April only adult broad-winged hawks are seen, with their black tails bearing two distinct white bands on the top sides. As the name implies, the wings are broad. Broad-winged hawks have the habit of circling very high into the air. They may fly so high as to be mere moving dots against the blue, even soaring upward until out of sight.

Even though the broad-winged hawks arrive in April, the females do not lay their eggs until May. Their nests are often located about twenty feet above the ground. Once the young are hatched, both parents assume responsibility for defense. If an intruder approaches, the hawks make a most peculiar sound, which by coincidence could easily be mistaken for the noise made by a tree as it creaks in the wind.

Bumblebees

Be sure to look for bumblebees (genus *Bombus*) in April. They are the largest and hairiest bees you will see. Their flight is relatively clumsy. Honeybees, which might be mistaken for them, are smaller, more slender, and their flight less clumsy. It should be mentioned, in passing, that bumblebees are native American bees, whereas honeybees were brought here from the Old World.

In the autumn, queen bumblebees are fertilized by males, but will not lay eggs until the next spring. With the onset of cold weather, queens enter special burrows, *hibernacula,* in the ground, where they will hibernate throughout the winter.

In April, queens leave these hibernacula to search for a place to start a colony. This will be a burrow in the ground, usually one abandoned by mice. Using old nesting materials also abandoned by the mice, she will pull off little bits of soft material for a nest and generally will fashion a new entrance into the burrow.

An observer in the woods, or in orchards and fallow fields, for that matter, will probably see the zigzag movements of the large queens moving back and forth close to the ground. This is the typical flight of a bumblebee queen searching for a burrow, seen only in April.

The queen will tend to another matter as well: she must collect pollen, and to do so, she will visit flowers. Queens will take the pollen back to the nest. There she will exude a wax from intersegmental glands on her abdomen. With it she will form a hollow cup. She will place pollen in the cup along with eight to fourteen eggs and seal the cup with more wax. At about the same time she will make a wax honey pot and fill it with honey from nectar gathered from flowers. This is the last chance to see a bumblebee queen until autumn. As soon as the eggs hatch, workers will be available to the queen. From then on, the queen will remain in the nest, out of sight, and the workers alone will appear in the countryside.

In autumn a change takes place in the colony. The colony begins to produce only queens and males. The males disperse widely and wait for new queens to emerge. The waiting habits of these drone males differ from species to species. Some hover near the entrance to the colony; they may fly back and forth for hours, even days, as they wait. Others wait farther away on branches of trees and shrubs or on fence posts.

When the queens emerge, the males mate with them. After mating, the queens will fly off and make hibernacula, and the whole yearly cycle will repeat.

The behavior pattern of the bumblebees fits in with the seasonal climate of the Northeast, with its warm summers and cold winters. Bees originated in tropical climates and migrated into the northern regions, while evolving species and behavioral patterns that allowed them to survive the winters. Of all the bees, the bumblebees are by far the most successful in adapting to cold winters. Two species of bumblebees even thrive on Ellesmere Island in the Arctic Ocean—a long way in time and space from the tropical lands where bees first appeared on earth.

FIELDS AND MEADOWS

In April we feel that the great wheel of the year has definitely turned and that a significant change has come to the land. Even with our eyes closed, we can feel and comprehend the April mood. This is especially so in the fields and meadows where the sun and wind have free play. New perfumes rise in the air and the light, as strong as in August, gives a fresh look to everything. The wind moving over the fields no longer feels icy cold. Instead, it carries a cool dampness, and perhaps the odor of distant rain.

Wolf Spiders

Before grasses and other plants become so high that they hide the ground from view, one can see wolf spiders (family Lycosidae) in action, running here and there over the ground. These well-named spiders mimic wolves in their hunting techniques. Unlike most other spiders, which wait passively for victims to be ensnared by their webs, the wolf spiders are actively on the prowl, searching for meals with their keen eyesight. Interestingly, they use several techniques while hunting for prey. A spider may wait in ambush and pounce on a passing victim, or stay in the open and run an insect down. It is surprising that an animal with such a small brain would be capable of such diverse hunting techniques. Most animals of its size have very rigid behavioral patterns, limiting them to one hunting technique, which they must use over and over again.

There are over one hundred species of wolf spider found north of Mexico. They all have stout, long legs and are gray or brown in color, but the best way of identifying them is by their actions.

Female wolf spiders often carry three dozen or more young on their backs. Even while mother hunts, the young go along. If a spiderling crawls over its mother's eye, she will brush it aside. If one falls off, it will crawl back up its mother's leg.

Meadow Mice

The meadow mice (*Microtus pennsylvanicus*), despite their name, are actually voles. Voles have shorter ears and tails than mice.

Meadow mice could be called the "hidden ones." For an animal that is so common and so widespread, it is not often seen. This is remarkable, for it is estimated that the average field, meadow, orchard, or cultivated land has 30 mice per acre. During a plague one field is known to have had 12,000 mice per acre!

Meadow mice are among the very few animals that have benefited from the coming of the Europeans. Meadow mice were previously restricted to meadows created when beavers cut down trees, producing grassy clearings. Unfortunately for the mice, these beaver-produced meadows were short-lived, for in a few years trees filled them up again. Once that happened, the only hope of the mice was that a few survivors could travel through the huge surrounding forests and find a newly made clearing that was not already full of mice. The chances of survival were very slim. To adapt to such a situation, the mice relied upon their extraordinary rate of reproduction. Therefore, as settlers cleared the forests for meadows, the meadow mouse population skyrocketed.

Meadow mice face spring in far better shape than most animals. Unlike almost all others, they thrive during the winter (See "Mice of the Fields," in December) because they are experts at hiding food in underground caches. In the autumn they make sure that their supplies will get them through winter. During the winter these rodents, which are hunted by every carnivore large enough to kill them, can then remain hidden. They do so by making tunnellike paths through the snow from food cache to food cache. Each individual mouse makes its own path. As winter progresses, thousands of paths are developed under the snow, crisscrossing every which way.

In April, after the snows have gone, someone walking in a meadow can easily find the little paths, which are exposed early in the month, where mice compacted the soil and grass. If you follow one, you will see where the mouse hid its food: at its cache there are often chewed branches and cut vegetation. If you are lucky, you will find a path leading to a mouse's winter nest, which is made of grass and roofed over.

In the springtime, mice make another type of nest. Instead of being above ground, it is built in a burrow and lined with grass, to make it warm and comfortable. Females give birth in the springtime, and before the cold weather returns a female might give birth to a hundred young.

Killdeers

Though killdeers (*Charadrius vociferus*) are wild, they are often seen on golf courses and in gardens. More frequently they are seen following plows as farmers work in their fields during April. Technically speaking, killdeers are plovers, which are shorebirds, but they are as likely to be found inland as at the seashore. They received their odd name from their cry, which goes "kill-dee, kill-dee." There is a piercing, plaintive quality to this cry, accented by persistent repetition. They often cry out as they move back and forth in flocks across grassy flatlands in search of insects, earthworms, or other small animals. Often they all move together, or stop together, in a nervous, restless manner. To an observer the birds often appear to be ill at ease.

Killdeer (*Charadrius vociferus*)

Killdeers are identified by the two distinct black bands across their chests.

In the Northeast, killdeers breed in April. The females do not construct nests but lay their eggs in slight depressions hollowed in the ground. The mottles and dots on the eggs mimic gravel so amazingly well that it is exceptionally hard to see the egg of the killdeer.

The actions of a nesting killdeer can be most disturbing to a naïve observer who happens upon a nesting site. The female will suddenly lurch forward with a cry, dragging a "broken" wing on the ground. Staggering away from the nest, she will pant, and if that is not enough to deter the observer, she may roll over on her back.

While the female is going through her histrionics, the male circles above, darting here and there with loud cries. It is a marvelous act and no doubt succeeds most of the time in drawing intruders away from the eggs.

Each bird and animal has its own best hour for being seen. The lighting and mood of a scene gives a setting to the qualities of a creature, who in turn partakes of the mood. Of course, that is a human reaction, but that is the point for an observer. The time for the killdeer is just after sunset, when the last fiery clouds of a dimming sky burn again in watery reflections, and the air fills with their haunting, piercing cries.

Red Foxes

Red foxes (*Vulpes fulva*) mostly live and hunt in the countryside where there are mixed woodlands and fields. Because much farmland is like this, they are frequently found in rural country areas dotted with farms. These foxes most often prowl the border between woods and open fields. Often, as they hunt, they stay partly or totally hidden among trees or thickets or behind stone walls. Such cover not only protects them from enemies, mostly humans, but allows them the opportunity to stay hidden from view while with keen eyes they search open fields for prey, usually mice. Once a fox sees a mouse in a field, it stalks it, pounces, and then kills it. Foxes may also catch rabbits or birds, may eat fruit and vegetables, and will not stop at eating carrion. Though red foxes may be seen hunting in the daylight, they do most of their hunting at night.

Red foxes mate in January and March. In March or early April, fifty-one days after she has mated, a female will give birth to four to ten young inside of a den, which has usually been made by some other animal. Though foxes are solitary animals most of the year, having little or nothing to do with one another, a male and female, both strictly monogamous, stay with each other from the breeding season until the pups are on their own.

While the mother stays with her young in the den, the father hunts for his family, bringing back food for them. If an enemy threatens the den, the male will carefully lead it away from mother and young. The male, exposed to the full view of his enemy, will move away from the den and let the predator pursue him. He does this even if it leads to his own death—a not uncommon occurrence.

WILD, ROCKY PLACES

Spring comes slowly to wild, rocky places. Cracks and glens stay in deep shadow, where the sun has no chance to bring its warmth. Snow often lingers there long after it has disappeared from the rest of the land. Moreover, rocks, being poor insulators, quickly lose to the night air whatever heat they may have gained during the day.

The joy of rocky landscape in April is the gushing water. Down through the narrow gorges flow roaring, fuming, splashing cascades. With the water comes an all-pervading smell of wet moss, of decaying wood, of ferns, and now and then the perfume of the trailing arbutus flowers. Tiny Canada mayflowers bloom. Rich purple colors enrich partridgeberry leaves.

Birches

Not many trees can survive in rocky areas, where their roots will be constricted and where soil is found solely in deep crevices. Yet among those trees that do have the right sort of roots are two species of birch: the **gray** (*Betula populifolia*) and **yellow birches** (*Betula alleghaniensis*).

Gray birches are small trees, rarely growing more than thirty feet in height. From a distance the bark of a mature tree looks much the same as the chalky-white bark of the **paper birch** (*Betula papyrifera*), also called the canoe birch. Standing half hidden by tall shadowy cliffs, the pale birch is a startling sight. In April, catkins decorate the gray birch, providing a greenish, mustard-yellow color, all dotted with brownish red.

Catkins, in spite of their appearance, happen to be true flowers. The petals are much reduced, and the catkins are dry and chaffy. They possess male parts: stamens, which produce pollen. Decorative catkins appear on many types of shrubs and trees, among them birches, willows, poplars, and alders.

Botanists long thought that catkin-bearing shrubs and trees were primitive plants and that catkins were more or less ancient flowers, but they have changed their opinion. Today it is believed that catkins evolved from rather advanced flowers that had ordinary-looking largish petals, which became reduced so as not to interfere with wind-blown pollen.

The slightest breath of air sets birch catkins swaying back and forth in a lively fashion. When you get close to a birch, you will note that the tree not only has long catkins, but also green cones, which are much smaller than the catkins. A birch cone is called a *strobile*, but is not quite like the cones found on conifers. When it matures, it falls apart. A birch has catkins—male flowers that produce pollen—and strobiles—female flowers that collect pollen and produce seeds. In the far-off winter the seeds will scatter across the white snow.

More interesting in many respects is the yellow birch (*Betula alleghaniensis*), which can easily be identified because its bark peelings are always either a silvery bronze or a golden yellow. Strips of bark readily peel from the tree. Campers find them useful, for they are so flammable that they serve as tinder and will catch on fire even when wet.

A yellow birch is a more finicky tree than the gray birch, which grows with a weedy vigor, even in urban vacant lots. At maturity a yellow birch can be far larger, sometimes topping out at a height of eighty feet. Most intriguing about the yellow birch are its roots, which often bulge here and there like long, muscular snakes among the rocks, seeking deep crevices at one point, slithering over barren rocks at another, clinging like lions' claws to cliffs at yet another. Those roots appear to have a life of their own, wiggling, snooping, poking, searching, holding, grasping, obtaining moisture from the most unlikely-looking cracks.

Saxifrages

Saxifrage is the name of a flower family (Saxifragaceae), and there are many species. The Latin word *saxifrage* means "rock breaker." There is some question why they got their name, but most likely it was because they grow in rocky areas, where their roots can actually split apart rocks. Saxifrage flowers most often bloom on tall, slender spikes, each flower being connected to the spike by means of a short stem. Such an arrangement is called a *raceme*. Most wild saxifrages have leaves growing only at the base of the plant. In wild, rocky places, saxifrages line long, narrow crevices in the rock. Their tiny flowers tremble on their stalks like white motes in the air.

In April, dainty white saxifrages called foamflowers (*Tiarella cordifolia*) are found in mountainous areas. The single plants have delicate shapes, but large masses of them produce whole dancing white areas. Their name suits them, for one can easily imagine that the flowers are flecks of foam dashed up from rocks.

No plants could demolish mountains or hills the way running water or freezing ice can. Nevertheless, lichens, saxifrages, and other plants do loosen stones. As delicate and dainty as they look, they play their part in the changing of rock to soil.

White-Footed Mice

The mice most commonly seen in wild, rocky places are the white-footed or deer mice (genus *Peromyscus*).These should not be confused with the common house mice, for their habits and looks are entirely different. One thing that sets white-footed mice apart from house mice is that their cleanliness is of paramount concern and they spend much of their time washing, combing their fur with their claws, and grooming themselves.

Moreover, their looks differ from those of the house mice. These mice are immediately seen to be more intelligent and more interesting. Their coloration is also different: the upper parts of their bodies are gray, brown, or golden-brown, whereas the underparts are white.

Although white-footed mice often live in hollow trees and under logs, they are equally at home in rock crevices, where they nest. They are among the few mammals of any sort that live most of their lives in wild, rocky areas of the Northeast. Stone is so cold and conducts heat away from the warm bodies of mice so quickly and efficiently that, to live in rock crevices, the mice must construct heavily insulated nests. This they do by packing leaves and shredded bark into the crevices and forming a comfortable warm hole within the nest. By taking advantage of the rock structures, they can have rainproof and windproof homes.

White-footed mice eat a wide variety of food: seeds, insects, berries, and occasionally carrion. As they go about their daily activities, they are fascinating to watch. Because they do not hibernate, they gather seeds and hide them. Even in the spring and summer they appear to be working with some plan in mind, as though everything were important.

Unlike house mice, which often walk, white-footed mice progress either by running or by means of leaps and bounds. Curious as it may seem, they can sing. Sometimes they make a buzzing sound that is easy to mistake for the buzzing of an insect. At other times they may squeak. If a white-footed mouse is startled, it may drum the ground with its forefeet.

White-footed mice are an important link in the food chain of wild, rocky places. They harvest seeds and berries and eat some of the insects found in those places; in turn they are prey for snakes, hawks, ermines, and other carnivores.

Rattlesnakes and Copperhead Snakes

In April a stirring takes place deep within the rocks. Timber rattlesnakes (*Crotalus horridus*), which have been entwined together all winter in their hibernacula, awaken from their hibernation. Finally the warmth of a new season, transmitted through solid rock, has reached them. Lethargically at first, they move with a strange stiffness. In slow motion, the snakes writhe and unwind themselves from their companions and struggle out to south-facing ledges near the entrances to the crevices containing the hibernacula. There they lie to soak up the warm rays of the sun.

Not far away, in other crevices, copperheads (*Agkistrodon contortrix*) also wake up and make their way out into the open. Occasionally both types of poisonous snake will have spent the winter together wrapped up in each other's coils. Even more surprising, they may at times hibernate with chipmunks. In hibernation, snakes are too stuporous from the cold to attack a rodent. Consequently a chipmunk is as safe as if it were sleeping next to its mother.

Snakes are exquisitely temperature-sensitive. The slightest chill in the air will send them back to the comfort of their hibernacula. On the other hand, a rise in temperature will fill their bodies with vitality. For days, perhaps weeks, they alternately advance out from and retreat back into rock crevices as the temperature dictates. During these successive advances and retreats they will not eat—just to be awake is enough.

At some point, when the weather has been warm for several days running, they will begin to feel hungry. When they become interested in food, the rattlesnakes and copperheads separate. The rattlers remain in the wild, rocky places all their lives. The copperheads, however, wander away, seeking the fields, swamps, and woods. Some will travel many miles and not return until the cool weather or autumn drives them back to rocky areas once more.

Both rattlesnakes and copperheads are pit vipers, so named for the pit located between nostril and eye on each side of the head. The pit is not just a mere depression: it is a specialized sensory organ. With it a snake can apparently "see" some sort of heat image. In the pit organ is a very thin membrane, the back of which bears numerous nerve endings that detect subtle temperature differences on the membrane. It is so sensitive that it can detect a heat difference of only 5/1,000 of a degree Celsius. No other animal in the world is capable of detecting such a slight temperature difference.

In essence, these pits serve as infrared eyes. Infrared waves lie just outside the visible spectrum of light (to humans) at its red end. Infrared radiation produces heat. We can feel infrared radiation from a hot iron, especially when it is just about to glow red. Because they possess pit organs, rattlesnakes and copperheads can "see" a mouse six inches away, perceiving it as a warm mouse shape against a background that is cooler than the mouse. Interestingly, the pit organs also allow the snakes to "see" cold-blooded animals. A cold, wet frog appears as a cold shape against an evenly heated warm background. Of course, it is only anthropomorphizing to speak of what the snakes "see." In actuality, no one can describe exactly what they see or experience, for we have no sense organ quite like this.

Rattlesnakes and copperheads are both poisonous. Of the two, the rattlesnake is both larger and more poisonous. Some large rattlesnakes may exceed six feet in length, although the majority are far smaller. Rattlesnakes and copperheads can be identified by their eyes, which have vertically elliptical pupils, their wide heads, their pits. Rattlesnakes, of course, can be identified by their rattles, located at the end of their tail.

Rattlesnakes strike when their bodies assume an S-shaped position. Their upper jaws possess fangs connected by ducts to glands containing poison. When the rattler strikes, it rotates its fangs down from a position where they are folded against the roof of the mouth until they are at right angles to its head. It grasps the victim's flesh with its lower jaw and pushes its mouth closed, driving the fangs into the flesh. Simultaneously the poison is forced through the ducts into the victim. To release itself, the snake relaxes all the muscles in its head. The whole process takes place in a wink of time.

Although a rattlesnake can kill a full-grown human being, the odds are against this. Someone who receives medical treatment has only one chance in thirty of dying. Even without treatment, the risk of death is not great, approaching one in eight. More people in America die from insect and spider bites than from snake bites.

Copperheads are more sluggish than rattlesnakes, and fewer people are ever bitten by them. They strike much as rattlesnakes do. Though its venom is like that of a rattler's, a copperhead injects less into its victim. In that sense, it is not such a dangerous snake. On the other hand, a copperhead stays well hidden in grass and leaves and never gives a warning before it strikes.

Few animals, in fact, are so well camouflaged. If seen on a paved road, the markings, which are like a series of black hourglasses, and its pink, brown, or copper-colored head are clearly seen. Once the snake gets into leafy debris, it disappears. Its ability along these lines inspired people in the North during the Civil War to call Southern sympathizers "copperheads," for they could, according to their detractors, remain hidden within the general population, increasing their deadliness.

Both rattlesnakes and copperheads are now endangered in the Northeast. As their habitats are destroyed, more die; furthermore, both, especially the rattlesnake, have been hunted almost to extinction. Nevertheless, some do remain in the wilder, rocky areas far from human habitation.

LAKES, PONDS, AND WATERCOURSES

In contrast to the greening of the world of trees and meadows around them, ponds and lakes appear lifeless in April. Appearances, however, are deceptive. In reality, pond water now teems with life. Every second of the day new algae, new bacteria, and new protozoan cells divide and form new cells, new lives. Though the casual observer will not see any of this, those equipped with microscopes and the skill to use them can experience this drama, as countless single-celled plants divide and reproduce and daughter cells break away and become the prey of microscopic creatures, such as stentors and paramecia. These, in turn, will be consumed by barely visible animals, such as hydras, copepods, and small insect larvae. Finally, this invisible chain will be consummated in the ponds and streams themselves by lean, winter-hungry fish.

Muskrats

By looking along the shores of April ponds, you will have a good chance to see some muskrats (*Ondatra zibethicus*). In April muskrats, eager for fresh plants, often hunt along shores for succulent roots of various plants, especially cattails. Because plants are leafless then, muskrats on or near dry land lack good hiding places and consequently become exposed to view.

Muskrat (*Ondatra zibethicus*)

At other times you might come upon a small pile of mussel shells, left on shore by muskrats. Any pile of shells might be a place where muskrats feed. They like mussels, but the strong shells give them trouble. It is very difficult for them to open up a shell, for the strong muscles of the living animal keep it shut. Muskrats overcome this problem by leaving the living mussel on the shore until it dies, the muscles relax, and the shell pops open. Muskrats can then enjoy their meal without any effort. Since muskrats return to their favorite eating spots, a stroller seeing a pile of shells should take note of it. Perhaps by waiting in a hidden location, you can see a muskrat come ashore with a new mussel.

A frightened muskrat heads for the water and dives in head first, even in shallow water. It propels itself through the water with its back feet, which are webbed, and uses its tail as a rudder.

Although a muskrat's life is always filled with turmoil and danger, no month carries more risk than April. Spring floods sweep many away, and unlikely as it may seem, many drown. With their lodges no longer protected by ice, year-round predators can capture them more easily. Also many hawks move in from the south and snakes become active.

During autumn and early winter, each muskrat finds its place within a social hierarchy and within the territory. Competition ceases in the dead of winter, but with the arrival of young in the spring, new adjustments must take place. No muskrat gives up his or her position without a fight. Fierce territorial battles ensue as females force excess males and females out. During April, squabbles among the muskrats rarely cease. There are forced entries, trespasses, constant evictions and takeovers. Though they put up a struggle, the old and weak are shoved aside. It gets to the point that, from sheer stress alone, many females flee and abandon their young. Few muskrats survive without scars. In the spring it is not uncommon to see wounded muskrats, some with ears torn, others crippled and broken. Forced to the fringes of the better territories, they must face life without concealment, without natural protection, and in exposed positions. Out on the margins of the better territories lurk minks, hawks, bobcats, feral house cats, foxes, and many other predators.

On one level, this sad reality is necessary. Without the predation, the muskrat populations would soar to the point where there would be mass starvation. A female muskrat can give birth to about thirty young a year, from April through late summer. If all the young survived and gave birth to more young, and so forth, one female could have a minimum of 24 million progeny in only five years.

Diving Beetles

Diving beetles (family Dytiscidae) are active the year round. Unlike most insects, they neither die off nor hibernate in the wintertime. Because of this, they can be seen, at times, during any month of the year.

These hardy beetles are oval-shaped and brownish black in color, with a highly polished, very smooth, streamlined body. They could be confused with whirligig beetles, which look much like them, but for their size. The diving beetles are twice as long—about one inch in length. The whirligig beetles have exceptionally short antennae, whereas those of the diving beetles are comparatively long.

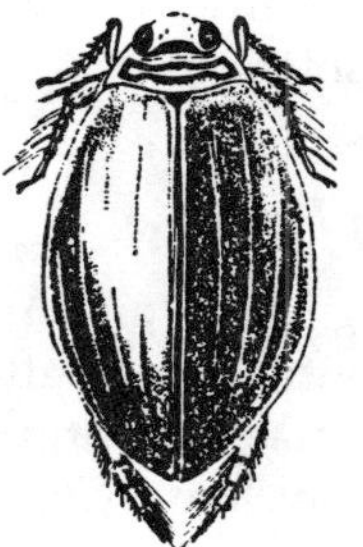

Diving beetle (family Dytiscidae)

The best way of telling the two beetles apart is by watching their actions in the water. Whirligig beetles, as their name implies, are often in motion; quite frequently one will spin around and around. The more sedate diving beetles often hang, motionless, just below the surface of the water.

A diving beetle, like all beetles, obtains oxygen from the air rather than from the water. It breathes through pores, called *spiracles*, located along the sides of its body. When it dives, it carries an external air supply in the form of a bubble held under its wing shields. Since diving beetles must return to the surface of the pond for air, it is often easy to see them appearing, disappearing, and reappearing.

The carnivorous diving beetles are capable of attacking anything their own size or, of course, smaller. They grasp their victims with their jaws and suck out the juices. They move with a remarkable grace through the water because their bodies are so streamlined. Their back legs are equipped with special hairs that aid in swimming. As the beetle moves its legs forward, the motion of the water against the hairs forces them flat against the legs. As it pushes its legs backward, the force of the water, moving against the grain of the hairs, pushes them outward so that they serve as tiny paddles. The hairs account for 68 percent of the thrust of the legs.

Diving beetles mate in April. After mating, a female goes to a water plant and cuts open a small slit where she lays between twenty and fifty eggs, which will hatch in about three to four weeks.

Once the eggs hatch, the wormlike larvae, which will live at the bottom of the pond, become dangerous predators in their own right. They have powerful jaws and can often overcome animals much larger than themselves. At all stages of their lives, diving beetles are effective hunters.

Marsh Hawks

During March and April, marsh hawks (*Circus cyaneus*) return from the south. Shortly after they have arrived at their nesting sites, at marshes, males perform a courtship flight for the females, displaying their marvelous flying abilities. A mating ritual will call for the male to rise above the ground and fly in very tight circles high above the female. When he has reached the apex of his flight, he drops like a rock to the ground. An observer would swear he is about to crash, but at the very last moment he opens his wings and rises from the ground. Over and over again the male will go through this aerial dance, displaying his talents until some female accepts him. From that time on, the pair is almost inseparable. Many of its activities are done together. An observer can often see the birds flying close to each other over marshes.

Males and females differ somewhat in color, the former being gray, the latter brown. Both have a highly visible white band on the rump, just above the dark tail feathers, which makes it easy to identify this hawk.

When marsh hawks hunt, they usually fly low over marshes. The hawks are very thorough, scanning back and forth as they cover every square foot of the marsh below them. As they fly, they have the habit of rocking back and forth on their wings, permitting an observer a chance to see the telltale white band.

The hawks hunt mostly for mice, but will also eat birds or snakes. When a cruising hawk sees a small animal below, it stops abruptly—so quickly, in fact, that it appears to have hit an invisible brick wall. The bird throws itself backward with a quick jerk. Then, in one smooth motion, it plunges to the ground and grabs for its victim. The hawk's average is far from perfect. Many times one will rise, with empty claws. But when a marsh hawk captures an animal, it will eat it on the spot.

Watching marsh hawks hunt is well worth the time because they are slower and more thorough than other hawks. As they return to cover the same ground repeatedly, one has a perfect opportunity to study their methods. Perhaps no other hunting bird or carnivorous animal is so accessible to view. Almost all others are too secretive or hunt too quickly on the wing, or on the run, to see at one's leisure.

Spotted Salamanders

Most people realize that there is something different about salamanders (order Caudata). Their slimy bodies, their protuberant eyes, their motions, and their dank habitats set them apart from all other four-legged creatures. At times, throughout history, people have been disquieted by their looks, believing them to possess supernatural powers.

Salamanders come down to us from a primeval time and are so little changed that they appear odd when compared to other four-legged animals that are far more modern. They are related, and not too distantly at that, to the ancient amphibians that waddled about the swamps some 395 million years ago, during the Devonian Period. Though the first amphibians arrived on earth before the dinosaurs, more time separates them from those giant beasts than from us.

In many ways, salamanders are unusual. Their larvae have external gills; the adults exude a slime; and they must live, except for brief periods, in damp places, such as under leaves and in damp cellars. Because of their need for dampness, the best chance of seeing a salamander out in the open is during a rainstorm.

Several species of salamander live in the Northeast. One is the spotted salamander (*Ambystoma maculatum*). Like other salamanders, its skin is slimy and shiny. One can identify it by its greenish black color and bright yellow dots.

Though adult spotted salamanders spend most of their time in damp places, they often roam here and there, although their gypsy life takes place within a given territory. Only in the winter, when they hibernate, do they cease their restless movement.

Like all amphibians, salamanders must lay their eggs in water, for only there will they hatch. Consequently all salamanders return to a pond, even a puddle, for the mating ritual. Though scattered in their own territories, male and females in a district will meet at one place at the same time. No one knows how they do it. It is known that a rainfall in April will serve as the signal to go and mate, but how can they tell which of several rainfalls? As yet there is no answer to this question. More puzzling yet is the meeting place. So many will congregate, from wide areas, in one pond that the water will be seething with salamanders. Sometimes they will all collect in one large rain puddle. How can they tell which of many puddles to meet at? It is a mystery.

When two salamanders get together to mate, the male will rub the female with his long tail. This gentle foreplay prepares both of them for their unusual and complicated method of mating. A male salamander does not have a penis. In order to mate with the female, he pushes out of his body a spermatophore, a gelatinous object that looks like a tiny mushroom, consisting of a stalk and cap. On top of the cap is a gelatinous mass in which the sperm is embedded. The female grasps the spermatophore with her front feet and carefully maneuvers it up into her cloaca, which is an opening for the intestinal, urinary, and reproductive canals. There the gelatinous material will dissolve, freeing the sperm, which fertilize eggs as they travel, one by one, down the reproductive tubes. The female will grasp the eggs as they emerge, and attach them to underwater plants.

After mating, the adults go back to their separate territories and once again become free-wheeling vagabonds. They will feed on earthworms, slugs, and snails and will likely hit a ripe old age of twenty years or more.

When the eggs hatch, salamander larvae will appear. These will look somewhat like the larvae, or tadpoles, of frogs and toads, which are also amphibians. There are, however, some major differences. Unlike the tadpoles of frogs and toads, salamander tadpoles have external gills. These do not resemble fish gills at all, being branched and bushy-looking. Frogs and toads actually have gills, but they are unseen, for they are internal organs. If you catch frog tadpoles and salamander larvae, you can notice that the salamander larvae have teeth, but the frogs have horny rasps. Furthermore, the salamander larvae grow all four legs early on, whereas frog tadpoles, at most, have only the back legs developed.

Golden Clubs

In April there is one most unusual plant in bloom in marshes, the golden club (*Orontium aquaticum*). Seeing it for the first time, you might be puzzled, because it looks like no other plant you've seen. The golden club is well named, for it resembles a large, smooth shiny club about two feet high, colored white for most of its length, and tipped with golden yellow. Seen at a distance, a group makes a most remarkable, even alien, sight. These clubs are nothing more or less than naked spadices, special flower-bearing stalks. Other plants that have a spadix, and belong to the arum family, have the spadices partly covered with a spathe, a leafy hood. Skunk cabbages (see March), for example, are arums that have both a spadix and a spathe that partly covers it. On close examination you can see that the golden club spadix has tiny flowers set in it in a mosaiclike arrangement.

CELESTIAL EVENTS

The Pleiades

No other star group is as jewel-like as the Pleiades. With the naked eye one can readily discern a prominent group of six stars, namely Alcyone (the brightest), Electra, Celaeno, Sterope, Maia, Taygete. They appear cloudy as they are surrounded by remnants of a nebula out of which they formed. The ancient Greeks saw six clear naked-eye stars and a dim seventh. Astronomers think the seventh dimmed in very early times. Today it can only be seen with a telescope, so can about 200 other stars.

The Pleiades are unmistakable and are found to the west of the constellation Orion, within the constellation Taurus.

Primitive peoples, in many parts of the world, have realized that the Pleiades demarcate the growing season of the year. In the northern hemisphere, at the beginning of the growth season, in April, the Pleiades set in the west just after sunset. When the Pleiades were in that position, primitive peoples in the northern hemisphere planted seeds, for the growing season had begun. Around the time of the solstice, in June, the Pleiades, which have remained unseen since April at any time of the night or day, rise just before dawn, so when people saw them rise then, they knew it was midsummer. When the Pleiades rose just after sunset in November, the growing season had ended and winter was about to set in. The Pleiadean calendar apparently is the oldest star-based calendar of all, but its genesis is lost in time.

The Big Dipper

If you look up at the sky at midnight on or about April 15, you will notice that the Big Dipper is high in the sky. It is not that high every midnight, and if you look at it every night at that time, you will observe its slow descent, the group of seven stars in the constellation Ursa Major moving counterclockwise, every night lower.

Six months later, on or about, October 14, the Big Dipper is as far down in the northern sky as it will get. After that date it will rise, always moving counterclockwise.

Though the Big Dipper, in the constellation Ursa Major, was known to the native Americans, it was not as important to them as the Pleiades as a star-based calendar. But the native Americans had a saying that the leaves of October were red because the wounded bear (their name also for the constellation) had bled upon them. After that the bear recovers and moves higher in the sky, and reaches its high point in April.

May

May is the proof that spring has fully accomplished its role of greening the earth. Countless leaves and blades of grass color the landscape, creating tapestries of meadows and woodlands. The growing season is in full force, and the pace of life quickens.

The light in May indicates that summer is almost here. In fact, May Day was considered to be the first day of summer by the ancient Celts. They called our May 1 *Beltane*, and their summer lasted until *Lammas*, our August 1. In some ways that old calendar of the Celts (see February "Celestial Events") was more logical than ours: their summer marked out the three months of the year that have the greatest amount of light. In fact, in the Northeast, May, June, and July have more than 400 more hours of sunlight than their opposing months, November, December, and January.

WOODLANDS

The birds' colored wings appear and disappear in dapples of flashing, varied colors in the May woodlands. One can tell that the height of the nest-building time is at hand. Racing against time, birds work on nests at a frantic rate. An oriole suspends its basketlike nest from a swinging branch, whereas a cuckoo throws together a haphazard platform. And all the while their woodland songs echo and reecho through trees.

Dogwoods

During most of the year, dogwood trees (*Cornus florida*) are inconspicuous. Though rarely tall, and often looking more like shrubs, they are true trees. Generally in May their flowers burst forth, in some areas dominating the forest landscapes. In fact, for most places May in the woodlands is really dogwood month.

Strictly speaking, dogwood "flowers" are not flowers at all, even though everyone calls them that. The white "flowers" we see are, botanically speaking, *bracts,* special leaves that grow near flowers and can turn a color or white. The dogwood bracts are pure white and look like thick-armed crosses, notched at the apexes. In the center of each bract lie the true flowers, which are remarkable only for being so unassuming.

A dogwood tree in full bloom is a stunning sight. First of all, the white bracts are intensely white, to the point of looking fake. Greatly adding to the odd appearance of the tree is the arrangement of the bracts, each parallel to the others. They look arranged. It is uncanny how orderly is the way they relate to each other. There is a reason for their unique appearance: each can, and does, move on its stem so that the face of the flower is aimed directly at the sun. The rays of the sun, 93 million miles away, are, on Earth, parallel because of the great distance; consequently flowers facing the rays are also parallel. Seen among May trees, in some deep forest glade, a dogwood tree appears, not wild, but like some misplaced ornament, some hybrid from a horticulture show. Adding to the effect is the fact they often appear ghostly because their leaves are not out nor often are those of the surrounding trees.

Jack-in-the-Pulpit

This plant (genus *Arisaema*) does indeed appear to have a pulpit. The "jack" pops out of it impudently and, because of its shape, is unmistakable. Jack-in-the-pulpits vary a great deal in color, but none wanders away from some sort of green. Most leaves are striped with pale green colors.

Jack-in-the-pulpits are closely related to the skunk cabbages, which appear much earlier in the springtime, even when snow still lies on the ground. In fact, the skunk cabbage announces the beginning of spring, whereas the jack-in-the-pulpit announces its end. Thus a season is sandwiched between these two close relatives.

Both the skunk cabbage and the jack-in-the-pulpit have flowers, which are hardly noticed, on a stalk called a spadix. In both, the spadix stands straight up within a hood, a leaflike *spathe*. But whereas the skunk cabbage has a gross structure, the jack-in-the-pulpit carries off these same features with a certain aesthetically balanced delicacy of form.

Raccoons

Few mammals learned the tricks of survival in suburban areas as well as raccoons (*Procyon lotor*). The urban sprawl that has been a disaster for so many mammals has not greatly decreased their numbers, if at all. Like the gray squirrels, woodchucks, rats, mice, and others, they have thrived, thanks to civilization.

Of the mammals that have made it in our world, raccoons are far and away the most skilled. Raccoons have many things going for them. There is every reason to believe that they are intelligent; they are opportunistic; and their habits are not so set by instinct as the habits of most wild animals. Moreover, the raccoons have forepaws that can easily manipulate objects. It is nothing for a raccoon to lift up the top of a garbage can by its handle, reach into a hole and pull out a nut, wash food, or pick up small objects.

Raccoons are so adaptable that science-fiction writers have on occasion described raccoon civilizations of the future. Hundreds of thousands of years from now, according to these writers, there will be cities built by raccoons. Farfetched? Maybe, but if some animal does inherit the earth from us in some far distant future, a raccoonlike one is definitely a possibility, since the great apes' populations are on the decline. Whales and dogs may be smarter than raccoons, but they cannot manipulate objects. Beavers can manipulate things, but they are not opportunists, as are raccoons, and appear to be too set in their ways.

Most raccoons of the Northeast live in forested areas near

streams or ponds. This ability to utilize two habitats gives raccoons great advantages, just as it does to other successful animals, such as foxes, which utilize fields and forests, and wood ducks, which utilize forests and ponds.

The woods offer raccoons hollow logs or natural dens in hills and riverbanks to use as homes, as well as holes high in trees. Being excellent climbers, raccoons can find meals in trees, obtaining fruits and nuts, and often spend a good deal of their time, especially in the daytime, up in trees.

Raccoons, however, obtain most of their food from streams and ponds. They hunt at night for crayfish, frogs, clams, and snails. Much of this hunting time is spent wading about in shallow water. Before eating food, raccoons place it in the water, but, contrary to popular belief, they are not washing it. They do this because wet food is easier for them to swallow.

Raccoons have distinct territories, rarely more than about a mile in extent, which they patrol, mostly at night. Raccoons often share their domain with skunks and opossums. The three species of mammal will cross paths in the night without bothering one another. When dawn threatens its night's activities, a raccoon will find a den to sleep in for the day, but rarely will it be the same den as the night before. In fact, a raccoon will probably use a den occupied the day before by a skunk or opossum. By the same token, those animals, in turn, will probably use a den that was used by a raccoon. Though the skunks always use ground dens and opossums tree dens, the more adaptable raccoon uses both types. These shared territories are passed on from generation to generation unless contested. Raccoons are not social animals, but solitary, and finally not strongly territorial either. They never fight for strict ownership of their territories. The home ranges of raccoons overlap, and when two raccoons meet, they evidently go their own way with hardly a nod.

The family life of raccoons might be called semisocial. The young, which are born from mid-April to mid-May, are finally seen walking about in May, following their mothers as they hunt. May is the perfect month for seeing them, when they look a little like puppies. Family units stay together a full year. After they split up, the yearlings may become den mates. This sharing of dens with each other is one of the few indications of a social structure.

Sometimes groups of raccoons will feed together at a feeder or favorite spot. If a solitary animal shows up, the group will push it aside. Even so, these groups are very loosely tied together; they exist only during the period when they are actively feeding. The social structure of nonrelated raccoons never becomes developed.

Spring Warblers

In May, bird migration surges to its peak, and at its height the arrival of the warblers occurs.

Most warblers are extraordinarily colorful birds, bright with yellows, oranges, blacks and whites. They are flitty, nervous little birds, which Roger Tory Peterson has called the "butterflies of the bird world."

Warblers are smaller than most sparrows and have thinner bills. They could be confused with vireos, but vireos are not nearly as nervous. Compared to warblers, vireos are sedate, sober birds.

In May at least two dozen species of warblers can be found in the Northeast. Some will stay for the summer; others are just passing through on their way to points north.

Warblers (family Parulidae) are songbirds. Songbirds, the most highly evolved birds, belong to an order known as the Passeriformes. They first appeared on earth during the Eocene Epoch, approximately 54 to 36 million years ago. They have vocal cords capable of songs or notes, a highly developed nervous system and a keen sense of sight and hearing. They can all perch. Warblers belong to this order, as do many other birds, such as swallows, wrens, and sparrows. Warblers are closely related to the Vireonidae, the family of the vireos, and the Icteridae, the family of meadowlarks, blackbirds, and orioles.

More than most types of birds, warblers stay in trees; few are ever seen on the ground or in open country. In spite of their name, they do not actually warble. Few would receive rave reviews as singers, although some—the ovenbird (*Seiurus aurocapillus*), for example—occasionally sing lyrically.

Warblers, being insectivorous, wait until May to return to the Northeast so that they are assured of a reliable food supply. Each species more or less stakes out its own territory. Some, such as the Blackburnian and black-throated green warblers, hunt insects in treetops. Others, such as the yellow-throated warbler, hunt in shrubs, while the ovenbird hunts for insects on the ground. It is a fine arrangement, because it keeps the vast numbers of species from actively competing with each other.

When we see so many warblers in the Northeast in May, we realize that trees, shrubs, and the ground must be swarming with countless insects to feed these hordes of highly active birds.

Though it is not difficult to tell if a bird is a warbler, it is very difficult in many cases to say which warbler is which and to name it. These birds are well known for being notoriously difficult to identify. However, there are a few common warblers which, thankfully, are rather easy to definitely identify.

The **yellow warbler** (*Dendroica petechia*) is unmistakable: it looks like a canary escaped from its cage. It is the only small bird in North America that appears all yellow. These common warblers are mostly seen in shrubs and the tops of small trees, such as apple trees.

Another common warbler is the **parula warbler** (*Parula americana*), which is common in almost any nature tree. The male is the only warbler both to have an orange-brown band on its yellow chest and also to be blue-colored above. Females lack the band, but have yellow chests and blue backs. Its call is "zeeee-up."

Even more abundant is the **myrtle warbler** (*Dendroica coronata*), a black and white and yellow bird, and the only warbler that has a white throat and yellow rump.

Ovenbirds are frequently seen hunting for insects on the ground. These birds have little red caps. As they are rather hard to see, the best identification is their habit of being on the ground and their call, which is "teacher teacher teacher," often given several times. Each time it calls the "teachers," its call gets louder and stronger.

One of the most abundant warblers is the **yellowthroat** (*Geothlypis trichas*), found near damp places, ponds, thickets, and the like. It is very easy to identify: it has a yellow breast and appears to wear a black burglar's mask. Its call is "witchity witchity." The **yellow-breasted chat** (*Icteria virens*), also a warbler, might be mistaken for it on sight, but its eyes have white circles around them and its mask is not as black as that of the yellowthroat. The yellowthroat's mask is intensely black and there is no white at all around the eyes.

These warblers are just about the only ones that are easy to identify.

Bird Migration

Hundreds of researchers have tried to understand how birds find their way about. Countless ingenious experiments have been performed on birds and with birds, yet much remains a mystery. A few things are known, however. To begin with, we have discovered that birds do not use just one set of clues for navigating long distances—or short hops. They have various techniques, and different species may use different sets of clues.

In order to navigate any distance over the horizon, birds must know how to find directions. Most, but not all, species use the sun as a compass. The sun can serve as a very efficient compass, but there is a problem: it constantly moves in the sky all day. The sun's apparent motion is fifteen degrees per hour. Obviously, to use the sun as a reliable compass, it must be timed. Humans time it with clocks and birds evidently have built-in biological clocks. They must couple their internal sense of time with their observation of the sun's location in the sky.

To see if this is the case, experimenters have placed birds that are ready to migrate in large circular cages. All day the birds trying to migrate toward a distant location will fly in one direction within the cage, no matter what the location of the moving natural sun may be. To fool the birds, the sun's image has been shifted by means of mirrors. If the shift of the sun's image is ten degrees, for example, the birds will shift their direction in the cage by ten degrees. Whatever the shift in the mirrored image, the birds will respond in the expected manner. For example, if the mirror moves the image sixty degrees the bird will move sixty degrees.

But a large majority of birds do not navigate by means of the sun. In fact, millions of birds migrate by flying only at night. These birds cannot use the moon as a navigational aide either, because its daily and nightly motion through the sky is too erratic and difficult to compute. Instead, these birds use the stars. Stars also move like the sun: fifteen degrees an hour from east to west.

Experiments with birds have been performed in large cages with an overhead dome. Star images are shown on the dome and moved as they are in a planetarium. As in the sun experiment, birds that migrate at night fly in one direction within the cage when the star images above are adjusted on the dome to duplicate their natural positions. When the images are moved, the birds also move. Birds use no single starts but certain constellations as navigational aides.

Finally, many birds migrate in cloudy weather. Unlike jetliners, they cannot fly high enough to get above weather systems. Most remarkable, as they migrate they are known to fly through dense fogs in the middle of the night. Radar has picked up a great many flocks of migrating birds winging their way through a pea-souper at midnight—following exactly the same routes other flocks had followed during clear nights.

How is it possible for such birds to fly in the correct direction? Many researchers think that they must use the earth's magnetic field to orient themselves. But can birds even detect the earth's magnetic field? NASA scientists H. Lindauer and H. Martin, in their work "Magnetic Effect on Dancing Bees," in S. R. Galler et al., eds., *Animal Orientation and Navigation* (NASA Special Publication 262, 1972), have shown that honeybees are so sensitive to magnetic stimuli that they can detect fluctuations of less than 10^{-4} gauss (approximately 1/10,000 of the earth's magnetic field). Experimenters at Cornell University have found that salamanders also detect magnetic fields. Can birds also detect a magnetic force? C. Walcott and R. P. Green, in their article "Orientation of Homing Pigeons by a Change in Direction of an Applied Magnetic Field," *Science* (184:180–182, 1974), write that homing pigeons can, and do, respond to magnetic differences.

Birds, as well as bees and salamanders, would not respond to magnetic forces the way a mariner's compass would. Such compasses show only the horizontal components of the earth's magnetic field. In reality, the earth's magnetic field is three-dimensional. Near the earth's equator the magnetic force is parallel to the ground; further north it dips toward the ground. At points yet farther north, it progressively dips more and more. Finally, at the north and south magnetic poles the magnetic force is perpendicular to the earth's surface.

If a bird actually uses the earth's magnetic field as a navigational aid, then it must make an adjustment between the force of gravity pulling downward and the earth's magnetic force: its dip on one hand and its horizontal direction on the other. Mathematically, the magnetic north is toward that point where the gravity and magnetic vectors form the most acute angle. If a bird can sense that, it will surely know where magnetic north is. Its direction can be established even on the foggiest, darkest nights of the year.

There is a problem with the whole subject of birds and magnetism. In spite of great efforts, not a single piece of solid evidence has been offered that would point to a sense organ that birds—or bees—could use to detect a magnetic field. Not even its approximate location has been discovered.

Birds use at least one other navigational aid for direction: the wind. On many occasions, birds have been observed waiting for the right wind to blow. Southward-moving birds will wait for a wind out of the north before migrating, whereas northward-moving birds will wait for a wind out of the south. How do they know which wind is which? More or less the same way we do. South winds are almost always warm and damp and accompanied by a drop in barometric pressure, which birds can easily detect. North winds are colder and drier and accompanied by a rise in barometric pressure. Not only do the birds use such winds to find direction, they also use them to save energy on long flights, for the winds can push them along.

A far greater mystery surrounding migration has to do with goal orientation, a mystery that makes all those mentioned above seem simple. To explain it, let us ask: How is it possible for a homing pigeon to be taken from its nest, placed in a dark box, driven in a van hundreds of miles away to a location that it has never seen or been to, be released, and find its way back home? How does it know what its goal is, or its orientation to it? Homing pigeons and other birds do know. Thousands have been released many miles away—even thousands of miles away from their nests—and have flown straight back home. A released homing pigeon will fly up, circle overhead a few times, then go directly toward its nest.

For one thing, it is positively known that these birds do not read clues in the landscape below them. In an experiment, homing pigeons fitted with frosted glasses that blur the land below but allow directional sunlight to enter have no trouble at all getting home. They evidently use the sun but not landmarks.

Someday a great deal more will be known about bird migration. But whether we understand it or not, the birds still know to fly into the Northeast each spring and leave each fall, guided by instinct, the celestial bodies, and perhaps, things unknown.

FIELDS AND MEADOWS

There is a feeling of expansiveness to large meadows and fields in May. They allow an open, unobstructed view of warm, blue skies filled with effulgent light, of soft clouds rising high, and of distances that fade away into diffused blue horizons. In May, dots of color appear and coalesce as meadows become flower-filled. Birds sing by their newly made nests. Spiders, which have recently appeared, weave luminous webs, and butterflies zigzag here and there in nervous explorations.

Monarch Butterflies

The famous pumpkin-colored monarch, at times called milkweed butterflies (*Danaus plexippus*), which appear in May are well known, for some flocks of them migrate across parts of America in much the same way as migrating birds. After wintering in Mexico or Florida, in their favorite trees where thousands may collect at once, they are on the move northward as early as March. It takes them until May to reach the Northeast. Some of the individual butterflies who have wintered over in the far south may actually arrive in the Northeast, but most, if not all, are monarchs that have hatched in broods along the way during the two-month migration. In other words, much of the migration northward takes place in stages between successive broods, rather than through individual endeavors. By June some in the northernmost groups will have crossed the border into Canada. They will not go much farther. All summer they will stay in the region that extends from the Gulf of Mexico into parts of Canada. In the autumn the monarch will move southward once more.

As monarchs migrate northward, they mate, and the mating behavior of the monarchs can easily be observed. Male monarchs will wait on branches for females to fly by. The males apparently cannot see very well, or are nearsighted, for they take off after any other butterfly that passes. Once a male realizes that the passing butterfly is not a female monarch, he goes back to his twig and waits. Eventually a female monarch will pass by, and the two of them will commence a mating flight.

He bumps into her several times, giving her a good nudge. Then they take off in a hectic chase, zigzagging wildly through the woods. As they continue, they rise to a great elevation, over a hundred feet above the ground. Up there, the male grasps the female and they move toward the ground in a long glide. The male holds his wings straight out, and the female occasionally flutters hers. When they arrive on the ground, they will seek out a weedy spot, usually well out of sight. There they will mate leisurely for from two to fourteen hours.

Flower Color and Scent

Because most plants depend on birds and insects for their pollination, flowers must do two things. First, they must "offer" some reward to the animals. The reward is usually nectar—a sugary substance, which not only tastes delicious but also provides animals with a substance—sugar—that gives them energy. The plants must further signal to the insects and birds that this reward is available. Therefore, flowers send out two types of signals: scent and color. Many insects, such as butterflies, can detect the smell of sugar and are drawn to it. But some creatures depend only on sight signals. Birds, for instance, have very poor olfactory organs, so they must depend on sight signals instead.

Strangely enough, insects, birds, and human beings all see the colors of the world quite differently. Humans are most sensitive to green-yellows, which is partly why we perceive so many different shades of green: apple, olive, avocado, moss, lime, and so on. Birds, however, see yellows, oranges, and reds better than we do. This helps explain why flowers that depend on hummingbirds are often (though not always) yellow, orange, or red. Those colors are about 30 percent more intense to a hummingbird than they are to us. Birds can see differences in reds that are invisible to us, but we can see blues that are invisible to them.

The color sight of an insect is more complex. Many insects—bees, for example—can see an ultraviolet light, which is made visible to us only with special films or certain devices, but never seen with the naked eye. Though they can see greens quite well, blues are, oddly enough, almost invisible to insects. On the other hand, red is invisible to them. The fact that insects cannot see a red does not necessarily mean that they avoid red flowers. But the insects that are drawn to red flowers are the ones that can detect an odor and are attracted by it.

Insects can also see a color that is impossible for us to even conceive of—a strange ultraviolet-yellow, that is to say, a color that is a combination of ultraviolet light and yellow. There are many flowers that are seen by insects as ultraviolet. Two interesting examples that researchers have tested are the charlock and treacle mustard flowers of Europe. These two flowers look identical in shape and color to us. But experiments have shown that bees see them as two separate types of flower because one, the charlock mustard, reflects ultraviolet light. The bees see charlock mustard as ultraviolet-yellow, whereas they see the treacle mustard as pure yellow, much as we do.

The sight characteristics of birds and insects explain why, on the one hand, there are so few all-blue flowers and, on the other, there are so many yellow ones. There are also numerous white flowers, because white flowers reflect all colors.

Later on in the year there will be many red berries. Perhaps one would wonder why berries are so brightly colored, since the seeds have already developed. Do the colors attract animals or insects, and if so, why? The answer is, they attract birds, which eat them, and later void the seeds in some distant locale. The colors of berries also serve as signals. They attract birds so that the plants, with their seeds, scattered far and wide by the birds' droppings have a better chance of survival.

Plant signals show that the interaction between plants and animals is not just a one-way street, with animals gaining all the benefits.

Fairy Rings

It is more than likely that someone walking the meadows or woods in May will see a so-called fairy ring: a circle of what appears to be dead or downtrodden grass. Not too many centuries ago, people in Europe called these fairy rings, believing that during the night fairies had danced round and round in the grass, killing it by treading it down. While dancing, they sowed the seeds of mushrooms.

Botanists have shown us that there is a much more mundane explanation for fairy rings. They are caused by mushrooms, usually the fairy-ring mushroom (*Marasmius oreades*). These are mushrooms that grow to be about four inches high, in a clump. They then begin to grow outward in a circle, for they deplete available food from the center. As the inner food supply continuously gives out, they spread outward, forming larger circles. Oddly enough, the opposite effect of the fairy rings can also be observed. When the mushrooms use up the food supply in the soil, grass will die, and so will the mushrooms. But once the mushrooms die, the nutrients within them are returned to the soil. The grass benefits and becomes green and richer. Both types of circle can be seen.

Brown-Headed Cowbirds

At one time brown-headed blackbirds puzzled a well-known American ornithologist, Alexander Wilson. On August 4, 1809, he wrote a letter to the naturalist William Bartram to ask, "Let me know if you have ever seen the nest of Gatesby's cowpenbird [cowbird]. I have every reason to believe that this bird never builds itself a nest, but like the cuckoo of Europe, drops its eggs into the nest of other birds."

Wilson's guess was correct. Brown-headed cowbirds (*Molothrus ater*), as we now call them, never build themselves nests, and they always lay their eggs in the nests of other birds.

In May these birds mate. The males, which are the only birds of the Northeast with brown heads and black bodies, perform awkward courtship dances in front of females, which are plain gray in color with no markings. Apparently the females can be satisfied with a rather perfunctory performance and will invariably accept a male. Indeed, cowbirds are noted for their promiscuous behavior.

When the time comes to lay a fertilized egg, the female will select the nest of some other bird, usually that of a vireo, sparrow, or warbler, each of which is considerably smaller than a cowbird. When the cowbird hatches, it is, of course, the largest hatchling in the nest, and it soon dominates the smaller legitimate hatchlings. When its foster parents arrive, it demands the most food and gets it, so little or no food is left over for the legitimate young, which usually die of starvation. Occasionally a potential foster parent will realize what has happened and will build a nest right on top of the old one in an attempt to smother the usurping cowbird. This rather desperate tactic usually works. At times, however, a cowbird will work its way up and get into the new nest. It may even be successful at getting into a third nest. At that point most birds give up and feed it.

Cowbirds are poor singers. One of their songs, heard while they fly, sounds like a squeaky hinge. Another is an odd but liquid "blub, blub, glee."

Otters

Otters (*Lutra canadensis*) mate in February (see February, "Otters"), and in April or May two or three pups are born. An otter mother spends some time teaching them needed lessons. All otters, after swimming or getting wet, dry themselves off by squirming and rolling in grass; they also groom themselves dry. Drying methods are taught to the pups by the mother, who puts on demonstrations for them. Until recently most people believed that otter mothers taught their pups to swim, but a British naturalist, Philip Wayre, writing in *The River People* (New York: Taplinger Publishing Co., 1976), showed that this was not the case. Although apparently astonished by being in the water for the first time, a pup immediately swims on its own. Nevertheless, its mother swims nearby. If she sees that things are not going right, she will grab the pup by the scruff of the neck and carry it to land. Wayre also noted that young pups will not recognize dead, motionless eels as food but will instinctively take out after living, moving eels, showing that they seem to have an instinct for pursuing only moving prey.

Mothers play with their pups, and physical contact is needed, for it gives the pups a sense of confidence.

WILD, ROCKY PLACES

Hard, cold rock slabs are juxtaposed against delicate floral petals, lacy ferns, and soft, furry mosses. The gross and the delicate meet in remote rocky places in May, as do the living and the dead, the gray and the colorful—contrasted in the starkest of terms.

Ferns

In May, ferns and mosses begin to subdue the harsh outlines of rocks. Ledges and fractures become hidden under leafy ferns so that many wild, rocky landscapes are softened.

Maidenhair fern (*Adiantum pedatum*)

It is odd, in a way, that any ferns have adapted to such a habitat. Ferns first appeared on earth during the Devonian Period, some 390 to 340 million years ago. For aeons they were tropical plants thriving in steamy jungles. Through evolutionary changes, some ferns evolved in such a way that certain species became well adapted to cool climates with cold, long winters, their roots now requiring damp, cool soil.

There are many species of fern found in wild, rocky areas. Look for the **maidenhair fern** (*Adiantum pedatum*), which grows on unbelievably thin black stems with a lustrous sheen. Its graceful stem and branches make perfect mathematical curves. Each stem is unequally forked to form a fanlike top of five to nine branches. You can identify the plant by the shiny black stem and fanlike top.

The **purple cliff brake** (*Pellaea atropurpurea*) grows on dry limestone cliffs. It is a rather small fern, identifiable by its purple stems and brittle leaf stalks.

Moonwort ferns (*Botrychium lunaria*) grow on many high, rocky ledges. They can be identified by their half-moon, fan-shaped leaves, which grow opposite each other on a stalk. The brown, dotlike, spore-producing *sporangia* look like clusters of grapes and are borne on a separate stem.

Hay-scented fern (*Dennstaedtia punctilobula*) is such a common fern that many people consider it a weed. Even so, it is a striking plant of brightest yellow–lime-green. Moreover, the leaves are delicately lacy. It gets its name because the crushed leaves usually smell like hay, although this is, unfortunately, not a totally reliable guide. If it does not smell haylike, identify it by its color, the sticky hairs that grow on the leaves (the waxy sticky substance will probably smell like hay), and the tiny sporangia (spore-producing organs) that grow like capsules at the indentations of the sub-leaflets.

Porcupines

Wherever there are trees, especially pines growing in wild, rocky areas, one is likely to find porcupines (*Erethizon dorsatum*). They live in either tree hollows or rock crevices. Though they may be abroad at any time during the day, they are most often seen at night. It is easy to induce a porcupine to come to a campsite by putting out salty food, for they find salt irresistible, even eating pack straps, gloves, boots, and the like to get the salt residue of perspiration.

The porcupine young are born from March through June. They are born with quills, but at birth these are very soft and will not hurt the mother. Shortly after birth the quills harden and become dangerous.

Porcupines appear to be lacking in intelligence, but they do not need to be very bright. Their survival does not, in any sense, depend on quick wits or an ability to understand what is happening in various situations. They survive because they are living fortresses. Few animals dare to attack a porcupine. The quills serve as effective, deadly weapons: any wild animal that gets quills in its mouth, intestines, or other vital area will probably suffer a terrible death. The quills have barbs pointed in such a way that they will work their way deeper and deeper through the skin into the flesh of an animal.

Contrary to popular belief, porcupines cannot throw their quills. They can, however, swat an animal with their tail, which is loaded with loose quills. Some may fly through the air as the tail moves, but they are not thrown, merely shaken loose.

Unlikely as it may seem, a few carnivores occasionally kill and eat porcupines. A fisher, which is a member of the weasel family can flip one over on its back and kill it by ripping open its quill-less stomach. Until fishers became rare, they were the porcupine's main predator. Bobcats can do the same, but kill porcupines only when driven by extreme hunger.

LAKES, PONDS, AND WATERCOURSES

A turmoil of life fills the ponds in May. Tadpoles that have recently struggled out of eggs, schools of dashing minnows, countless nymphs of dragonflies, and damselflies scurry back and forth. On the surfaces of thousands of ponds scattered throughout the Northeast, the pond lily leaves are unrolling. On the shores, cattails in new leaf move in the wind, their spikes turned an emerald-colored velvet. Insect swarms are growing: blackflies, dragonflies, midges, damselflies, crane flies dart and hum and buzz in the air over the glassy waters. At night the bats arrive. The deer, alert to every danger, come to eat the succulent new water plants, as do the porcupines.

Duckweed and Wolffia

A stroller near a pond will probably see two very small floating plants. One is large duckweed (*Spirodela polyrhiza*). It is about 1/3 inch long and looks like a floating leaf. On close examination, one can see that it is a complete plant, with roots and even tiny microscopic flowers. Duckweeds often trap an even smaller green plant called *Wolffia* among them. *Wolffia* (genus *Wolffia*) is so small that it is often called watermeal. The life cycle of this perennial is most unusual. During autumn months it produces starch grains. As starch

Large duckweed
(*Spirodela polyrhiza*)

Watermeal
(genus *Wolffia*)

is slightly denser than water, they sink the *Wolffia* to the bottoms of ponds. All winter the plants are nourished by the stored starch. In the springtime, when the starch has been used up, the plants, no longer burdened by the heavy starch grains, float to the top of the water. This singular yearly cycle not only protects the plants from being frozen and killed in the ice on the top of ponds during the winter but also allows them to absorb needed sunlight during the remainder of the year.

Wolffia is known as a botanic oddity because it has the smallest flowers on earth. *Wolffia* plants are only about 1/25 inch long, and the flowers are so small that one needs a microscope to see them.

It is not uncommon to see masses of duckweed and *Wolffia* floating about on ponds in the Northeast. Do not mistake *Wolffia* for pollen. Though small, it is nevertheless larger than pollen grains—and greener, too.

Dragonflies

In May, dragonflies (order Odonata) appear not only in huge numbers but in all sizes and colors. The behavior of some species is fascinating and, moreover, easy to watch. Take the white-tailed dragonfly (*Plathemis lydia*), for example. The males have an amber stripe across the middle of each three-inch wing and a flattish silver-bluish-white tail. Females are darker. These dragonflies, belonging to a

Dragonflies (A–B: genus *Aeschna*; C–E: genus *Libellula*)

group called skimmers, spend most of their time in sunlight over pond water. One can easily see them almost any day in May as well as throughout the summer.

They dart here and there, apparently with little plan. But studies have shown that, contrary to appearance, almost every movement has its reason.

Male whitetails mark out an area of the pond or lake that is their "territory." Each male will find a perch within his territory, usually a stone or stick. He will often rest on it and always return to it. If he spots another male whitetail approaching, he will dart toward it. The two will struggle for the territory. They may approach one another until one backs away, or they may fly up into the air, one hitting against the other, or they may chase each other back and forth. If no other male is in sight a whitetail may leave his perch and fly slowly and leisurely about in his territory searching for any intruder. If none is spotted, he will perch again and raise his tail. That is a signal of ownership. If, on the other hand, a male has been defeated, he will hold his tail down, a sign of submission.

When a female whitetail comes to the pond, the swift, dominant male will quickly grab her by the thorax with his legs. Once clasped, she will raise her tail and they will mate. The male and female will fly, clasped together, to a spot where the female will lay eggs. The male holds her so other males cannot mate with her; the action aids the female as well. If other males interrupted her, her attempts to lay her eggs would be thwarted. She will lay them on rocks or floating plant leaves.

Wood Ducks

Of the many birds that nest near ponds and streams during May, none is more striking than the wood duck (*Aix sponsa*), the most colorful of all ducks. The large heads of the males are patterned with complicated red, green, brown, and white markings. They also have swept-back crests. The male's bright red eyes add to their glamour. These cannot be mistaken for any other ducks.

Of all the perching ducks, wood ducks are best able to perch on tree limbs. They are, as their name implies, as fully at home in the woods as on the water. Because their nesting sites in hollow trees are not always near water, they are at times found deep in woodlands, a good distance from water. They may fly back and forth from their nesting area to water, or they may just as likely walk through woodlands, a sight that can give a hiker pause.

For a long time the ducks presented naturalists with a mystery: How did the little ducklings get out of holes in trees where they are hatched at least ten feet above ground? Audubon decided that they rode to the ground on their mother's back; other ornithologists were positive that mothers carried them in their bills. Motion pictures now show that the ducklings, coaxed by their mother's cooing, hop out of holes high above ground and flutter, with a flurry of wingbeats, to the ground. Though they cannot fly on this first descent, the whirring of their wings works well enough as a parachute, and they land safely. How they get back up to their nests has never been a mystery: wood ducklings have very sharp claws that can dig into the bark of a tree. With their aid, they climb up the trees into the holes.

Painted Turtles

On warm days in May it is possible to see various species of turtle basking in the sun. Among those sunbathers are the painted turtles (genus *Chrysemys*). Groups or, as they are called, floats of them may be seen near and among water lilies or duckweeds. More timid than most turtles, painted turtles slip away and disappear underwater at the slightest disturbance. These turtles can be identified by their dark olive-green shell with "painted" red marks around its edge.

When a male painted turtle is about to mate, he swims backward toward a female and, when he gets near, tickles her face with his claws. If she accepts his gestures, they will both turn around and mate. In May, females lay eggs in specially prepared nests, which are holes in the ground, sometimes next to tree stumps. The nests are rarely, if ever, located more than ten yards from a pond. About five to twenty soft eggs are laid at one time. After laying them, females go back to the water and never pay attention to their young.

There is some evidence that painted turtles are more intelligent than most reptiles. Experimenters have discovered that they can learn complicated mazes very well—remarkably enough, as well as rats can. Such abilities no doubt help them find their way about in the complicated three-dimensional space of a weed-filled pond (see October, "Wood Turtles").

June

Whatever the calendar may say to the contrary, we feel on the first day of June that summer has arrived. At the very least the long spring feels over. The pace of life—to outward appearance—has slowed down. There is a settling. Basically, the clouds, the sky, the look of leaves will not change until far-off October. June brings with it a sense of completion.

THE LIGHT OF JUNE

If June has a sign, it is the light. For a while in this month the sun is higher in the sky over the Northeast than it is over the equator. This means that each acre of land is receiving more radiant energy from the sun in these northern regions than in equatorial Africa. It is downright tropical: Uganda come to Connecticut. We also receive a bonus, which even Uganda misses out on—the long hours of daylight.

In the Northeast the changes in the length of daylight hours during the year are dramatic: from a mere nine hours in December daylight at Boston, Massachusetts, it increases a little over fifteen hours in June. Of course, the hours of sunlight depend on latitude. Life responds in many ways to the varying hours of daylight. The long hours of summer promote the development of mating behavior in birds, just as the shortened days in the autumn will trigger their migration southward. The life cycles of many insects are timed by the length of daylight; some dragonfly nymphs, for example, are affected in a remarkable way. As long as the sun is gaining at a rate of more than three minutes a day, as in early spring, some will change over into adults before the summer solstice. If a nymph does not mature during that period however, it will remain as a nymph until the next spring, when it will finally emerge as an adult dragonfly.

But this influence is most noticeable and striking among flowering plants. As we noted in March, each flowering plant blossoms in its own season, based on its own biological clock. During the last sixty years a great deal of effort has been spent trying to figure out the nature of that clock. Scientists at the U.S. Department of Agriculture discovered that plants use a substance called *phytochrome* to time the daylight hours. This chemical, which is a bluish protein pigment, regulates the course of plant growth and development, as well as the flowering time of plants, by responding to the presence of light during the day, the absence of light at night, and the brightness or dimness of light as well.

From this discovery it was found that all flowering plants, that is *angiosperms*, can be classified according to the way they respond to daylight. Long-day plants, as they are called, bloom when the days are lengthening, in the springtime. Short-day plants bloom as the days are shortening, in the late summer or fall. Some plants may bloom at any time during the growing season, from early spring to late fall; they are called day-neutral plants. There are many cases in which plants fall into other groups, such as the long-short plants, those that bloom in early summer after the days have first lengthened, then shortened.

Some plants are amazingly sensitive to the slightest changes in the length of daylight. It is known, for example, that a variety of rice is able to detect a ten-minute difference in the length of daylight and respond to it. This sensitivity determines not only when a plant will grow but also where it might grow. Some plants, for example, can flower only in the higher latitudes near, or in, the Arctic, where the summer sunlight hours are very long. Many plants, in fact, will grow only in certain latitudes. An extreme case of this is seen in certain varieties of soybean, which must grow within a fifty-mile-wide belt of a given latitude. In many cases the daylight hours, far more than a climate, determine the geographical location of plants. This also explains why many plants from either southern or northern regions will not grow very well if transplanted to the temperate zones.

WOODLANDS

The woodlands of June stand thick with leaves. Dappling light trembles through the foliage. Here and there masses of flowers appear in the forest gloom: rhododendrons, catalpas, black locusts, and others. Fragrances permeate the shaded groves. Bees, attracted to them, especially to the linden flowers, zip through the woods on a blur of wings. Now and then the forest echoes with a call, a chirp, a twitter of birds, so well hidden in the depths of trees and shrubs. A bird may flash into view. A redstart might flutter about in nearby branches. A scarlet tanager may call "kip-purr" from a tall tree as it spreads its red wings and darts to another branch. Far below, an ovenbird might scratch up old dead leaves as it searches for insects.

Woodland Lights and Shadows

The essence of a June forest is in its shadows. To go, for example, from a bright sunlit meadow into a dense forest can be quite an experience—the light inside the forest may actually be so dim that it takes considerable time for one's eyes to adjust. It is very like walking into a dark cellar. At no other time of the year is the effect so pronounced as in June, for then the sun is at its highest. Ross Hutchins, a well-known naturalist, has calculated that the shady parts of a forest, where ferns, mosses, wild ginger, and violets grow, get only 1/3,000 as much light as the tops of the high trees above.

Trees of June

Trees have great advantages over other plants, for they can reach the light, where their branches and leaves will spread. Tree leaves are placed in mosaic patterns so that each leaf can obtain the maximum amount of light. Many young trees show this need for light, for their leaves are much larger than those on a mature tree. The larger the leaf surface is, the more light it can gather. The leaves, of course, will transform the energy of sunlight into food energy, and June is the best month for capturing solar energy.

At the same time that all trees are gathering light, many are in flower, for example, the basswood.

White Pines

To know how white pines (*Pinus strobus*) fit into the ecology of the Northeast is, in a way, to know the social history of the region as well. When Europeans first set foot on the Atlantic shore, and inland, they noted with interest these tall, stately trees, some of which at that time had trunks with diameters of 3 feet or more and rose 220 feet into the air—perhaps higher. The tallest and straightest were reserved, by law, for the British Navy and were marked with government marks. Right after the Revolutionary War, the trees were cut down. No trees grow to such dimensions today. Some at Cathedral Pines, Cornwall, Connecticut, do reach 150 feet in height.

Settlers realized that the pines were rather widespread in the region, but nowhere common, and they wondered why. Today, because more is known about the ecology, we know the answer. White pines are among the very first trees to take over abandoned or burned fields. Their seeds blow in and sprout. White pines thrive on open air, open surroundings, and plenty of sunlight. Once established, they provide shade for hardwood trees, such as oaks. Once hardwoods grow tall, they deprive most of the white pines of their needed sunlight, and the pines die. Given enough time, only the hardwoods remain.

Few people on first seeing a white pine can imagine why it is called a *white* pine, for the tree has a distinctly dark appearance: dark foliage and almost black trunk. It receives its name from the pale, almost white color of its wood.

You can identify it by the needles, which grow in bundles of five and are flexible. The pine has a gracefully bent cone, which when mature is dry, open, and about five inches long. Unlike many pine cones, it lacks spines. When a white pine grows free in the open, its branches, five at a time, grow in whorls; one whorl a year is added as the tree grows.

White pines bloom in June. The flowers look like catkins, a dry taillike flower. The male flowers grow at the base of the new shoots and are yellowish, with yellowish pollen. The purplish female flowers, at the end of branches, will develop into cones. As the flowers bloom, the pollen sometimes covers the trees and ground near them with a "gold dust."

American Basswoods or Linden Trees

If you have never noticed it before, the flower of the basswood or linden tree (*Tilia americana*) is a surprise. It grows directly out of a special leaf, called a *bract.* From a short, springy stem hangs a cluster of tiny star-shaped flowers, which bloom in June. The flowers exactly balance the bracts, so that when the wind moves them, they swing with an easy, rhythmic motion. Later, in the fall, when the flowers have produced seeds, they and the bracts will fall, and drift easily in the wind.

Linden trees are at their best on a warm June night, when the perfume of the flowers lies heavy in the air. A moonlit forest is noticeably sweetened by this odor. During the day the perfume guides honeybees to the nectar-dripping flowers; the bees pick up the scent with sensory organs on their antennas. In the opinion of many, the honey made from linden flowers tastes the best of all, for it has a rich, tangy flavor.

Red Maples

Three months have passed since the red maple (*Acer rubrum*), alone of all the trees, gave color to the leafless groves of March. Much has happened since: many trees have flowered, and leaved, and taken center stage since then. Yet the red maple has still retained its dramatic qualities.

Touched with crimson, twin winged seeds hang down from the branches. Some are blotched, and others have turned a pale brown. June is a good month to look for young red maples. Their large leaves—so much larger than those of the adult trees, hang down, bending the petioles that support them. You will see the petioles first, for they can be bright red. Young trees, in particular, look as though hundreds of red wires hung on them. Yet don't be surprised if you come across a red maple that lacks the red petioles, for a good percentage have green petioles instead.

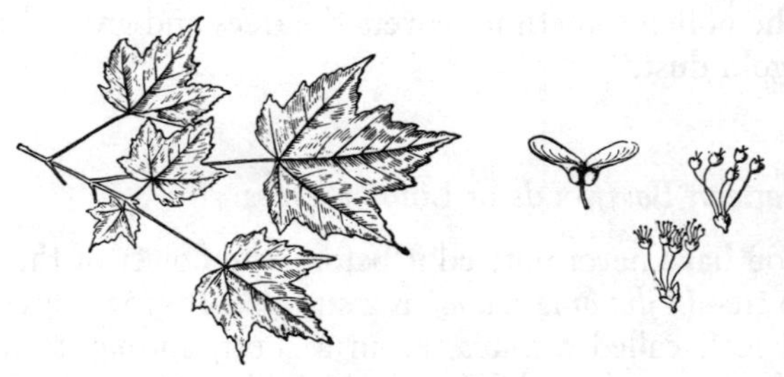

Red maple (*Acer rubrum*)

Ferns

While the trees seek light, other plants, such as the ferns for the most part, seek the shadows, the dim recesses of the forests, marvelous fern-haunted corners where the still, damp air of perpetual twilight is cool.

Many people who are good at identifying flowers shy away from

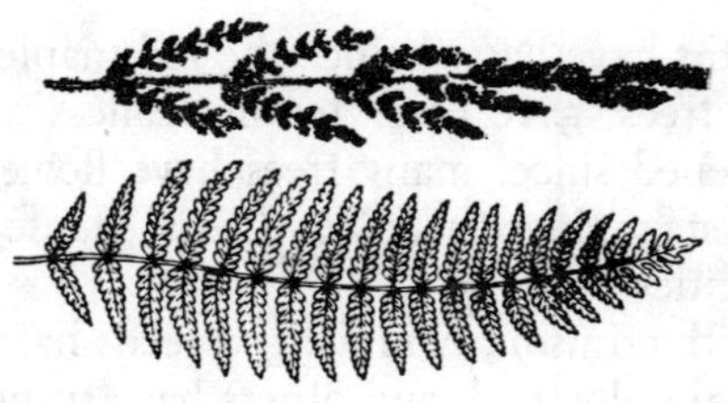

Cinnamon fern (*Osmunda cinnamomea*)

the ferns, considering it difficult to tell them apart. Though it is true that some ferns are difficult to identify, many are quite easy.

When full grown, the **ostrich fern** (*Matteuccia pensylvanica*) is marked by its size. The largest fern in the Northeast, it may reach a height of eight feet. Ostrich ferns grow with two sets of leaves. The inner leaves are the fertile ones: they have spores, reproductive bodies, in little modules that dot the back of the leaf. Growing around them in a circular fashion are the sterile leaves, which lack the spores. As the name implies, there is something plumelike about these lovely ferns.

Another common fern of the Northeast is the **cinnamon fern** (*Osmunda cinnamomea*), none of whose leaves has spores. Instead, the fertile fruits are all carried on a central stalk, which has no resemblance to a leaf and is unmistakably cinnamon-colored. Though these ferns are not as big and as dramatic as the ostrich ferns, they do grow to a height of three feet. This popular fern is perhaps the best known of all. The spores of both the cinnamon fern and ostrich fern ripen in June.

Wild Flowers

In June, the jack-in-the-pulpits are still growing strong. Their large leaves have grown, risen over them, until they serve as an umbrella over the flower.

The azaleas are still blooming. The **mountain laurels** (*Kalmia latifolia*) have opened their odd-shaped buds. Their unique pentagonal flowers are open, the stamens held back, ready to be triggered by an insect. Once an insect enters the flower, the stamens will snap down over it and spray it with pollen.

The shy **wood sorrels** (genus *Oxalis*) are blooming. These frail-looking flowers rise up above the leaves, which look for all the world like shamrock leaves and make identification easy. Wood sorrels are actually Old World flowers that were brought here by settlers. Because of their ancestry they have a distinction, rare among our wild flowers, of appearing in paintings by Fra Angelico and Sandro Botticelli. The latter artist was one of the first to draw and paint precise, accurate pictures of plants. It is not surprising, of course, that he turned his attention to the wood sorrel, because of its pure, delicate, and precise form and unusual coloration.

Tent Caterpillars

It is almost impossible to walk a mile in a northeastern forest in June without coming upon a tree that has in its branches an odd tentlike structure made of silver-white, silklike threads. It is the work of the tent caterpillar (*Malacosoma americanum*). All spring, since they first hatched, these caterpillars have been at work on their tents, which they place in the crotch of two or more branches.

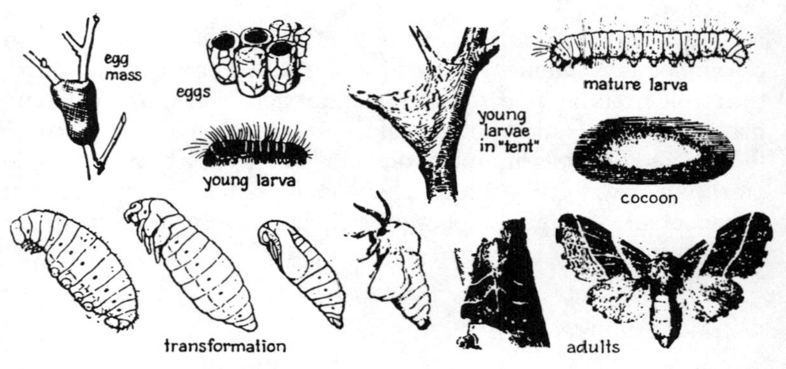

Tent caterpillar (*Malacosoma americanum*)

The caterpillars are black, with a continuous white stripe down the back. They build up the tent in layers, so that in reality there are tents within tents. Apparently they do this is for sanitary reasons, for once the inner tent becomes filled with their droppings, they build another around it, using the old tent as the floor for the new. So that they can get in and out, the tent has at least one entrance and may have several.

Even experts are puzzled by why caterpillars build the tents. Perhaps, as most people believe, they afford protection from enemies such as birds. This would make a good deal of sense if the caterpillars stayed in the tents all of the time, or left them only at night. However, this is not the case, for in the morning, around noontime, and just after dusk the caterpillars leave the tent and go to feed on leaves of the tree bearing the tent or tents. Like cave explorers who leave long pieces of string behind them so they can find their way back out, a caterpillar leaves its own silk thread on the path it takes from the tent to the feeding ground to guide it home.

The caterpillars do not kill the tree that feeds them. If they built too many tents in the tree or ate too many leaves, the tree would die. Its death would soon be followed by the death of all the caterpillars in it. They may damage trees, but the trees usually survive so that the needs of the caterpillars may be met.

Whippoorwills

The call of the whippoorwill (*Caprimulgus vociferus*), heard on a warm moonlit night, is not easily forgotten. Extraordinarily melodic and eerie, it has an almost human sound. Once people thought it was the call of death.

But then, many superstitions have surrounded these birds, which are of the goatsucker family. That name comes because some thought their big mouths were used to suck milk from goats. Of course, no bird on earth would have the slightest interest in milk, goats' or otherwise. The large mouths are, however, effective for catching night insects on the wing.

In their pursuit of insects, whippoorwills may fly near buildings. In most cases the lights attract insects, which in turn attract the birds. These birds are marvelous fliers, easy and buoyant, their long wings taking them effortlessly through the air. If you want to see them, it is best to look for them in flight at twilight.

During the day, whippoorwills are masters at hiding. They can sit among leaves and stones and you can easily walk right by them, never noticing them at all. They may also sit flat on the bark of a limb and not be seen. Occasionally someone with a flashlight may shine the light in the bird's eyes—more by accident than intent—and be quite startled to see two red eyes looking at him in the dark. If the bird is startled and flies upward, you'll be surprised at how soundlessly it can fly.

FIELDS AND MEADOWS

Plants in the June meadow compete for each square inch of land. Flowers, weeds, grasses all try to shoulder one another away. The tall plants—meadow rue, tall mulleins, spirea—all reach for the sun. The spiderworts continue to bloom; the oxeye daisies look like miniature suns in the green sky of surrounding herbage. The jewelweeds, big but still flowerless, grow with a jungle vigor. On giant, rank stems, the green dragons poke out peculiar-looking flower spikes. The orange Canada lilies hang down like bells. The strangling growth is so lush that it often hides from sight little meadow brooks, which slowly trickle over moss-covered rocks, by banks of forget-me-nots.

Grasses

Throughout the long spring the grasses lagged behind all the other herbaceous plants, but in June they show their power. In many places, especially in drier areas, they rise high, covering fields, ruling over slopes; their heads, like spearpoints, poke up along fence lines. By June, the grasses in many fields sway their tops to give visible shape to the wind.

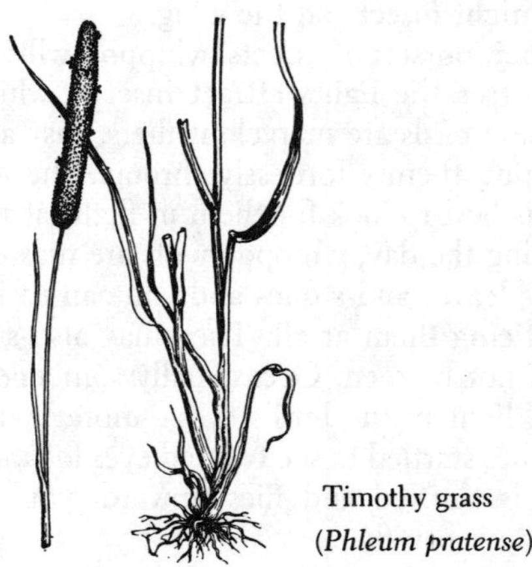

Timothy grass
(*Phleum pratense*)

Grasses thrive in open, windy places. In fact, they need the wind, for it, far more than insects, pollinates the grasses by blowing the male pollen to female flower plants. The grass flowers lack encumbering petals that could block the wind-borne pollen.

Poets often write of the odor of flowers in June, but their fragrance is not the one that stands out: it is actually the smell of grass and hay that is memorable. When the first cutting is made, the air will be heavy with grassy perfumes.

Mankind has always felt a simple familiarity with grasses. Their names give that away: bromegrass, cheatgrass, holy grass, bent grass, bluegrass, poverty grass, and quake grass—direct and simple, nothing highfalutin.

But several grasses become showy in June in their own way. The most noticeable is **timothy grass** (*Phleum pratense*). By June its flowering head, called a *spike*, is in the shape of a long cylinder, which has the feel of stiff fur if you spindle it between your fingers. In June the bright green spikes have risen high above most plants. If you look closely at the spikes, they sometimes reflect light as though they were decorated with tiny sequins.

Vanilla grass (*Hierochloe odorata*) is one of the most fragrant of all. Unlike timothy grass, which has but one spike, vanilla grass has many spikelets, which are an off-brown color. Sometimes, at a distance, vanilla grass will appear as though it were staining the field with this color. The leaves of the grass are very fragrant. The grass is sometimes called holy grass, for it was strewn at church entrances in northern Europe because of this fragrance.

Dandelions

If dandelions (genus *Taraxacum*) were not so plentiful, they would be treasured for their flowers. The blooms certainly have everything: a perfect sun shape of the richest color, placed on a shiny silver stalk. The dandelion is one of the most highly evolved dicotyledons seen blooming early in the summer. Flowering plants are either monocotyledons or dicotyledons—monocots and dicots for short.

The *monocotyledons* include grasses, lilies, irises, and orchids. They all have certain basic characteristics. When a shoot comes up from a seed, it comes up as one leaf. Almost all the leaves of monocots have parallel veins, and most of the flowers have three or six petals.

The *dicotyledons* include magnolias, buttercups, roses, morning glories, sunflowers, dandelions, and thistles. When a shoot comes up from a seed, it comes up with two leaves. The leaves have branched veins, and the flowers usually have four or five petals or multiples of those numbers. Some flowers, though, are tube-shaped.

As flowering plants evolved, they have often become less complicated and their flowering parts become more simple in shape. Primitive dicot flowers such as magnolias have numerous petals, stamens, and other flowering parts. As dicots have evolved, they have fewer petals. In fact, the petals fuse into one tube-shaped flower; flowering parts become reduced in number.

As a rule of thumb, one can tell how highly evolved a dicot flower may be: the most primitive have many petals; the most advanced are tubular. There is a wide range in between, but it is usually not difficult to tell just where a flower might be in that range.

It takes less energy for a flower to produce a simple tubular flower than one with many petals, so a plant with such a flower is energy-efficient.

But let's return to the dandelion. If we simply glance at one, we might easily make the mistake of thinking that it is a primitive flower—one with many petals. But if we look at the flowering head of a dandelion through a magnifying glass we can see that the dandelion has two types of flowers. Each of the outer flowers, called *ray flowers,* which are sterile, has one long petallike ray. This outer circle of rays attracts insects. The inner flowers are tubular and fertile. It is not at all uncommon for a dandelion to have three hundred such flowers on the flowering head.

The dandelion is in the composite family (Compositae), all the plants of which have similar flower arrangements. The composite family is the most highly evolved dicot family on earth as well as being the largest family of plants on earth. There are perhaps 20,000 species in this family. Other typical members of the composite family are thistles, ragweeds, sunflowers, asters, and goldenrods. Composites are almost always short-lived herbaceous plants.

A unique relationship exists between the seasons and the degree to which plants have evolved. If you watch flowering plants bloom, month after month, you will notice that the most primitive bloom early in the growing season. On the other hand, most members of the composite family bloom late, in September, even October. The dandelion is an interesting exception to the rule.

Blue False Indigo Plants

The blue false indigo (*Baptisia australis*) is in the same family (Leguminosae) as the true indigo plant, famous for its deep blue dye.

This rather scrubby-looking plant may reach about three feet in height and has a blue flower whose color reaches an almost unimaginable deep perfection of blue. The false indigo has a dye in its sap. When the plants die, the chemicals in the dye react with air and become oxidized, causing the plant to turn black.

Milkweeds

In June, milkweeds (genus *Asclepias*) become common in many places. These dramatic, hefty tall plants display extraordinary flowers.

Milkweeds receive their name because of their milky sap. Though it looks like milk, the sap can hardly be called benign. It can easily kill sheep and cattle, for it contains a chemical, *cardenolides,* allied to digitalins, a cardiac medicine. When an animal, or a human, eats the plant and ingests the cardenolides, it can fatally interfere with the animal's heart rate.

Few flowers on earth possess such complicated and special

Common milkweed (*Asclepias syriaca*)

structures for depositing pollen on insects. A milkweed flower has at its center a column surrounded by five nectaries. An insect that visits the flower to obtain the nectar must step into the flower. When they do so, their legs slide down a V-shaped slit in the central column. Arranged along the slit are odd horseshoe-shaped structures. When the insect leaves the flower, as it drags its legs up, it will hook one of these structures, which will cling to a leg. The structure, called a *pollinium*, has on it a tiny bag of pollen. When the burdened insect flies to another milkweed flower, the pollen in the pollinium will fertilize the flower. During the time that the milkweed flowers bloom, a great percentage of insects flying about over meadows will have pollinia attached to them because of one of the cleverest arrangements found in any flower.

Yet, for all its ingenuity, no intelligence devised it. The "cleverness" of the pollinium came about wholly through evolution.

Monarch Butterflies

By June, monarch butterflies (*Danaus plexippus*), are arriving from their migrations from Florida and Mexico. Held aloft on fragile-looking pumpkin-colored wings, they seek milkweeds below. Once it finds one, a butterfly will alight and, if a female, will most likely lay eggs on the milkweed. These eggs are tiny cone-shaped objects. Once the caterpillars emerge and have gone through several molts (becoming large enough to observe), you can see that they are zebra-striped, in orange and black. The caterpillars also have thread-like horns. Once fully mature, they make chrysalises, which will hang from milkweed leaves, looking something like greenhouses with gold markings. They resemble semitransparent jewels. After remaining a chrysalis for about two weeks, the familiar orange-colored butterfly will emerge, dry its wings, and fly on.

The larvae of the milkweed butterflies eat the sap of the milkweeds, but they do not become poisoned by it, for they possess a natural tolerance. As the larvae change into adult butterflies, the poison stays within the insect. Because of the poisonous cardenolides, these butterflies will either sicken or kill birds that eat them. Over the ages, birds have come to the point that they instinctively avoid eating milkweed butterflies. Protected in this way, the butterflies fly about with a great deal of impunity.

Interestingly, birds also stay away from the monarch's look-

Monarch butterfly
(*Danaus plexippus*)

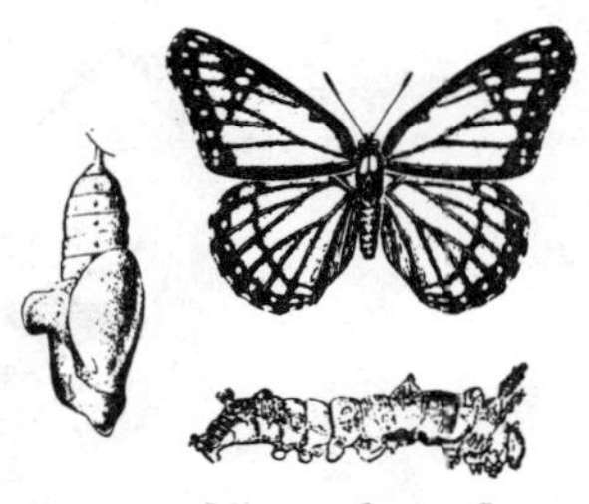

Viceroy butterfly
(*Limenitis archippus*)

alike, the viceroy butterfly (*Limenitis archippus*). Even though the viceroy is nontoxic and probably would serve as a fine meal, it is protected. An observer will have a difficult time telling the two butterflies apart. A viceroy looks almost exactly like a monarch, except that on the hind wing there is a black line parallel to the butterfly's body, whereas there is no such line on a monarch's wings. This case of mimicry is one of the best known and probably the most easily observed, for both butterflies are common.

A newly emergent monarch butterfly will fly northward. It will probably lay eggs farther north, and its offspring will also move north. Many northward-moving butterflies die. When survivors reach Canada, they will move on until there are no more milkweeds growing for their eggs. When it gets cold, those butterflies, which have never been south before, will head toward far-off Mexico and other southern regions. Very few will make the round trip from Canada to Mexico and back again.

When people say that monarch butterflies migrate, they really mean that the butterflies, for the most part, fly in waves of newly hatched butterflies, always moving northward, until they reach Canada.

American Goldfinches

It is not at all surprising to see small black-and-gold birds flitting about near country roads and paths in June. Of course, they can only be male American goldfinches (*Spinus tristis*). They are the only birds in all of America that have gold bodies and black wings. A female is, by comparison, drab; her body is a yellowish-brown-olive color.

The colors of a male goldfinch vary with the seasons. Only in

American goldfinch (*Spinus tristis*)

June is the yellow so bright—in the spring, fall, and winter, the male will look drabber. The bright colors of the male in June form its war flag. The male, stalking territory for himself and his mate, displays the bright colors as a warning to other goldfinches to stay away. Furthermore, the bright colors serve as part of his courtship ritual, so that a female will accept him. The male's bright colors later become drab as a protective measure against predators.

It is quite interesting to see the changes in color, for they reveal that the goldfinch has varying priorities during different parts of the year. Most of the time, protection from predators is paramount. In June, however, reproduction and the rituals associated with it are more important than even protection against the fangs and claws of enemies. Other birds, such as warblers, also go through similar changes—indeed, their changes are even more dramatic.

Bats

Bats (order Chiroptera) are no more common in June than in May, July, or August, but we are more likely to see them in June because of the long twilights. Bats can be startling, popping out of the darkness, their wings spread for a fraction of a second just like those Halloween cutouts. A split second later, the bat has angled off in another direction quick as a flash, to disappear. In spite of these quick appearances, the odds of identifying a bat can be pretty good. The Eastern **Pipistrelle** (*Pipistrellus subflavus*), the smallest American bat, appears earlier in the evening than most other bats. The flight is extremely erratic.

In spite of their names, **big brown bats** (*Eptesicus fuscus*) are not much larger than pipistrelles. More than any other bats, they frequent buildings. If a bat flies in a window and enters a room, nine times out of ten it will be a big brown bat.

The **hoary bat** (*Lasiurus cinereus*), whose fur does look frosted, is a forest dweller and is rarely seen anywhere outside the woods.

The **silver-haired bat** (*Lasionycteris noctivagans*), whose features are much less grotesque than those of most bats, is usually seen flying over lakes and streams.

Bats are fascinating to watch as they twist and turn in the air while seeking insects. Their flight is a marvel. Though difficult to describe, it is unlike a bird's flight: the movements appear loose, much more complicated, jerky, and erratic.

Unlike bats, birds, especially long-winged birds such as gulls have bodies and wings perfectly suited for gliding. A balsa model made in the shape of a gull, for example, would glide. Moreover, birds can, to a great degree, guide themselves by means of their tails. In contrast, bats' wings are poorly shaped for either gliding or soaring. A model of a bat could not glide. Also bats' tails are not used for any flight maneuvers. Because of the shape of their wings and tails, bats fly in quite a different manner from birds. They never soar upward or glide horizontally. They must always move their wings, pushing themselves along through the air. And because they cannot rely on their tails as rudders or elevators, they must change the shape of their wings by bending one or both, to steer. Consequently their flight appears more erratic than that of birds.

This does not mean the flight of a bat is second-rate. Quite the contrary, in the air a flying bat can turn sharply to the right or left, put on bursts of speed, and in all ways perform maneuvers, especially in acrobatics far better than most birds. They also have the great advantage of being able to fly in absolute darkness, guiding themselves by listening to the echoes of their high-pitched squeaks, which bounce off even obstacles. This ability allows them to fly in dark areas where even owls—which need some dim light—could never go.

Tiger Beetles and Ground Beetles

Of the many hundreds of species and types of beetle one can find in June, the tiger beetles and their close relatives the ground beetles are definitely among the most interesting.

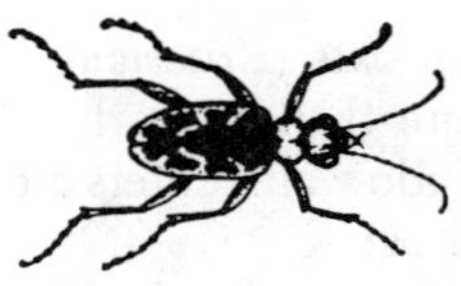

Tiger beetle
(family Cicindelidae)

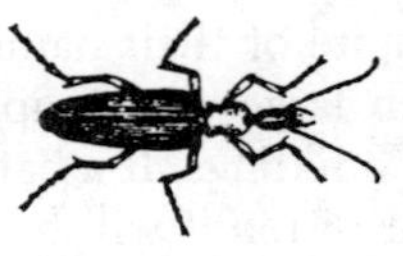

Ground beetle
(family Carabidae)

The well-named **tiger beetles** (family Cicindelidae) stalk the June meadows. Ounce for ounce, they are as fierce as Bengal tigers, and for their weight they are far stronger. They ruthlessly prey on other insects by running them down, grabbing them, and eating them. On almost any sunny afternoon in June they can be seen in a meadow, especially on paths and in open areas, racing across the ground. They are also seen in open areas near streams and beaches of lakes; at other times they are seen flying.

It is the colors of these beetles, ½ to ⅞ inch long, that are so fascinating. Most have metallic, iridescent bodies, which transform them into living jewels. There are many species of tiger beetle, and many have their bodies marked with dots and stripes. All tiger beetles have, for their size, extremely long legs, which help them run swiftly. Their heads are prominent, and they have medium-length antennae and noticeable jaws.

It is a challenge to search on paths or barren places for tiger beetles, for they are so extraordinarily wary. Try to sneak up on one. Be wary of actually touching it (although you probably can't), for it can bite good and hard.

Closely related to the tiger beetles are the **ground beetles** (family Carabidae), but they are considerably larger, usually 1½ inches in length; their bodies are wider and their jaws much larger. Ground beetles lack the speed and in most cases the bright colors of the tiger beetles. On the other hand, they are large, dramatic-looking beetles, and a few of the many species shimmer iridescently.

The best known of the group are those curious beetles called the **bombardier beetles** (genus *Brachinus*). Their defense against enemies is unique: from anal glands they can squirt an acrid mixture of gas and liquid at their enemies. Their smoke screen deters most predators. A research team at Cornell University showed that this mixture is composed of two chemicals: hydrogen peroxide and hydroquinones. When they come together quickly, they literally explode by turning into steam and gas. The split-second expansion of the gas forces the rest of the mixture to be ejected. One can even hear a tiny "pop" when the beetle ejects the chemicals.

WILD, ROCKY PLACES

Changes slow down in June in the wild, rocky places, and the vines have gained control. Tendrils grasp upward, reaching for a grip among the rocks. For the first time during the year, these rocks become hot to the touch—a proof positive of summer. In some of the trees, gray squirrels may spend the day lying on branches, bellies against the bark, feet hanging down. Panting, made lethargic from the heat, they may not move for hours.

Hobblebushes

If any flowering plant is at home on rocky cliffs, it is the hobblebush (*Viburnum alnifolium*), a shrub that may grow to a height of six feet or more. In June flattened, snowy masses of flowers decorate it, offsetting barren rocks with a needed touch of flamboyance.

If you look closely at the cluster of flowers—the *inflorescence*—you will see that the plant has two different types of flowers. The outer and larger flowers have five rather large, petallike rays. The expression *petallike* must be used, for they are actually sepals, parts of the outer bud covering before the blooms opened. These outer flowers are white and showy. They do not produce seeds and have only one purpose: to attract insects. The inner flowers possess a different shape. If you look at them under a magnifying glass, it will be apparent that they are tube-shaped—they belong to the honeysuckle family. These are the flowers that are fertile and produce seeds. Like all honeysuckles, they attract bees, whose humming noise near these flowers is often the only sound heard in deep ravines.

The name *hobblebush* must be explained. When the branches bend over toward the ground, the ends often take root and form loops resembling large croquet wickets, which can easily trip up a hiker. Impenetrable and notorious thickets often form "hobble hells."

Staghorn Sumacs

The staghorn sumac (*Rhus typhina*), found in dry, open rocky areas, admittedly comes into its own in the autumn, when the clumps of odd-shaped berries turn a rich brownish red color. Few plants enhance the October countryside more successfully than these small trees.

But before berries can exist, flowers must bloom, and it is in June that clumps of flowers tinted a greenish mustard yellow appear.

The trees grow into unique, kinky shapes, and sumac groves epitomize the rank, wild, and untamed. They are at their best on moonlit nights, when the odd, misshapen branches mingle with their own gnarled shadows.

Ruby-Throated Hummingbirds

For the sheer joy of bird-watching, probably no bird can surpass the ruby-throated hummingbird (*Archilochus colubris*). Always on the go, this tiny powerhouse has energy to burn.

The ruby-throated hummingbird is absolutely unmistakable. To begin with, it is the only hummingbird seen in the Northeast. Its tiny size and metallic green back give it away. The bird gets its name from the ruby throat of the males; the females have a few reddish streaks on a white throat.

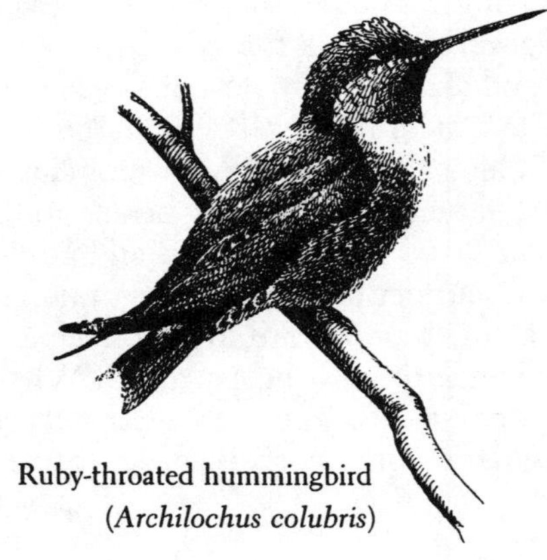

Ruby-throated hummingbird
(*Archilochus colubris*)

Hummingbirds nest in a wide variety of places, but orchards and wild, rocky places are favored locations. They are probably attracted to rocky places where they find the lichens with which they build up the outside walls of their tiny nests, which are then held together with spider webs. Rocky places supply both materials in abundance, if they are far enough away from the air pollution around cities for the lichens, which are sensitive to pollution, to have a chance to live. Hummingbirds, unlike many birds, do not hide their nests, which are often seen near the exposed tips of branches.

Few birds dare attack hummingbirds, which are much too quick to be caught on the wing, for they can hover, move backward, dart forward at high speed, and in all cases outmaneuver any other bird. Hummingbirds can be aggressive in defense of their territory and will go after much larger birds, such as crows, hawks, and even kingbirds. Not only does the hummingbird have quickness, but it is armed with a thin, needle-sharp bill, which it will use like a dagger in wing-to-wing combat.

One cannot help but admire the audacity of hummingbirds when these insect-size creatures take out after a jay. Feathers may fly, but they won't be those of the hummingbirds. It is interesting to note that the survival of these tiny birds depends on swift movements and courage.

Hummingbirds must pay a price for their actions: they burn up so much energy that they are forced to eat almost constantly. There is hardly a moment when hunger does not drive the little birds onward in quest of yet another meal. Most of the time they depend on the nectar of flowers. They will also eat insects and are often seen snapping up bees on the wing.

Hummingbirds have such long bills that it is impossible for them to groom themselves properly. To make up for this and to keep their feathers clean and in top shape, they take numerous baths. One might see humingbirds in the morning rubbing themselves against leaves so that the morning dew washes them off. At other times they may stand in shallow flowing water, grasping moss with their feet to keep themselves stable.

There is a peculiar delight about hummingbirds in the twilight. After most birds have roosted for the night, the hummingbirds are out among the flowers, sipping nectar, finding yet another meal. The steady hum of their wings produces a sleepy summer song.

LAKES, PONDS, AND WATERCOURSES

When one looks at the green algae globs, the tall cattails, the arrow arums, and the impenetrable thickets of willows along the edges of June ponds, it is hard to remember that only a few weeks earlier the pond looked so barren, so unpromising. Now it is crowded with life. No place, aside from the estuaries of the sea, contain so much life in such a little space and volume of water.

A Pond at Evening

After the heat of a June day, a pond comes to life in the evening and at night.

It is while the big orange sun sets, casting sparkles on the water, that one will see the splashes of fish feeding. Some, such as the bass, may jump high out of the water to nab a passing insect. Others, such as the yellow perch, cruise near the surface hunting for floating victims.

Swallows dip and sway over the waters, searching for hovering clouds of insects. As the twilight arrives, the swallows retreat back to their mud nests built inside of barns, under bridges, or on cliffs, or to holes in stream banks, and the bats take over. Guided by high squeaks, most of which we cannot hear, they locate the insects as sound bounces off them, radarlike. A few moths fool the bats by jamming the airways with their own squeaks. Even so, this is the time when the flittering bats feast.

It is at night that the raccoons come to the water's edge. After napping most of the day in hollow trees or in dens, they are awake. Warily on the lookout for foxes, wildcats, and other predators, they search for fish, which they can flip out of the water with their hand-like paws. Crayfish can be found along the shore and a few mussels discovered.

Porcupines lumber down from conifer forests to visit nearby ponds to search for water plants. In fact, June is the one time in the year when they do this. Porcupines, not used to such travels, are rather slow and awkward.

Owls float soundlessly through the night air as they search for mice, voles, and lemmings, scurrying about in the grass. The barred owl, most commonly seen near ponds, picks up on the slightest sound below with its acute hearing; its eyes, which can see in very dim light, pick out the rodent. With a swift plunge, it will try to get a rodent and take it back to a tree, where the roosting owl will eat it. At the foot of the tree are pellets of bones and fur—sure signs that there is an owl's roost above.

If you have a waterproof flashlight, you can shine it into the shallow waters along the shore and see fish asleep on the sand. They will blend into the background so well as to be almost invisible. However, they slowly wave their fins back and forth and open their gills, and these motions give them away. Even if the light shines into the eyes of the fish, they will not move. Fish possess no eyelids, so in spite of its open eyes, the fish can be asleep.

As evening progresses, a male frog chorus is bound to start up. Each species has its own say in its own time, but none say it louder than the bullfrog, which croaks a healthy, resonant "jug-o-rum." Many people believe that there is a large head bullfrog who leads the chorus of croakers, but actually each bullfrog is on his own. He calls out whenever the mood hits him, not in response to any of the others.

Water Lilies

The glory of June ponds are the water lilies (family Nymphaeaceae). Standing on shadow-haunted, dark green water, their pure white sharp-petaled flowers open each morning to the sky. At their centers lie clusters of thick, pulpy yellow stamens.

To live in the water as they do, water lilies have had to make many adaptations. Unlike many water plants, which have stems covered with leaves, sometimes hundreds of them, water lilies possess large leaves: the lily pads. The reason they are so large is that they must catch as much sunlight as possible to produce enough food for the plant. They have the further advantage that out on a pond or lake the sun, from horizon to horizon, is theirs. The lily pad leaves are unique in that the *stomata*—the holes through which gases such as oxygen and carbon dioxide pass—are on top of the leaf so that water will not restrict the free passage of the gases. Almost all other plants in the world have stomata on the underside of the leaf.

To help the heavy flowers float, water-lily stems enclose long air-filled tubes. Most land-based plants must keep as much air as

Water lily (*Nymphaea odorata*)

possible out of any tubes inside of the stem, but the water lily needs air not only to float the stem and flower but also to bring oxygen down to the roots.

As the long stems sway back and forth in water currents, they may meet and rub against each other. If it were not for a slimy mucus covering them, they would saw each other in half as kite strings sometimes do.

These adaptations have been worked out slowly over millions of years, for the water lily is a primitive flowering plant, as its many-petaled flower would indicate. The water lily's ancestors first appeared on land, and then gradually took up life in the water, and made adaptations to that environment. By moving to a new frontier and escaping competition from land plants, the water lilies did well for themselves.

We know lily pads are used as resting places for basking frogs and landing pads for insects, but it is the underside of the lily pads that can be crowded with life. Water mites, tiny bright red animals closely related to spiders, may be seen crawling about in the water or on the leaves. Fresh water sponges may cling to the outsides of water-lily stems, and many insects lay their eggs inside the stems, where the air tubes will supply them with oxygen.

Great Blue Heron

Great blue herons (*Ardea herodias*) epitomize the wild and savage. They are striking-looking birds, a full four feet tall. In fact, they are the largest herons in America, as well as the largest wading bird in the Northeast. They have white faces, with black plumes on top of their heads and gray bodies.

Great blue herons are difficult to approach, for they are exceptionally wary and sharp-eyed, but they can be examined through a pair of binoculars as they hunt. Unlike many birds, they hunt not by chasing their prey but by stalking it. One can watch a great blue heron slowly, ever so carefully, lift up one leg, put it down, equally slowly, then do the same with the other leg. Once it gets to an advantageous place, it will stand perfectly still for a very long time, even for hours, its neck drawn back into an S shape. All the while it watches the shallow water in front of it with its keen eyes. Once a frog, fish, or snake is within striking range, it shoots its head forward, its neck straightens out like a spring, and its beak grabs the prey. Most of the time the heron will swallow its catch on the spot. If, however, it sees a large fish, the heron may spear it, take it to land, and thrash it to death on the ground.

Giant Water Bugs

For sheer size and power, no other American insect matches the giant water bug (*Lethocerus americanus*), some of which grow over three inches long. Their large, strong forelegs are capable of holding fish and frogs, as well as insects, in a viselike grip. Once they capture a victim, they simultaneously inject venom into its body, which quickly kills small fish and insects.

Giant water bugs have flat bodies, streamlined enough that they can easily move through the water in a gliding motion as they search for a meal, their long back legs pushing them along. Their large eyes keep watch for both enemies and victims. As they hunt for prey, larger fish hunt for them.

Many giant water bugs are also strong fliers and go aloft each summer night. Lights often attract them; so many that they are often called electric light bugs.

From May to August, water bugs lay their eggs on water plants.

Most insect eggs are much too small to see, but as one would expect, those of the giant water bug are large, for insect eggs. It still must be admitted that a hand lens helps a great deal in spotting them. Water bug eggs resemble the tiny sunflower seeds in shape and stripes. The eggs hatch in about one to two weeks, and the young look just like miniature giant water bugs.

July

With the arrival of July comes a heat for which we can never be fully prepared. Above all, it will be the high temperatures that will dominate the moods and substance of the month.

Green July afternoons, heavy with humidity and heat, lie still and bird-silent. Vines, branches, leaves—millions of leaves—smother all. July brings with it a slight sense of exhaustion and something overdone. Plants may be so thick as to kill themselves in a suffocation of leaves. And even when the wind moves wearily through the trees it hardly brings relief.

WOODLANDS

During July one naturally gravitates toward the woodlands, where shadows and deep shade offer a relief from the heat. There it becomes apparent how different July is from April, May, and June. With the flowering season over in July, one now becomes aware of the patterns of leaves: silver-green fountains of willow, feathery clusters of sumacs, and the highlights on shiny magnolias. The shapes of individual leaves are also fascinating: the strange mitten shapes of the sassafras, the remarkable variety in various oaks, the prominent-veined beech, the triangular poplars; the singular, four-lobed tulip tree; and the star shapes of the sweet gum trees.

Leaf Shapes

Looking at many different sizes and shapes of leaves, you might well wonder why there is such variety. One reason has to do with monocots and dicots again (see "Dandelions" in June), which are the two major types of flowering plants. Each has its own type of leaf. Typical monocots have grasslike leaves with parallel veins; they include lilies, palms, and grasses. The leaves of dicots have radiating veins with many branches. Typical dicots are roses and maples. As a monocot plant sprouts, it shows just one leaf. As a dicot sprouts, on the other hand, it has two leaves.

Other factors influence leaf shapes. In general, plants that live in the shade have large leaves, to collect more sunlight. Conversely, plants in full sunlight usually have smaller leaves. It is believed that some leaves—those of some oaks, for example—have pointed lobes so that water runs off them more easily, just as water runs off fringed shirts such as those worn for that very reason by native Americans and plainsmen. Small, thick-shaped leaves have evolved to meet drought conditions. Others, such as grass leaves, can withstand high winds.

The Effects of the Heat

In July, heat dominates the world. Heat is much more than a mere feeling or heavy weight: it is an energy—the energy of molecular motion. As such, it has the power to bring about important changes in the living substance of plants and animals. Its major effect is its influence on chemical changes. The higher the temperature, the faster chemical reactions take place. In living cells the rate of biological processes are directly influenced by heat. As pointed out by George G. Simpson of the American Museum of Natural History, in his book *Life*, there is a tendency for the average rate of biological processes to double for every 10° C (18° F) rise in temperature.

We can see the effects of this indirectly. Take the rise of insect populations during July heat waves as an example. Cold-blooded insects have a limited ability to regulate the heat of their own blood and must depend mainly on the heat of the surrounding air to warm the cells and blood of their bodies. Once warmed up, insects, most particularly mosquitoes, respond by flying about more, feeding more, mating more, and laying more eggs. The eggs will hatch faster in hot weather, new swarms of insects will appear, and their populations will soar.

Not only cold-blooded animals are influenced by the heat; plants are too. Their internal chemical and biological processes also become more activated, which explains why so many weeds shoot up all over the place in July.

The heat does not, however, affect all living things in the same way. Since birds and mammals are warm-blooded and under normal conditions their blood and cells stay at the same temperature whether the surrounding air is hot or cold, they have the problem of staying cool during heat waves. We are quite capable of staying cool, for humans are basically tropical animals. We keep cool by sweating, and our hairless bodies allow breezes the freedom to evaporate our perspiration. Some other mammals—horses, for example—also perspire, but most birds and mammals stay cool by panting, allowing their breath to evaporate the wetness in their mouth.

Most warm-blooded animals also take other means beyond the physiological ones for keeping cool. Most, for example, rest during the heat of the day. Squirrels lie belly down on tree branches, woodchucks shuffle down into the cool depths of their burrows, and birds rest beneath the shading foliage.

Hawks, buzzards, and other similar birds escape the heat by taking to the air and circling above rising thermals to reach cooler air. For every thousand feet of altitude, the average temperature drops about 5.5° F. By soaring two thousand feet above the ground a large-winged gliding bird can thus be in air 11° F cooler than the ground. Not all large birds seen wheeling high above us in the noontime summer sky are searching with eager eyes for prey. Some are just trying to cool off.

Forest Birds

Not only do July woodlands lack flowers on the trees, they also lack birdsong. How quiet they are after the springtime and June. Few birds still breed in July; consequently most no longer sing their territorial or mating songs.

July is fledgling time, and the small-sized, young birds appear in force, awkwardly trying their new wings. Fledgling birds receive no help from their parents. They fly when ready. In preparation for its first flight, a young bird will stretch its wings and do other similar exercises—you can sometimes see young birds doing this in their nests. When the time comes to fly, off the young birds will go, out of a high nest, right into the air. Almost always the first flight, guided by instinct, proves successful. The fledglings may fly and move in unexpected ways: one moment fluttering up in surprise, pausing until you are almost upon them, they then escape in a clumsy, nervous flight. They appear confused and perhaps they are, since their behavior patterns have probably not yet been integrated into their nervous systems.

Each set of parents has on the average more than two offspring, often many more, so the bird population in July at a minimum is twice what it was in the early springtime. This dramatic rise in the bird population indicates that the yearly death rate must also be high, because by next spring there will be about the same number of birds as last spring: more than half the birds will die before the year is out.

Yet as you take a walk in July you will note only that birds seem scarce. It is surprising how well hidden they can stay on a hot July day, among the leaves of trees and shrubs.

Pepper Bushes

If you frequently walk in the woods from springtime until July, you will come upon the dead seeds and husks of the pepper bush (*Clethra alnifolia*) and probably wonder when, if ever, the bush will bloom.

But in July pepper bushes finally become heavy with snow-colored flowers, clustered on long spikes. Often you will smell the heavy fragrance of the flowers before finding the bush itself. Most pepper bushes grow in moist areas of woodlands, hidden down in the hollows. In such a gloomy, shadowy place you will usually immediately notice the glow of their white flowers, from a good distance.

Pokeweeds

Here is a plant that displays its tropical origins by its vigorous growth, its probing branches moving helter-skelter as they grow.

Nothing can stop this plant from having its way. In the South it is considered a terrible weed. Whereas in the Northeast the winter and shorter growing season keep it at bay.

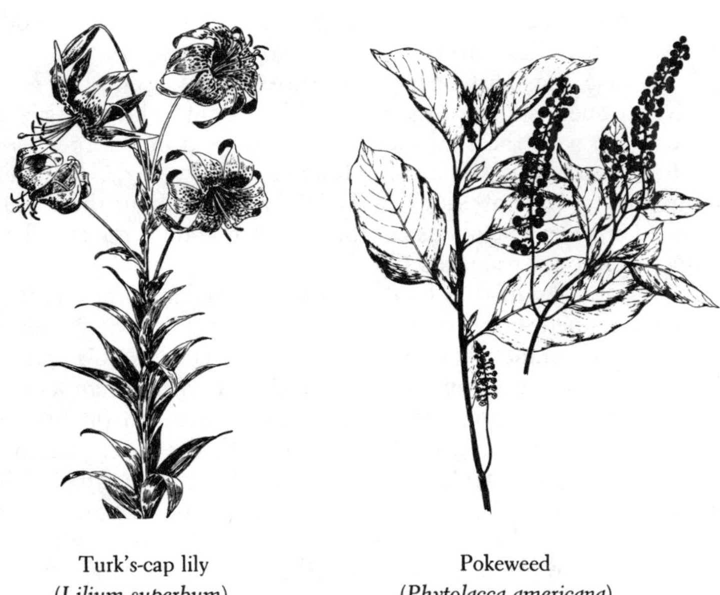

Turk's-cap lily
(*Lilium superbum*)

Pokeweed
(*Phytolacca americana*)

With its red stem and branches, bright green leaves, and spikes of white flowers, there is an undeniable tricolored gaiety to pokeweed (*Phytolacca americana*). Later, when the berries develop, they will be a rich, semi-translucent black. The deadly poisonous berries contain a natural dye that was used by Indians, such as the Algonkians of Virginia, who called the plant *puccoon*, "dye plant." English settlers picked up on the word, calling the plant *pokeweed*, and also used the juice of the berries for both dyes and inks.

Woodland Flowers

For more delicately shaped, more colorful flowers, we must look to the wild flowers that thrive on the forest floor.

No one could miss the dramatically large **Turk's-cap lilies** (*Lilium superbum*), which are formed, as though sculpted, into graceful shapes enhanced by back-curving petals and huge anthers. The nodding flowers hang down from tall, gracefully curved stems. The lilies add a needed dash of orange-red to the woodlands to complement the monotonous greens, especially those of the moist woodland thickets where they grow.

Unlike the Turk's-cap lilies, **sneezeweeds** (genus *Helenium*) thrive in open, sunny areas. Looking like giant golden daisies, they dare to vie with the sun, their flowers swaying in the breezes atop six-foot-high stems. One cannot ignore sneezeweeds, for there is something impudent, saucy, and slightly vulgar about these brightly colored flowers. The plants got their odd name from the fact that the leaves were once used as a type of snuff.

In most woodlands two rather similar-looking vines, both with trumpet-shaped flowers, can often be found weaving their way through tree branches. One is the **trumpet creeper** (*Campsis radicans*), the other the **trumpet honeysuckle** (*Lonicera sempervirens*). The former has orange flowers and leaves arranged opposite each other; the latter, much redder flowers, with the stem piercing the leaves. These spectacular flowers often attract ruby-throated hummingbirds, for unlike many insects, which cannot maneuver their long proboscises down into the flower, the birds can work their long bills down into the nectar-filled depths.

In spite of their look-alike appearances, the two flowers are not related. The honeysuckle belongs to a family that thrives in the Northern Temperate Zone, whereas the trumpet creeper belongs to the Bignoniaceae family of tropical plants. Ever since the retreat of the last glaciers, several tropical plants, such as pokeweeds and trumpet creepers, have managed to make their way north, surviving in most cases through rapid summer growth. The trumpet vine is such a fast grower and so dramatic that one can buy "trumpet vine" seeds from most seed catalogues: such are its abilites as a beautiful invader.

Another red flower, of even deeper, richer reds than that of the trumpet honeysuckle, is the **bee balm** (*Monarda didyma*). It is also called Oswego tea, because settlers and, of course, Oswego Indians used the leaves for a tea. The bright red flowers resemble the heads of gaping dragons sticking their tongues out. These, too, are a favorite with hummingbirds.

Bee balm is a member of the mint family. It is usually easy to tell if a flower is a mint or not: mint plants have square stems, opposite leaves that smell aromatically when crushed, and tubular flowers with two lips. Common and colorful mints found in July woodlands are the orange-and-yellow horse balm; purple-blue ground ivy; pink motherwort (the odd name comes about because folk herbalists once used this heart-stimulant plant for menstrual problems), and pink-colored wild basil; there are many others as well.

In woodland thickets, look for the intensely blue **Asiatic dayflowers** (*Commelina communis*), which look for all the world like blue-winged, yellow-bodied butterflies that have just landed. These flowers are small and especially dainty and would be overlooked but for the penetrating blue that cuts through the gloom and can be seen at a considerable distance.

Indian Pipes

Of all the flowers you might see in the woodlands of July, none are more curious than the Indian pipes (*Monotropa uniflora*). At first sight they are extraordinarily puzzling because of their white, translucent stem.

Unlike the vast majority of flowering plants on earth, Indian pipes lack any chlorophyll—hence their anemic appearance. Most

Indian pipe (*Monotropa uniflora*)

plants depend on chlorophyll for their food production, but not the Indian pipes; they obtain nourishment from decayed plant matter. Apparently they do not get it directly, for it seems that a fungus is needed for the manufacture of nutrients. Scientists have yet to discover the fungus's exact role in this process, even though they have determined its necessity.

Although Indian pipes live without functioning leaves, they do produce true flowers. These are pinkish white bell-shaped ghosts with a touch of blood-colored pigment.

Mushrooms

Mushrooms, like Indian pipes, lack chlorophyll and live on decayed matter. Instead of making their own foods, mushrooms break down organic matter found in decaying vegetable materials such as wood. By chemical means they can, for example, break down cellulose and turn it into starches and sugars. These can be used by the mushrooms as their own food. This process is of great benefit to wooded areas, for mushrooms and other fungi rid forests of old logs and stumps. By clearing them away, they give vigorous trees more room for growth, at the same time returning nutrients to the woodland soils.

Fly amanita (*Amanita muscaria*)

July is mushroom month. They are easier to find in this month than in any other. Among species appearing in the woodlands are the **destroying angels** (*Amanita virosa*), which range in color from a pure white to pale olive. How dainty and harmless they look. Yet, these rate as the most poisonous of mushrooms. A match for their fatal abilities are the colorful red and orange **fly amanitas** (*Amanita muscaria*), also known as fly agarics. As Pliny, a Roman naturalist, put it so slyly, fly amanitas "were very conveniently adapted for poisoning." He should have known, for some were supposedly used to kill the Roman emperor Claudius. Magenta-colored **russulas** (family Russulaceae) thrive with their close relatives, the green-colored russulas, on decaying logs. Their colors, which pale with age, and their sunken caps identify them. The caps of the brightly colored orange-yellow **chanterelles** (*Cantharellus cibarius*) are even more sunken, so much so that the gills are lifted up and exposed. No mushrooms are more fragile-looking than the **parasol mushrooms** (*Lepiota procera*). Their name gives them away, for they do look like living parasols. These and many other mushrooms grace forest floors during the month of July.

Skunks

The striped skunk (*Mephitis mephitis*) is a truly beautiful animal with its black coat of fur, white stripe, and to all appearances a blissful, refined face. Actually, skunks are known to have a gentle disposition. They are docile, for there are only a few animals that dare attack them and face their powerful sprays. Of the hunters that will take on skunks, owls rate as the most notorious. Apparently the chemicals in the spray that temporarily blind other animals do not bother the owls.

Skunks mate in February or March. The young, which in northern areas are generally born in May, do not go out into the world until July, when they follow their mother, and sometimes father, on leisurely woodland walks. The family marches single file. Like bears or elephants, they walk in a peculiar manner, with an odd swaying gait, because they place their feet down on the ground flat-footed. Most other animals walk on their toes, not the soles of their feet as skunks do.

Skunks, being nocturnal animals, rarely make an appearance in broad daylight. The best time to see them is at night. They are not hard to find, but be careful. They are good hunters, as are all members of the weasel family. Their prey for the night might be some insects, mice, or shrews.

Screech Owls

The night woods of July belong to the screech owl (*Otus asio*), whose plaintive call echoes among the dark and silhouetted trees. Its call is not a screech at all but a long-drawn-out "oooh." Thoreau wrote that the call was "Oh-o-o-o-o that I had never been bor-or-or-or-orn." In the South the screech owl is often called the shivering owl, because its call may very well give one the shivers.

This robin-sized owl searches for prey as it glides on soundless wings through the woods. Its large eyes can see in the very dim light because more light enters through their large lenses. You can see this same effect easily by looking through binoculars (sometimes called night glasses) with large objective lenses. With such binoculars one can easily see various objects in the nighttime that are hidden from the naked eye.

Thanks to its large eyes, the owl flies in the semidarkness and watches for the slightest movement below. A dashing mouse, a jumping grasshopper, a spider inching its way over the ground, once seen, will be pounced upon with an astonishing savagery. For its size, a screech owl has fearsome abilities.

FIELDS AND MEADOWS

The past and future meet in the July fields. Many grasses are dead, even whole hillsides are pale and dry; sometimes only straw is left. While many grasses are dying, clovers bloom, and their dainty pea-like flowers crown many stalks with pinks and whites. Down in the damper areas the jewelweeds carry their yellow and orange dangling flowers on their branches like earrings. The flowers of the pokeweeds pour over the fences. Meanwhile the Joe-Pye weeds show that they will shortly bloom.

Queen Anne's Lace

Queen Anne's Lace (*Daucus carota*) is to a meadow as white-caps are to the ocean, giving it dabs of white frothy color. The numerous shallow, saucer-shaped flowers in a cluster, the inflorescence, all ooze with an easy-to-reach nectar. The naturalist, Richard Headstrom has observed as many as sixty different insect species come and go from just one inflorescence. Curiously, the many small flowers of Queen Anne's lace are all pure white except for one, right in the middle and, surprisingly, it is purple, or even close to black.

Thistles

Many thistles, which will become more dominant as time goes on, bloom in July. The **pasture thistle** (*Cirsium pumilum*), which has light magenta flowers, has the largest flowers of all the thistles, up to three inches across. If you find them, smell them for their fragrance. The nodding, swamp, and field thistles are among the tallest of wildflowers and may reach nine feet in height. Many naturalists, such as F. Schuyler-Mathews, claim that the nectar of thistles is so sweet that bees actually become intoxicated from it. Of course, this effect must have been due to alcohol, produced by fermentation, rather than sweetness as such.

Ladybird Beetles

Probably everyone can identify ladybird beetles (family Coccinellidae) or, as they are often called, lady bugs. Their shiny round red or yellow bodies covered with dots set them apart from all other beetles.

Apparently they received their odd name during the Middle Ages, when they were dedicated to the Virgin Mary. Obviously, they had to be very special to receive such a honor. They showed the people of the Middle Ages, as they do ourselves, their beneficence in that both the larvae and adult beetles will eat almost any soft-bodied insect. Ladybird beetles attack many species of harmful insects: aphids, Colorado beetles, alfalfa weevils and bean thrips, and eat the eggs of asparagus beetles. So effective are they that they are sold to farmers by the pound to clear their fields of insect pests. About three thousand of them can protect an acre.

Ladybird beetle adults overwinter in grass roots. In April they come out of hibernation and search for food. In July the larvae appear. You will need to use a magnifying glass to see them, they are so small. They can almost always be found near an aphid colony. Warts, spines, and dots cover the larvae. Quite unusual for insect larvae, they have legs—six, all covered with spines.

Adult ladybird beetles have a unique defense system against enemies. Their bodies are so hard and slick that the only way an enemy can grab a ladybird beetle is by a leg, but each leg has a joint that easily ruptures when grabbed. As it does, drops of a most disagreeable fluid come out of the broken joint. Faced with the horrid stuff, the attacker backs away. At other times, ladybird beetles play dead, and as many predators attack only living, moving animals, they leave them alone.

Butterflies of July

With good reason, July is often called the butterfly month. It is almost impossible to look anywhere in a field or meadow without seeing at least one bouncing along on an erratic flight.

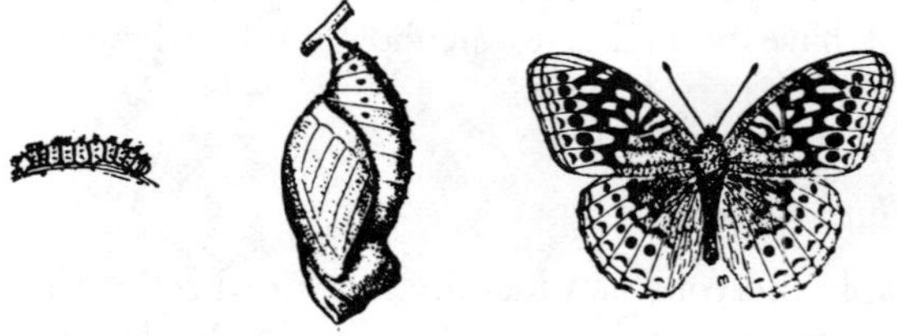

Great spangled fritillary (*Argynnis cybele*)

Adding to the butterfly populations, which have been building up since March at a steady pace, are the newcomers such as the **fritillaries** (family Nymphalidae), which are usually orange-colored and bear small black dots on the wings. Also appearing in July are the **anglewings** (genus *Polygonia*), named for the wings' edges, which are ragged and notched, forming angles. Many others also appear, including the **painted lady** (*Vanessa cardui*), which is one of the most common butterflies in the whole world.

Though we might expect all butterflies to act in a similar manner, a closer look will reveal a number of singular activities. Take the **buckeyes** (*Junonia coenia*) for example. Whereas most butterflies fly alone, buckeyes circle about together. They often circle up into the air, and if you watch closely, you will see these born fighters actually buffeting each other. Some butterflies are always busy, flying about looking for a meal. Others will spend much of the day resting on flowers, taking leisurely sunbaths. Many will head in a very businesslike manner directly toward plants where they will feed. Yet **American coppers** (*Lycaena xanthoides*) are easily led astray and will actually chase after shadows. Though sulphurs will gather by the hundreds around puddles of water, others, such as monarchs, seem to be content to be left alone.

Bobolinks

July is hardly the month when one would be thinking of bird migrations, yet now bobolink (*Dolichonyx oryzivorus*) flocks restlessly gather together. The hours of daylight are slowly changing, and they detect the shortening days. Bobolinks will not leave in July, but they are already preparing for August takeoffs.

Well they might, for they have a long, difficult, and even dangerous journey ahead of them. These small birds, the size of purple martins, will head for the interior grasslands of Brazil, Paraguay, and Argentina. To get there, they will fly nonstop across the Caribbean Sea. For many long hours, as they cross the water, their small wings will flutter hundreds of thousands of times, until they finally are above the coasts of South America.

No bird is more at home among the open grassy fields and meadows of the Northeast during the summer than a bobolink. The males are unmistakable, for they have light colors on the top of their bodies and black on the lower parts, reversing the shading seen on every other land bird of America. Moreover, they have a distinct yellow patch at the back of the head. The females, on the other hand, are distressingly difficult to identify because they are so drab. They are more or less brown with speckled feathers, which makes them look like any number of sparrows. They do, however, have a richer buff color than most sparrows and a buff stripe down the middle of their head.

Bobolinks are more often heard than seen. Their song is crisp and cheery, truly the song of summer meadows. William Cullen Bryant wrote that the bobolink's song went "bob-o-link, bob-o-link, spink, spank, spink." This delightful, bubbling song rises every summer over the northeastern meadows, until quite suddenly, in August, the nervous bobolinks fly south.

Fireflies

Though it is true that there exist other bioluminescent animals on earth, such as those of the deep sea, virtually nothing rivals the fireflies (family Lampyridae) on land or in the air. They are unique. If fireflies did not exist, only science-fiction writers could dream them up.

Flying males flash lights as sexual signals to females who wait near or on the ground—the females of some species lack wings. Once a female sees the light of a male above her, she will respond with her own blinking of lights. The male will then descend and mate with her. Species identify each other in the dark by particular systems of flashing lights, as well as by the intervals between flashes.

Male fireflies blink their lights just as they ascend. This light is produced by special organs in which a chemical, *luciferin,* is quickly oxidized to oxyluciferin when it comes in contact with oxygen and the enzyme luciferase. The insect can control the reactions with its nervous system.

The reaction is remarkably efficient: to get the same amount of light as a candle of the same illumination, the insect uses only 1/80,000 as much energy. No man-made light is anywhere near that efficient. If such an efficient means were developed for a candle, a candle that burns for one hour could be made to burn for a little over nine years, nonstop night and day.

Some fireflies appear early in the evening before it is really dark; others come out much later. Moreover, different species often have different colored lights: yellow or green, with shades in between. To watch these lights is to be in the very depths of a warm summer night, for the blinking lights intensify the soft velvety, warm quality of the July darkness.

WILD, ROCKY PLACES

Everywhere, all summer long, life struggles for existence, testing every single niche, every patch of land, reaching into the depths of ponds and grasping upward toward high crags of broken granite. Few places stay unconquered—only the cold, dark depths of some lakes and barren slabs of rock. It is not so much the hardness of the rock that keeps the plants from winning out, as the Sahara-like conditions of dry heat. The proof of this is wild, rocky places near waterfalls where foam and spray keep the steep cliffs damp. The ferns and mosses climb up the rocks and smother them.

Black Widow Spiders

Rocky areas, especially high ridges, are good places for spiders. Winds circulating around such exposed places form downdrafts and updrafts of air. Many insects are caught in these winds and find themselves helplessly driven against the rocks. There they will be caught in the webs of waiting spiders.

Among the spiders that build webs among rocks, especially in remote, undisturbed places, are the black widow spiders (genus *Latrodectus*). Many spiderwebs are not only beautiful but amazingly symmetrical and well engineered. Such is not the case, however, with the web of the black widow. It would be difficult to find a more irregular, messy-looking web. The spider is usually hanging upside down in it. The most common black widow (*Latrodectus mactans*), found north to New York, is all black except for a distinct scarlet hourglass-like mark on its abdomen. This and related species of worldwide warm climates are found in the southern parts of the Northeast. The northern widow (*Latrodectus variolus*) is found in all of the Northeast. It looks exactly like *L. mactans*, but the red hourglass is not so distinct and appears broken at the neck.

If you come across such spiders, leave them alone: they are very poisonous. About 10 percent of all people who are bitten by them are in grave danger of dying and even survivors suffer terrible pain.

Male black widow spiders look very much like the females, but are much smaller and recognizably thinner and have extra red markings on their bodies. They never eat or bite; in fact, their whole time is devoted solely to reproduction. When a male is mature, after about five molts, he spins a web. On it, he deposits drops of a fluid containing sperm. This he will transfer to his clawlike pedipalps; after that he will search for a female. Once he finds one, he is faced with a tricky problem: he must mate with her, that is, he must place sperm in her genital opening, without being eaten by her. To subdue her, he goes through a complicated courtship ritual. If all goes well, which is rare, he will mate and escape with his life. If not, she will assuredly eat him. Black widows receive their name because of this habit, but in reality they are no worse than many other female spiders, who also eat males after mating with them.

In June or July, just before females lay their eggs, they make cocoons to lay them in. After the eggs are laid they will hatch in ten to fourteen days. For the next two to six weeks they will live in an egg sac, which their mother has made for them with her silk. While in the sac, the strongest will survive by eating the others.

Although their life history appears to be a brutal example of the survival of the fittest, adult black widows are actually rather passive as spiders go. They rarely bite or attack unless pushed into doing so. For days, even weeks, they will patiently wait for some windblown insect to be dashed against the rocks and land in their webs.

Common Juniper

The common juniper (*Juniperus communis*) has the distinction of being the most common of all trees in the northern hemisphere of both the New and the Old World. The tree—often of shrub size, even when full grown—is quickly identified by its shrubby look, its very dark blue "berries," and especially its sharp needles, which grow in radial clumps of three around the branches. Juniper can grow in forests, on dunes, and in abandoned fields, but nowhere is it more at home than in wild, rocky places. The low, compact, shrubby junipers fit comfortably between rocks in a way that makes them natural partners, as if the juniper "knows" exactly what shape it should take to make the best mosaiclike fit. In fact, the tips of its branches stop growing when they touch rocks. Though those branches stop, others will extend farther outward until they touch a rock, then stop in their turn, and so on until eventually a perfect fit is made.

Ruffed Grouse

This large bird, often called a partridge, is a true denizen of wild places. The ruffed grouse (*Bonasa umbellus*) is a hardy bird, able to withstand the rigors of life either in the woods, during the winter, or in rocky places during the summer. Though not colorful, being mostly brown, the male, at least, can look very dramatic when he displays a collarlike ruff by extending his feathers. At the same time he will fan out his banded tail and strut like a peacock. But more than anything, male ruffed grouse are famous for their drumming, a sound made by beating the wings rapidly. Though called *drumming,* the word conveys the wrong impression, for the sound may be curiously like that of an outboard motor, so much so that many people hearing it mistake it for an engine noise. The sound is very odd, for at times it is so low and heavy that one thinks one is hearing a disturbance in the air. If the wind is right, the sound can carry a mile. Because of the grouse's peculiar ventriloquistic skills, it is often difficult, if not impossible, to know where the drumming is coming from. The extension of the ruff, tail display, and drumming are made by males for the benefit of the females they hope to attract. Unlike most birds, ruffed grouse will copulate long after the nesting season is over, often into the fall.

The best place to look for them is in dry, sunlit sandy areas, for they frequently take dust baths to get rid of lice. To do so, they dig hollows in loose, sandy soil. In the hollows they will get sand all over themselves, rubbing it into their feathers and going through all sorts of contortions as they do so.

Polistes Wasp

For some reason, the common polistes wasp, such as the *Polistes annularis* (*polistes* in Greek means a "city builder"), has no common name. Yet almost everyone is familiar with these wasps, which are black with red dots and yellow stripes and almost an inch long. Certainly everyone has seen their open-celled, paper nests, though polistes nests are not nearly as large or as elaborate as those made by the white-faced hornets. The smaller polistes nests are more

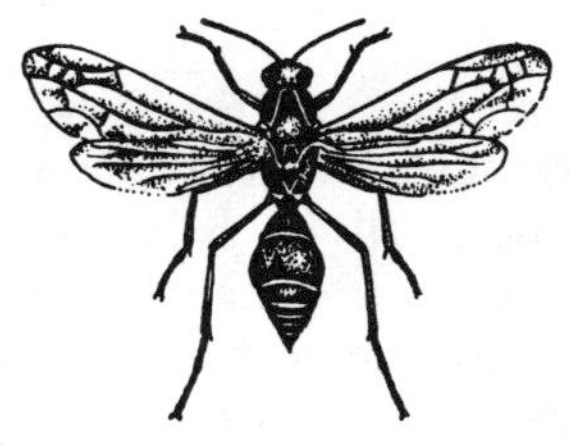

Polistes wasp

frequently found and may be seen hanging from garage ceilings, rafters in barns, back-porch windowframes, bridge supports, and many other similar places.

One might easily wonder where the polistes located their nests before people built the types of structures they now utilize. After all, the wasps have been on Earth at least since Permian times, over 230 million years ago. It is thought that before humans appeared, the wasps built their nests under tree branches and overhanging rocks. When in a wild, rocky place, look for their nests in such sheltered places.

The nests are built only by queen polistes wasps, who begin them in the springtime, usually in April, when the queen awakens from her winter hibernation and searches for a place to start a nest. Because she mated in the autumn, she carries fertilized eggs, which can be laid only in a nest. Once a queen begins a nest, she may be joined by other queens, who will work on the nest with her. This sharing of tasks by insect queens is an oddity among insects. No others, whether bees, hornets, ants, or termites, have this custom. However, not all queens are equal. They struggle for dominance, and there is a rigid pecking order among them.

When the queen or queens start a nest, they first make a stem, which hangs downward from a support. To it they add open cells, placing them in such a way that the nest will be balanced on its one stem. Stem and nest are all made of a type of paper. The queens chew up decaying wood, bark, or even cardboard to make their paper, and their saliva makes it very tough—so tough that it once was the preferred material used as a plug to hold musket balls in barrels. As the cells are built, eggs are laid in them. While the young develop they are daily fed with insects ground-up in the jaws of the adults. The first adults to appear are the workers, who will then aid the queen or queens.

The best time to see the nests is in July, when they reach maximum size and there is much activity going on in and around them. Young are being fed, more cells are being added, and eggs are being laid. Be careful! The wasps can sting.

No nest survives until the next year. All the wasps will die before winter begins, except the fertilized queen, which will hibernate for the winter under bark or in the wall of a house. Eventually the nests will all crumble away. Even if they survive, they are never used again. Each spring a new cycle begins.

PONDS, LAKES, AND WATERCOURSES

Ponds are filled not only with wiggling, swimming, lurching, floating life, but with a wide-ranging diversity of it as well. Actually every single phylum of animal, aside from the echinoderms (the phylum that includes marine starfish), lives in ponds. In July, if you're determined and have the right equipment, you can find such oddities as sponges, mollusks, flatworms, flukes, ribbon worms, and segmented worms. You may also find strange creatures called *moss animals* (bryozoans), which look similar to coral, and may even happen upon a rare surprise: a freshwater jellyfish.

Plant life is also varied, and up the scale of the plant kingdom, one can find all the plant phyla: single-celled diatoms, algae of many shapes and sizes, fungi, club mosses, a few ferns, up to and including wild flowers such as water lilies.

The Daily Temperature Cycle of a Pond

Life's activities fluctuate in a pond. Mornings and late afternoons are busy times, but during the heat of the day, life slows down. Fish do not jump; salamanders drift; tadpoles lie motionless on rocks. Early in the afternoon one has the feeling that all the animals are taking some aquatic substitute for a siesta. This may strike one as odd, especially as heat is known to activate cold-blooded animals, but another factor has come into play. Warm water cannot hold dissolved gases, including the life-giving oxygen, as well as cold water. Warm water, as everyone knows, tastes flat, because it lacks gaseous sparkle. During the day, as the sun heats a shallow pond, the gases that were dissolved in the night-cooled water escape back into the atmosphere. By late afternoon, pond animals suffer from partial suffocation caused by the oxygen depletion; consequently, all efforts become difficult.

At sunset the temperature of the water drops and the water rapidly absorbs gases from the air again. The oxygen content climbs, as does that of other gases, such as nitrogen, and carbon dioxide. Thanks to the increase in oxygen, the fish become active again, tadpoles swim away, and insect larvae hunt for food once more. At night more oxygen is absorbed in the cool waters, but most fish will sleep, for they hunt by sight. Unable to find prey, they wait, asleep, for daylight.

For pond animals, dawn is the time of maximum activity. They all have light to see by and an adequate supply of oxygen. This explains why fishermen have far better luck during the early hours of the morning than do their late-rising competitors. The roving fish will take advantage of their new energy and be on the prowl, ready and willing to snap at a passing lure. It is not only the fish that are refreshed: virtually every animal in the pond benefits from the increased supply of oxygen and finds energy for its own activities.

All through the summer, but most particularly in July, ponds rhythmically warm and cool, losing and gaining gases during each twenty-four-hour day, and pond life responds accordingly.

July Lakes

The daily heat cycles of a deep lake during the summer are very different from those of a shallow pond; they are even different from those of a very large but shallow lake.

Sunlight cannot penetrate into water beyond about thirty feet, even in the clearest of water. This means that a lake well beyond that limit in depth will contain a lower strata of water that will only very slowly warm up during a summer. In fact, even at the end of a very hot summer the lower layers may remain colder than 40° F, even though the upper layers near the surface may be 75° F.

The cold and warm layers of water, for all practical purposes, do not and will not mix because the cold lower layers are more dense. The cold layers cannot rise, nor can the less dense warm upper layers sink.

During the summer, when winds sweep across a deep lake, they push some of the upper layers in front of them; this water piles up on the downwind side of the lake. A hill of water can thus be built up. Eventually the water in it will push downward because of its weight. But instead of going toward the bottom of the lake, it merely circulates back toward the upwind side of the lake, just beneath the surface layers of water. Although the current and countercurrent may move for days on end, they do not disturb the cold lower layers of water. Density keeps them apart.

Fish living in such a lake have it far easier than those living in shallow bodies of water. During the day they can move downward from the warm upper layers of water and cruise in the cold, oxygen-rich lower layers. When the upper layers cool down late in the day and at night, the fish rise and feed on surface insects.

But it is not just fish that move up and down during the day. Many other animals also do the same. Planktonic crustaceans, for example, make up-and-down migrations during the entire twenty-four-hour day.

Pond Algae

The first thing most people notice about a July pond is its murky appearance. Some may think that it is dirty because the brownish green murk resembles pollution. The murk can in fact be so dense that if you stick your arm into it, you will not be able to see your hand.

This murk is formed by thick algae. In some ponds near urban centers or near industrial sites, the murk may be thick because the algae thrive on pollution. But some country ponds, which are 100 percent free of pollution or dirt, may also be thick with algae. Even in the cleanest of lakes a dense murky discoloration may come about because of countless millions of the tiny algae plants.

Algae are very primitive plants that come in a surprising variety of shapes and forms. Over 10,000 species of algae are known in the world, and many thousands can be found in the Northeast.

Some, such as certain types of blue-green algae (class Cyanophyceae), are single-celled plants, which drift in the water. Many float on top of the water forming scums, such as grass-green algae (class Chlorophyceae), among them *Spirogyra*. A few, such as stoneworts (genus *Chara*), resemble higher plants, though they are really very large green algae (class Charophyceae). Diatoms are also algae (class Bacillariophyceae). Diatoms have glassy cases, which enclose them, and can be seen only under a microscope. Massed together, they may form slippery, jellylike strings that can be seen with the naked eye.

In spite of remarkable differences, all algae have a few things in common. They lack complicated structures such as roots, stems, and leaves. Most reproduce by simple cell division. Many are microscopic, but many others grow large enough to be seen, such as the stoneworts and others. Actually some Pacific Ocean algae, namely kelp, may be longer than coastal redwoods are tall.

Algae can influence ponds in two ways. First of all, they glue together silt, in some cases keeping inside a pond silt that might be washed away. By doing so, they allow clay, silt, and sand to accumulate in a pond until it eventually becomes filled with dirt and ceases to exist.

But algae can also serve an important and beneficial function. They form the base of the food chain for the animals of a pond. Snails, copepods (tiny pond crustacea), tadpoles, and various other animals eat algae almost exclusively. These animals are, in turn, eaten by fish, giant water bugs, snakes, and so on.

Snapping Turtles

From April to October female snapping turtles (*Chelydra serpentina*) lay their eggs. To do so, they must, awkwardly and slowly, make their way overland until they find some suitable spot, usually a sandy place. There they scoop out a hole and deposit twenty-four to thirty eggs. Once her job is done, the female turtle will find her way back to a pond or lake, sink down into its muddy depths, and wait for prey.

Snapping turtles deserve their reputation for being dangerous. On the other hand, they are not particularly aggressive and do not necessarily strike out at each passing object that could become a meal. They are apt to ignore swimmers or wading feet. When they do strike, however, with their mouths like parrot beaks, they move with astonishing speed.

One can easily identify snapping turtles by their beaks and also by their large tails, which are proportionally far larger than those on any other freshwater turtle seen in the Northeast.

During July the first brood of young snapping turtles appear. When the eggs hatch, about ninety days after being laid, the young, which will never know their own mother, much less their father, will immediately be on their own. Until they are almost full-sized adults, they will spend their time at the edges of ponds, lakes, and streams, where they can be hidden by cattails and pickerelweeds. They hunt night and day for insects, frogs, shellfish, dead fish, or even garbage, as they can, and will, eat almost anything. When they reach a larger size, they will dare to go into the water itself, where many new dangers lurk. Swift fish may catch them, water snakes might find them, and in fact their own parents pose a danger, for snapping turtles have no hesitancy about cannibalizing their own young.

Belted Kingfishers

The colorful blue-crested belted kingfisher (*Megaceryle alcyon*) could hardly be better named. No other bird is better at fishing; none dares imitate its methods. In looking for fish, kingfishers usually fly about fifty feet above a body of water, in an undulating flight. As they pump themselves along on their short wings, they call out with a loud and peculiar rattling noise. Many ornithologists believe that kingfishers have the keenest sight of any birds, perhaps surpassing hawks and eagles in this. Kingfishers can see a two-inch fish swimming underwater from a height of fifty feet, even though they are moving, the water is moving, and the angle of refraction of the light through the water displaces the fish, which is also moving. The bird must see all that at once and adjust for each motion, pull to a sudden stop in midair, and then plunge like a rock. A fraction of a second after hitting the water with a blow that would probably knock the brains out of most birds, it grabs the fleeing fish with its long, powerful bill.

Belted kingfisher (*Megaceryle alcyon*)

In July, kingfishers will hatch a brood of young from eggs laid on the ground far back in a burrow, often as long as fifteen feet. You might be able to tell where the burrow is by watching a female kingfisher taking a fish back to it.

The female has two bars across her chest: one blue, the other a rusty orange. The male has only one bar, which is blue. Any kingfisher seen in the Northeast will be a belted kingfisher, named after the bar.

Kingfishers tend to have favorite perches: a limb on a tree, a particular section of a telephone wire, or the top of a dead tree. If you can locate a kingfisher's perch, you can return to it day after day with a good chance of seeing the bird.

CELESTIAL EVENTS

The Summer Triangle

Above us in the summer sky during the night are three bright stars that form a large triangle. Each of these stars is of the first magnitude. Often this triangle is seen at its best in a city where a haze of pollution hides all the stars in the sky but them.

This triangle is called the summer triangle and is formed by the stars Vega, Altair, and Deneb. They belong, in order, to the constellations Lyra, Aquila, and Cygnus. Vega is one of the brightest of all summer stars seen in the Northeast.

Though the summer triangle itself is not a constellation, it forms by far the most interesting group of stars, readily seen in July. At midnight on or about July 15 the summer triangle can be seen directly overhead above the Northeast.

Look for the constellation Cygnus, which derives its name from the Latin word for swan. Deneb, which is in it, is the farthest north of the three stars that form the triangle. The constellation Cygnus contains five stars that form an easily found cross in the sky, which outlines the body and wings of an imaginary swan.

Near the edge of the summer triangle, and almost in it, is the constellation Delphinus, meaning "dolphin." Look for four stars that form a rhombus. Attached to the rhombus are two more stars—in fact, the arrangement looks like a kite with a short tail. Delphinus is one of the loveliest of the summer constellations.

Sirius

No chapter on July would be complete without a mention of the star Sirius, the brightest of all stars, except of course the sun, seen from Earth. It is located in the winter constellation Canis Major, which in Latin means "Greater Dog." Because of this, Sirius is often called the Dog Star.

The "dog days" of July, curiously enough, refer to Sirius, not, as so many people think, to living dogs or their rabid behavior during the heat of the summer.

The ancients, particularly the Egyptians and Greeks, thought that the earth received heat from Sirius (the Greek word means "scorcher"), which it does—it receives 1/25,000,000 the heat from Sirius that it gets from the sun! For the earth to be warmed as it is from the sun there would have to be twenty-five million Siriuses in the sky. This belief came about because ancient astronomers noticed that Sirius was away from the sun during the winter, but constantly moved closer to it during the spring and summer, then away from it again in the autumn. In July, Sirius is in conjunction with the sun, and on or about July 19 they rise together. In the clear skies of Egypt, priests noted this heliacal rising of Sirius with the sun. By a strange coincidence, the Nile also flooded on or about that date. Because of these events, the Egyptian New Year was July 19.

There are a number of subtle changes in August. To begin with, the sounds are different. Many birds have ceased singing, but as their songs decrease, insect choruses rise. The air hums with flies and bees and wasps. The grasses tremble with cricket songs, while katydids rattle in the trees. Leaves begin to look worn. Some yellow because stems have broken, many hang ragged and perforated from insect damage. A great many have been dried out by the relentless heat of the sun. All, except the recently sprouted, are dirty and long gone is the fresh yellow-green look of early summer.

The days are shorter and sunsets arrive a little earlier. No longer do tree shadows appear like dark pools beneath noontime trees. Instead, they stretch across paths. There is a threat of autumn in the light.

WOODLANDS

In the woodlands, August is the time of deep summer stillness. During the month one does not sense change taking place. Few flowers bloom, fewer yet die. Aside from some sumac-berry-like fruit, elm seeds, and sycamore buttons, few fruits or nuts change color. Indeed, their monotonous green gives an eerie static quality to the woodlands. There are weeks during the year when time seems to stand still, when change seems but a dream, when the world appears caught in a trance. Such are the long weeks in August forests.

Mushrooms

On the forest's floor, mushrooms are still popping up. The boletes (family Polyporaceae) are at their peak, looking round and fat, like toadstools seen in fairy tale illustrations. Some are pale, some the color of toast, some dull pink-purple in color, and yet others creamy white. Their range of colors is wide and delicate, from pastel to lurid.

Lurid boletes (*Boletus luridus*), which are poisonous, have green caps and yellowish stems covered with a singular netlike pattern of bright blood-red lines. If a lurid bolete is cut, its yellowish flesh turns blue.

A stroller in the woods should keep an eye out for the pumpkin-colored **jack-o'-lantern mushrooms** (*Clitocybe illudens*), which often grow at the base of the hardwood stumps. They may grow to a height of about seven inches and their caps measure from two to five inches in diameter. The gills are attached to the stem and extend a good way down. In spite of their color, the mushrooms really received their name because they glow at night. In damp weather their eerie light is at its best.

***Cortinarius* mushrooms** are so violet that they appear as though they had been dipped in a brilliant dye. They look much like the store-bought field mushrooms, except, of course, for their color. They are also covered with tiny hairy scales. When mature, their gills turn a rust color, giving the mushrooms a striking color combination.

Puffballs (subclass Basidiomycetes), looking like white balls, may be huge and weigh up to thirty pounds. The large ones are unmistakable, but the smaller ones may be confused with immature amanita buttons, which are deadly poisonous. Puffballs lack any gills. When ripe, their spores escape out of a hole at the top of the mushroom. Probably no plant on earth could in theory have so many progeny. A large puffball can pour out, like smoke, over 7 trillion spores. Each spore is a small reproductive structure that can grow into a new individual. If all grew into mushrooms, they would take up more space than 800 planet Earths. As they drift away in the wind, most fall on barren soil. Others decay or are eaten by various animals.

Many other types of mushroom appear in August, a good month for discovering them in woodland areas.

Great Lobelias

Great lobelias grow to be large plants, reaching a height of three feet, and are covered with many blue-purple flowers. Their appearance in August is a sign of change: summer is on the decline.

Great lobelias grow mostly in swampy areas and wet woodlands. At times they may grow near or with wild phlox and white snakeroots. When they do, the results are dazzling, the color combinations next to perfect.

The scientific name for the great lobelia is *Lobelia siphilitica.* Like so many flowering weeds, it was used at one time as a medicinal plant. In this case people used it as a medicine for syphilis, probably at times with fatal results, as the plant is poisonous.

Luna Moths

No moth is more distinctive than the luna moth (*Actias luna,*), and in August a second brood appears. The colors of the moth are singular pale greens of the softest, most delicate tones. Its great soft wings end in gracefully curved, long trailing tails.

Two broods of luna moth appear each year, the first in May or June. After that the moth population declines; none appears in July, but in August, moths appear again. There is a curious fact about the two broods: moths from one have a slightly different appearance from moths of the other, in spite of the fact that they are the very same species. The spring brood has pink to purple wing margins, whereas the late summer moths have yellow wing margins.

Luna moth caterpillars, which are seen in early spring and in July, are apple-green and are mostly found on sweet gum, walnut, persimmon, and hickory leaves, for those are their favored foods.

Luna moths belong to a group of moths called *giant silk moths.* Although these moths can, and do, produce silk, they should not be confused with the true silk moths, those that have been used, at one time or another, in the manufacture of silk; these are much smaller, with wide bodies and white wings. The silk from true silk moths is

Luna moth (*Actias luna*)

far easier to work with and to spin into threads. The moths are not native to North America. Though some were once brought to this country, few, if any, can be seen in the wilds here.

Robber Flies

Anyone walking in the woods on a summer day may very well see large, dark insects darting here and there in short quick flights. The insects are probably robber flies (family Asilidae). You may mistake them for a few other darting insects or for some sort of bee or wasp, but robber flies, although they do resemble bees and wasps, are quite different. To begin with, they are swift-flying insects, which hunt on the wing. They are so successful that they could be called the hawks of the insect world.

An easy way to distinguish a robber fly is by watching it in action. Its behavior is distinctive. Unlike bees or wasps, robber flies often perch motionless on twigs and wait for prey to fly by. As a robber fly waits, it does something most unusual for an insect: it turns its head. Anyone coming upon a beelike insect on a twig can often tell if it is, in reality, a robber fly by wadding up a piece of a leaf and flicking it by. If the insect turns its head and watches it go by, it is a robber fly. It may even go further, take off, and attack it on the wing.

Robber flies do not chase their prey; instead, they intercept it—a far more difficult maneuver than a chase. To intercept, the robber fly must see that its course and the course of its prey stay at a constant angle to each other. Once the robber fly meets up with its prey, it grabs it with its legs and quickly pierces its back with beaklike mouthparts, injecting a chemical that paralyzes the victim. The robber fly then lands with its victim and sucks out its innards. On the ground a robber fly cannot turn its prey over. To do that, the fly must once more lift the prey into the air, and then turn it over in midair by moving it about with its legs. Once the robber fly has arranged everything properly, it will once more land and continue eating.

Robber flies are not too successful on their hunting forays: 85 percent of the time they are unable to capture an insect. If they fail, they return to their perch and wait for another chance. Obviously a 15 percent success rate is good enough, for robber flies survive on it. Indeed, they are rather common.

One might wonder what happens when one robber fly passes by in front of another one, hungry and waiting. Will it be attacked? It will. To protect themselves from cannibalism, robber flies have therefore worked out various signals to warn one another: wing movements, body positions, and a high-pitched buzzing. All robber flies warn each other. The signals are especially modified when males and females meet during sudden attacks. The signals usually successfully inform each other which sex is which so that they may mate instead of devouring each other.

Flying Squirrels

Flying squirrels, which are most unusual animals, escape observation by casual observers, especially during the day, by being animals of the night. To see them, you should make an effort to go into the woods on a bright moonlit night when enough light fills the gaps between shadowy trees.

The northern flying squirrels (*Glaucomys sabrinus*) live in the mountains and northern region. The southern flying squirrels (*Glaucomys volans*) live south of Massachusetts. The two species resemble one another very closely.

It is certainly worth a moonlight walk to see a squirrel hurl itself from a high branch into space. Once in the air, it spreads its four legs, so that a flap of skin between them on either side deploys and

Flying squirrel (*Glaucomys volans*)

serves as a gliding surface. As the squirrel glides along, losing altitude, it never moves its legs up and down to flap the skin stretched between like a wing. In spite of the name, flying squirrels do not fly, but glide, guiding themselves by means of their busy tail. Squirrels have been known to glide over one hundred fifty feet, but most glides are shorter. At the end of a glide, a squirrel raises its front legs up and drops its back legs down. This position slows it down, almost to a stall, so that it can safely grab the bark of a tree trunk with all four feet.

The young flying squirrels are born in March or April. Unlike most rodents, they develop slowly. They do not glide from tree to tree until August. Even then, their mothers must help them, which they do with considerable diligence and care. To teach the young to glide, mothers leave their nests and encourage them to follow. First the mothers with the young move along the branches of a tree. If they master that, groups cross over from the branches of one tree to another, where the branches touch. Slowly the mothers encourage the young to the point that they will leap, then glide. Some young are fearful and freeze; others may cling helplessly to a tree and "chur" for their mothers, who always come to the rescue and either help them or carry them to safety. Occasionally a young one falls to the ground. If it does, its mother will take it and roll it up into the shape of a furry ball and carry it by holding its stomach skin in her mouth. As the mother gallops up a tree, the young will wrap its head and tail around its mother's head. Once up a tree, the mother will, sooner or later, encourage it to try again.

If you want to see a flying squirrel during the day, try an old trick: find a tree with numerous woodpecker holes in it, and scratch the tree. A flying squirrel may stick its head out of a hole that it is using for its nest to see what is going on below.

Flying squirrels are much smaller than the common gray squirrels (*Sciurus carolinensis*). The biggest difference is their eyes: flying squirrels, being nocturnal animals, have large eyes. So if a small, large-eyed squirrel pokes its head out a hole, that's it: a flying squirrel.

FIELDS AND MEADOWS

By August there is an increasingly desiccated look to meadow landscapes because of the natural drying out of mature plants. Plants, especially annuals, have but one purpose for living: to have flowers and produce seeds. Once those functions are completed, there remains no biologic reason for a nonperennial plant to continue living, so it dies. Once its life's mission is accomplished, it is genetically coded for death. Many animals also die on the completion of their reproductive duties. Many fish, such as certain species of salmon, die after spawning. The nuptial flight of a male bee ends in death. Death immediately follows the mating act of many insects.

From the standpoint of a species, reproduction is far more important than the survival of an individual. Nature may be harsh, but at least it is logical, efficient, and effective. The world, seen in biologic terms, has little waste or slack in it. Nothing useless is retained.

A yellowing field in August is a product of these realities of life and death. Even so, there is a blond, bright look to those fields with their grasses moving in the wind. In nature, death can have its own aesthetic.

Weeds and Seeds

Another difference seen in fields and along roadsides is the presence of tall weeds. Countless tall, spiky weeds stand high above grasses and wild flowers. Mulleins, Joe-Pye weeds, goldenrods, tall thistles, and many others dominate the fields.

By August many have gone to seed. Clinging to the plants are thousands of seedpods. Some plants are prodigious: one pigweed, for example, can have as many as 200,000 seeds. Such numbers give one pause. What would happen if they all turned into plants? In three short years 8 quadrillion pigweeds, the progeny of just one plant, would blanket a field. Obviously very few seeds ever become fully grown seeding plants. In the case of pigweeds, only about one seed in 200,000 ever grows into a mature plant. All the others are eaten or become nutrients of the soil. Either birds, mammals, insects, worms, protozoans, or bacteria will devour them.

New York Ironweed and Joe-Pye Weeds

Not every acre of meadowlands and fields in August becomes yellow—far from it. Many plants are still flowering. Of all the plants that may cover the fields during the month, two are tall and dominate others, namely New York ironweeds (*Vernonia noveboracensis*) and Joe-Pye weeds (genus *Eupatorium*). None matches them for color. The magenta-purple flowers of the New York ironweed have a penetrating color that can be seen for long distances. Few flowers can achieve such effects, few are stained so brightly. Moreover, the thistlelike flowers, held high in clumps on stalks that often reach a height of eight feet, tower over a field or meadow.

Quite by chance, Joe-Pye weeds, which are also very tall, are often found growing near and, at times, in the middle of patches of New York ironweeds. Because they, too, bear purple flowers, the two weeds together can make a colorful contrast: where the New York ironweed colors are strong, those of the Joe-Pye weed, look pale, dusty, and tentative. At a distance, the purples seem shadowy.

You might wonder why the Joe-Pye weeds received their odd name. Many believe it derived from Joe Pye, an Indian who helped sick colonists by making up a concoction of the weeds to be used as a medicine for those suffering from fevers, probably typhus. The medicines must have worked, or appeared to work, for since that time the weed has been named after Joe Pye.

Goldenrods

There are many varieties of goldenrods (genus *Solidago*), but only a trained botanist could identify all of them correctly. Of the numerous types, some have flat-topped flower clusters, some spikes, some plumes of flowers, and some flower clusters arranged in branches that look like elm branches. Goldenrods also have many different sorts of leaf: lance-shaped, toothed, smooth, oval, and so on.

In August whatever goldenrods are blooming will be showy and brightly colored. Before the month is over, there will be hardly a field in the Northeast without one species or another in it, flashing its rich colors.

Some people appreciate the goldenrods' colorful addition to the landscape, but others hate their very existence. Few plants are so thoroughly detested, with good reason, for their pollen can produce severe cases of hay fever. Yet, contrary to popular belief, they are not the worst offenders: actually, the pollen of ragweeds is far worse.

Ragweeds

There are two types of ragweed, the common (*Ambrosia artemisiifolia*) and the giant (*Ambrosia trifida*). Both are rather nondescript-looking plants, for they appear to lack any flowers. Actually they do have flowers, but they are green and difficult to see. Both types of ragweed are hairy, and there is a rough, coarse look to them. The common ragweed reaches a height of about five feet; the giant may reach a height of fifteen feet. Its leaves resemble, to some degree, fern leaves and are three-lobed. In both plants the male flowers, the ones that produce the harmful pollen, grow near the tops, with the female flowers beneath.

Unfortunately, ragweeds are rather common and found in waste places and fields throughout the Northeast. The only good thing about them are their seeds, which are relished by birds, for they have a high oil content and are nutritious.

No pollen causes so much suffering from hay fever as the ragweed pollens. The allergy begins when a person breathes in pollen. It lands on the lining of the passages in the lungs and more often in the nostrils. The antibodies of an allergic person will react to proteins in the pollens. As they do, various substances will be released from the tissues and blood cells in the immediate vicinity of the pollens. The chemical reactions are complex; however, basically, they release histamines, which cause the blood vessels to dilate and an outpouring of mucus also takes place. Antihistamines are commonly taken by hay-fever sufferers because they stop the histamines from forming and

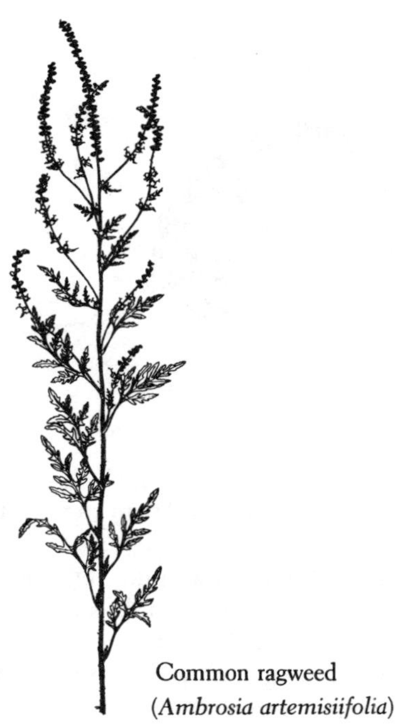

Common ragweed
(*Ambrosia artemisiifolia*)

the symptoms are relieved. Hay fever is not caused by most pollens. We breathe in numerous types of pollen from hundreds of species of plants all during the growing season. Ragweed pollen has a particular chemical structure and, most especially, proteins that cause hay-fever reactions in many people, usually from mid-August into September.

Jumping Mice

Jumping mice (family Zapodidae) are small mammals that resemble mice. They may be seen from spring to fall, but they are best viewed in August when hayfields are newly mown and when these animals go in search of new homes. As they do so, they often jump high in the air and become visible to the casual observer.

Size for size, no mammal can jump as high or as far as a jumping mouse. Its long back legs are muscular and of enormous power. When startled, they leap forward in a direct line, taking three or four leaps each eight to ten feet. As they do so, they seem hardly to touch the ground. If pursued, they quickly dodge back and forth. In an in-

Meadow jumping mouse (*Zapus hudsonicus*)

stant they can make a hairpin turn so tight that most pursuers are left behind as they try to turn back.

In spite of their name, jumping mice are not related to either mice or rats, so their name is misleading. Odd as it may seem, their nearest relatives in North America are porcupines. They are also related to jerboas, which are jumping rodents found in parts of North Africa, southern Europe, and Asia. But neither porcupines nor jerboas could be considered to be close relatives. The only close relatives happen to be jumping mice found in parts of China.

Jumping mice are solitary creatures, and aside from mating, they have little to do with one another. Each goes its own way, often searching in damp meadows for seeds and berries. On occasion they may be seen swimming across a pond. Good swimmers, they have no hesitancy about getting into the water.

Unlike true mice, jumping mice are never very common. Apparently there are never any population explosions. On the other hand, they cannot be called a rarity.

The best way of identifying one is to see it jumping. Otherwise its exceptionally long back legs and very long tail will serve for its identification.

In the winter, jumping mice disappear, for, unlike true mice, they hibernate, spending the winter in deep holes underground. Their hibernation period varies: the farther north they are, the longer they hibernate.

There are two genera of jumping mice. The genus name of the woodland jumping mice is *Napaeozapus.* The *Napaeae* of Roman mythology were woodland nymphs. *Za* means "sure" and *pous* means "footed," as if, seeing a jumping mouse floating through the air from graceful leap to graceful leap, one might associate it with a fleeing, sure-footed wood nymph. The closely related meadowland jumping mice are of the genus *Zapus*.

Spiders

During the month you will doubtless notice many spiders running about in grass, bushes, and other places. From all appearance, there seem to be more in August than in other summer months, but actually that is rather unlikely. Spiders do become more noticeable however, for late in the summer they have gone through several molts and become much larger and consequently more easily seen.

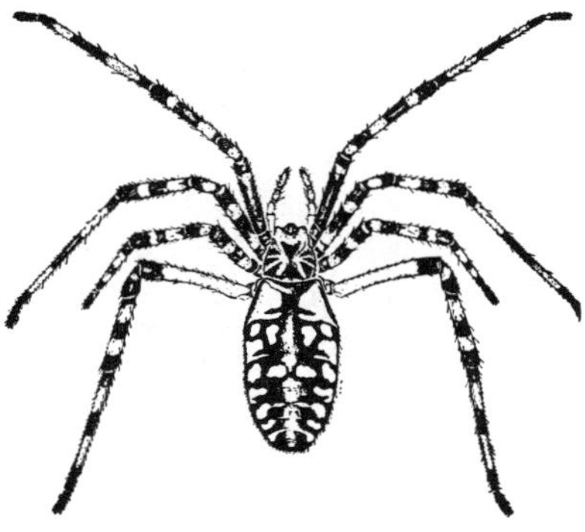

Orange garden spider (*Argiope aurantia*)

When we think of spiders, their webs come to mind. The most remarkable webs are made by spiders that belong to the group called orb weavers (family Argiopidae), several hundred different species of which live north of the Mexican border. The commonest are the **garden spiders** (*Argiope aurantia*) and **shamrock spiders** (genus *Araneus*). The garden spider is yellow and black. The shamrocks are brownish red and their abdomens are mottled with black-and-white patterns. Both are about 7/10 inch long.

The best time to see spiderwebs is early in the morning when there is dew on the ground and dewdrops outline the webs with countless silver beads.

When an orb weaver spins or wraps a web between two plant stems, it begins by crawling up the stem upwind from the other. The spider releases a line of silk out into the wind. If the line touches the other branch, it sticks to it, forming a bridge. If, however, the line never touches the other stem, the spider pulls back the thread and eats it.

If an attempt fails, the undaunted spider attaches the end of a silk thread to the first stem, walks down, and crosses the ground to a second stem, which it climbs. Once up, the spider pulls the thread tight and makes a bridge from stem to stem. When this is secured, the spider walks back and forth several times, spinning out more threads until a silken cable is formed. When the cable is strong enough to act as a support for the future web, the spider attaches a single thread to one end of the bridge. Leaving the thread somewhat loose and hanging below the bridge, the spider crosses the bridge and attaches the single thread to the other end. Then the spider walks back out on the single thread to its midpoint, where it attaches another thread and descends to the ground on it. Once on the ground, the spider pulls the threads tight until they form a taut Y shape.

The intersection of the threads becomes the hub of the future web. After the Y is formed, the spider then attaches numerous spokes to the hub, reaching to the stems, the upper bridge, and a lower bridge that will eventually be made. A few other supporting threads are added as needed. Eventually a web made primarily of radiating threads is formed. All the threads in it are more or less inelastic and nonsticky.

Once all the radiating spokes are spun, the spider goes to the hub of the web and starts laying down a thread from spoke to spoke. As it goes around and around, its legs constantly feel the thread that is already laid down. By its doing so, the space between the turns of the silk thread remains constant as the spider covers the whole web. Mathematically speaking, the spider constructs an Archimedean spiral.

Once the spiral reaches the circumference of the web, the spider turns around and goes back over the spiral, following it back to the hub. As it does so, it lays down a new spiral of a different type of silk. This is a sticky silk, and when insects touch it, they are caught. The spider must not only be sure that it does not step on the sticky silk, but at the same time rolls up the silk thread of the first spiral.

Once the spider arrives back at the hub of the web, it is finished.

Some spiders wait for prey by remaining quietly at the center of the web. Others walk to the edge, being careful not to step on the sticky silk. Wherever a spider may wait, it will constantly feel the web for vibrations. It discounts those caused by the wind or by inanimate objects, such as seeds, hitting the web. It knows when an insect is caught, for it will struggle, setting up characteristic vibrations. As the insect struggles, the spider will race to it, avoiding the sticky threads as it does. It may wrap the victim up in more silken threads or eat it on the spot.

In spite of all the work involved in the making of a web, most spiders make a new web every single day. Because of these daily activities, it is usually not difficult to find a spider at work.

WILD, ROCKY PLACES

By August, the dry, hot summer has taken its toll in wild, rocky places. The mosses are often dry, lichens probably shriveled, and many exposed areas covered with a film of dust. Balsam firs drip warm fragrant resins down their rough bark. The leaves of a gray birch tremble in the wind to produce dry rustles. And, the only sound in that silent world may very well be the constant hum of insects.

Mountain Ashes

Few shrubs or trees are as much a part of the mountain scenery as mountain ash (*Sorbus americana*). These trees grow near the highest, most rugged, rocky mountaintops and apparently thrive on harsh conditions, howling winds, long winters, deep snows, and the hot, drying sun of summertime, on the arid summits.

Mountain ash trees have pinnate leaves. The word *pinnate* comes from a Latin word meaning "feathery," and the leaves of the trees certainly look feathery. In July and August these shrubs are in bloom, and dense clusters of white flowers appear on them. In spite of the name, a mountain ash is not a true ash—that is, a member of the genus *Fraxinus,* which contains the white ash and black ash. Instead, it is a member of the rose family (Rosaceae), as a close look at the small flowers will indicate: like all roses, they have five petals and many stamens.

Mountain ashes are among the last large shrubs or trees to bloom during the summer. This is because of their location, high in the mountains. The air is cooler up there, and both spring and summer arrive much later than in the lowlands. In the mountains, August is more like late spring than late summer.

For wildlife, mountain ashes are valuable trees. In the fall and winter they are weighted with clusters of bright red berries that are devoured by deer and birds.

Brown Snakes

Brown snakes (*Storeria dekayi*) are hardy little creatures able to live under conditions that most animals would find intolerable. Many city dwellers, especially children, know of these snakes, for they thrive in trash-filled vacant lots where they slither about under and over broken bricks, rusted tin cans, and shattered glass.

Before there were any cities or vacant lots, these snakes lived, as many still do, in wild, rocky areas. Instead of working their way through trash, they maneuvered among stones, roots, logs, and crevices in granite slabs. It is remarkable to consider that the wildest of all northeastern habitats is more or less duplicated in our cities.

Brown snakes are, of course, brown; their bellies are pinkish in color. They are the only brown snakes that have two rows of black dots on their backs. These gentle, nonpoisonous snakes are never large, growing to about nineteen inches at the most, and actually the majority are far smaller.

In August the young are born alive. They are very small, only about four inches long and only 1/16 inch in diameter. Most earthworms are considerably larger.

As brown snakes go hunting, they constantly flick their tongues. This motion of the tongue is not an aggressive act. A snake's tongue bears sensory organs that allow the snake to "taste" the surrounding air. Because the sensory organ is quite different from those that allow us to taste and smell things, it is impossible to describe exactly what it does, though apparently the sense is close to our sense of taste. Like all snakes, brown snakes have good eyesight. They hunt, as their size would indicate, for small game: spiders, slugs, insect larvae, and earthworms.

Veeries

A veery (*Hylocichla fuscescens*) is a bird of secretive places. Few birds can stay so well hidden. If found at all, it is discovered only in the deepest, darkest thickets, often those of remote, wild, rocky places.

By some strange quirk of fate, the bird is also known as Wilson's thrush. As any bird-watcher can tell you, Alexander Wilson is almost as famous among American ornithologists as John Audubon, but the odd part is Wilson appears never to have seen a veery. In none of his books or papers is the bird even mentioned. The only connection Wilson has with the bird is that it was named after him. Apparently, during Wilson's time (1766–1813) the veeries were in such remote, difficult places that even such an intrepid naturalist as Wilson could not find one.

Now the expansion of civilization has forced the veery more out into the open. Moreover, the bird benefited from the second growth of forests and the increased numbers of thickets. It is a much commoner bird now than two hundred years ago, though still rarely seen out of the wilds.

The veery is a type of thrush, closely related to the wood thrush and also the bluebird. It is a sparrow-size bird, but can be distinguished from sparrows by its longer, thinner bill. It has a rust-brown back and buff-colored undersides.

The bird gets its name from its song, which consists of a series of "veery, veery, veery," but this explanation does not do the bird justice, for it has one of the most interesting and lovely songs of any bird, one that truly reverberates. At times it is as though the veery were singing into some silver tube, filling its song with tremors and echoing depths.

Veeries make their nests on the ground in exceptionally well hidden places deep in dark, impenetrable thickets. In the nests, made of grasses and twigs, the females lay four greenish blue eggs. The males play an active role by vigorously defending the nests.

Veeries are rarely seen elsewhere than close to the ground. Never walking, they jump about, at the same time keeping an upright posture. Unlike the vast majority of birds, they may sing while moving about on the ground in the course of their search for beetles, weevils, and caterpillars. At times they may also eat seeds and berries.

Though one will rarely come across a veery, it is worthwhile to listen for one.

LAKES, PONDS, AND WATERCOURSES

In August the appearance of most ponds has not changed dramatically since July. Dragonflies still dart above the waters. Small young turtles sun themselves on logs or stones. Duck chicks have grown and lost their downy look. Leopard frogs hop away from ponds and head for woodlands. More algae have grown, clogging the surface in many places. A few ponds may suffer from an explosion of life, until the water is thick and murky with microscopic life. Some ponds, too filled with plants, may have become thick with decay.

When Ponds Go Dry

The most dramatic change seen is in ponds that have gone dry. In August many, heated all summer long by the hot sun, may have lost so much water through evaporation that they have finally dried out. Some may have completely changed, leaving behind nothing but slabs of baked dry clay, like poorly fitted tiles with large gaps between them. In places these slabs of clay may be curled up at the edges and as hard as dry adobe bricks and crumbly as cookies.

This is so much a part of the yearly cycle for many ponds, and waterways, that animals have adopted ways of coping with the extreme desiccation. Those that can, escape by crawling, walking, or flying. Others, such as the hapless fish, die. On the other hand, a surprising number adjust. Microorganisms lie embedded in the mud as spores. They can endure in a viable form for months, even years, until rains once again fill the depressions and form ponds. Some species of frogs and toads dig down into the mud and simply await whatever fate brings them. Within a few months—or years—a good heavy rain will release them. Not only must many small organisms, such as clams, water fleas, and leeches, become dormant, but they are faced with the problem of dehydration. The animals deal with this by allowing the mud to dry around them. The mud seals them, and water loss is at a minimum. Some water fleas and fairy shrimps have been known to remain in this estivation for years, some surviving for over twenty years.

Estivation is, for all practical purposes, exactly the same as the hibernation of animals. The same physical and physiological changes take place. Heart rates and breathing rates fall dramatically. The animals remain in a profound stupor.

Mosquitoes

Mosquitoes have various ways of adapting to dehydration. The common *Culex* mosquito lays eggs in ponds as well as in more temporary locations, such as rain-filled gutters and ditches. Showers that fail to bring a pond to life may be enough to leave puddles that can be utilized by mosquitoes. Nothing short of a desertlike drought could defeat them.

In addition to finding small and temporary water supplies, mosquitoes survive so well because the eggs hatch and larvae develop rapidly. Depending on the temperature, eggs hatch within three to five days and larvae mature to the pupal stage in one or two weeks.

Mosquitoes face a problem when they lay their eggs on the water. This problem has to do with the surface tension of the water, which produces a film. The water film is tough enough to support a mosquito; in fact, a mosquito cannot break through it by itself. You may wonder, then, how mosquitoes manage to ensure that their larvae, which must grow beneath the film, get there, since the female cannot lay eggs beneath the surface. The problem is solved by the presence of hydrophobic regions on their eggs. As the eggs float on the water, their lower ends, being wettable, pierce the film. When the larva hatches, it leaves the egg by emerging through its lower tip and passes directly into the water.

Mosquito larvae, living under the film, are also faced with a problem, for they must breathe air. They obtain air by piercing the film with a sharp tube like a snorkel that is located at the rear of their bodies.

Because an adult mosquito, which, of course, has wings, cannot make its way up out of the water through the film, a new problem arises. Once hatched, the adult mosquito must rise above the film of water. This problem is solved because the comma-shaped pupa floats just beneath the surface. A bubble of air produced by the adult comes to surround it. The inner surface of the pupal skin is hydrophobic so that water does not enter the interior, sinking the skin "boat." During emergence, the adult rides in the open skin as in a boat.

Male mosquitoes have bushy antennae. They do not suck blood; instead, they feed on nectar and the juices of fruits. The females feed on nectar, too, but also suck blood from various animals, including you and me. The blood is used about once a week for egg production. In fact the blood serves as a nutrient for the yolk of the eggs.

Female mosquitoes are attracted to their host animals by several means, including moisture (mainly perspiration), lactic acid, carbon monoxide, body heat, and movement. Given so many redundant signals, it's no wonder they find blood.

Nothing is as annoying in its own way as the hum of a mosquito, a sound produced by the wings. If one listens to the vibrations of various kinds of mosquitoes, it becomes apparent that vibration rates differ. Those of the female are lower and serve to attract the male. His bushy antennae are precisely tuned to the sound produced by his mate's wings.

Most of us at one time or another have had a dream of a mosquito-free world, but the reality is not what you would expect. The myriad of mosquitoes that fill the summer air are absolutely necessary for the survival of many important wild animals. They serve as a major food source for such animals as bats, nighthawks, gnatcatchers, trout, and dragonflies. Many of these animals, in turn, are prey for carnivores—hawks, mink, bears, and many others.

Long-Billed Marsh Wrens

If you travel by boat along sluggish waterways, deep into marshlands, you will have a good chance of seeing long-billed marsh wrens (*Telmatodytes palustris*). Actually, they are common but not too frequently seen, for they stay well hidden among thick growths of cattails.

Long-billed marsh wrens look much like house wrens, especially

Long-billed marsh wren
(*Telmatodytes palustris*)

in outline. The bill, however, is longer, and the black back has white stripes on it; no other wren has similar markings.

Few birds are so energetic or quick, nervous or fidgety. It is thought that they keep constantly on the go because they are such prolific breeders. They are locked into a perpetual search for food for their young.

In spite of their parental chores, they also have the unusual habit of building numerous nests. No one knows for sure why, for the majority are never used for laying eggs or raising young. It is most likely that they are fake nests used to decoy predators away from the real nest. Some observers have seen male birds lure predators such as snakes to a fake nest. The birds even go so far as to fight for them. Even if they are not lures, predators have the problems of figuring out which nest, among many, has eggs. Their problem is multiplied because the nests have only a small entrance in the side. Because of that, the hunter cannot merely glance into a nest; it must take time to investigate, and is forced into inefficient tactics.

The nests, both fake and real, are well made of grasses. About the size of a softball, they are built in cattails, supported by the forks where the leaves meet. In them the females lay five to nine speckled, chocolate-colored eggs.

The most interesting aspect of the birds, for most people, are their songs—not that they are beautiful. The naturalist Laurence Palmer likened them to singing sewing machines, which is hardly a rave review. There is a sewing machine–like "weadle, weadle, weadle" quality to their song, which serves as a good identification. Nervous during the day, insistent and poignant at night, the wrens add their strange presence to the summer marshes.

Swamp Rose Mallows

In August, many swamps and ponds of the Northeast, especially those near the coasts, are endowed with dramatic blooming swamp rose mallows (*Hibiscus moscheutos*), which have all that one could desire of a flower. To begin with, they are exceptionally large—far larger than almost any other wild flower and actually very few cultivated flowers are larger. The colors seen in swamp mallows are the most wonderful pinks and reds and whites. The petals have colorful streaks on their interiors. In shape and structure, they look much like their close relatives the hollyhocks.

Swamp mallow shrubs are big and tall and have large, broad leaves. They often grow in shallow water, sometimes forming such masses that they create small islands.

The pink-red flowers are the perfect complementary colors for green marshes. Their images reflected on stagnant waters produce the mood of a summery world, self-contained and balanced in stillness.

Swamp Milkweeds and Milkweed Bugs

Someone can rarely get a good close look at the flower of a swamp milkweed (*Asclepias incarnata*) without getting his shoes muddy and sustaining some mosquito bites. Swamp milkweeds have small flaming-pink flowers of a peculiarly vigorous color. The plant grows to a height of about four feet and has clusters of flowers. Unlike most milkweeds—a large family—it has long, narrow lancelike leaves.

Despite the less than ideal conditions, the plant should be examined for milkweed bugs (*Lygaeus kalmii*) and (*Oncopeltus fasciatus*), which, by the way, are true bugs. They have sucking mouth parts and forewings that thicken at the base. They are brightly colored, the *O. fasciatus*, the large milkweed bug, being black and yellow and the *L. kalmii*, the small milkweed bug, black and red. To find them, you must look carefully under the leaves, being sure not to disturb them. If startled, they will quickly drop to the ground and disappear in the grass.

Their mating rituals and behavior are quite unusual and, moreover, are easy to observe. When a male is about to mate, he crawls onto a female's back. After being there a moment, and not copulating, he gets off and moves around behind her until he is facing away from her, then they connect their abdomens in an unusual end-to-end position. Once copulating, they continue for long periods of time: in hot weather maybe for ten to thirty minutes; in cold weather maybe for more than a day.

CELESTIAL EVENT

The Perseid Meteors

Meteors, commonly called shooting stars, light up the night sky by the hundreds every year for several nights around August 11 to 13, when they peak in frequency. The meteors are the lights of incandescent rock particles, properly called meteoroids. As they move toward the earth from their journey in outer space they hit the fringes of the atmosphere, fifty-five to sixty-five miles above us, and burn up. What we see is their fiery deaths, as short-lived blue trails of light. During the August showers they appear to come toward us from the constellation Perseus and are consequently called the Perseid shower. The meteoroids are very small, mostly the size of gravel or smaller. Millions of them orbit the sun in a group. Each year, in late July and August, the earth's orbit intercepts theirs and the earth travels through a cloud of meteoroids. It is thought that the meteoroids are rocky debris of a comet, namely one called Swift-Tuttle 1862 III.

At the height of the showers it is possible to see, on the average, about sixty-five meteors per hour. This is the second largest of the yearly meteor showers. The largest occurs on or about January 4. During that shower, called the Quadrantids, one can see, on the average, about a hundred meteors per hour. Because of the weather, it is far better to try to catch the August meteor shower. It may be the second best, but you won't freeze watching it.

September stands alone in the year somewhat like a season unto itself. The year seems to pause this month. Stilled warm air fills meadows and woodlands, mired in the doldrums, but imperceptibly the world begins to cool down. Reluctantly, September lets go of summer.

Because of the amount of dust and pollen in the air, imperious sunsets blaze on western horizons. The sun, like a hot ruby, sinks behind the horizon. Later an incandescent magenta gloom enfolds the still and silent landscape in a lukewarm purple as darkness slowly claims it.

WOODLANDS

In September, in spite of fall's arriving, a summer green continues as though it clung to the trees. In fact in September, throughout most of the Northeast, the woodlands look just about the same as they did in August. One would be hard put to find a tree that had turned red. Change moves slowly, and the woodlands in September appear immune to the fact that summer is ending.

Instead, the difference shows up in the blooms that dot woodlands. Many varieties of asters foretell autumn, as do the brightly colored phlox that line the sides of roads. Pure white snakeroot flowers glow, almost as though with a light of their own, from the dark recesses of thickets. In wet areas, fringed gentians, probably the bluest flowers of the whole year, bloom with vigor.

Doll's-Eyes or Baneberries

White baneberries (*Actaea pachypoda*) ripen in September woods and thickets. The word *bane* comes from an old word that meant "to kill." The odd-looking white berries, which have one distinct black dot on them and ripen on scarlet stems, could easily kill a person, for they contain a powerful poison. Few berries exhibit such spectacular color combinations; they are a study in red, white, and black. The common name for them, doll's eyes, is perfect.

Closely related to the doll's-eyes are the red baneberries (*Actaea rubra*). They are, of course, red, as red as the stems to which they are attached. They also look beautiful and also contain just as much poison as their death-dealing relatives. Both types of berries are to be looked at only.

Asters

Asters (genus *Aster*) certainly are the flowers of autumn. Like other members of the composite family, they come into their own late in the growing season. No month is better for seeing them than September. The raying petals of asters surround the centers of the flowers. They look like and are related to both sunflowers and, especially, daisies. No place on earth has so many asters as North America, and the best of them grow in the Northeast. They come in several colors—whites, blues, and yellows—and often the colors come combined in soft, pastel hues.

Of the many asters of September, you should try to spot the unique calico asters (*Aster lateriflorus*). Unlike most wild flowers, different-colored flowers may be seen growing on one plant. The centers at any rate differ widely in coloration, even on adjacent flowers. These wildly colored flowers add gaiety to any woodland scene.

The New England asters (*Aster novae-angliae*) can hardly be missed. They grow on high plants, which can be seen almost any-

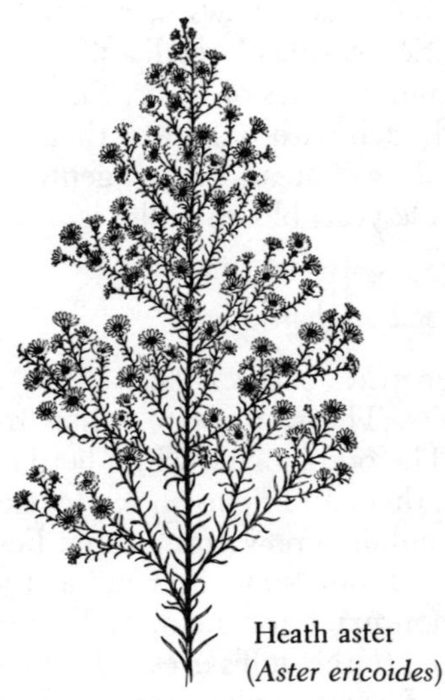
Heath aster
(*Aster ericoides*)

where in autumn woodlands. Their colors are variable, ranging from the purest of pinks to baby blues to whites. Whatever shade appears, it is perfection. These flowers serve as the heralds of the northeastern autumns.

Fortunately for the casual stroller, asters of one species or another simply cannot be overlooked. They cluster together at the sides of almost any woodland path.

Moths and Butterflies

In September there is often a second brood of various moths and butterflies. The adults of the new generation float on colorful wings, taking advantage of late summer warmth and early autumn quietude.

Among the second-generation moths seen in September are the **dagger moths** (genus *Acronicta*), so named because they have daggerlike marks on the outer edge of their fore wings. The moths are grayish in color and have a wingspan of a little over an inch. They can be seen flying about in woodlands.

During September, **fall webworms** (*Hyphantria cunea*) construct silken tents on countless trees. Unlike the tent caterpillars

White admiral (or banded purple) butterfly
(*Limenitis arthemis*)

Wanderer butterfly
(*Feniseca tarquinius*)

which feed outside of their tents, the fall webworms feed inside. Tent caterpillars usually enclose only the fork of a tree branch in a tent, but the fall webworms always construct their tents so that they will cover some leaves. The adult moths are white in color; most varieties display a few dots on their wings. One variety of *Hyphantria cunea* is the spotless fall webworm moth, one of the most beautiful of all moths. Because these moths are attracted to lights, they can be easily seen.

White admiral butterflies (*Limenitis arthemis*) frequently pay visits to meadows in August and September and can be identified because their black wings have two prominent white bands, parallel to the moth's body. The wings have green edges. These large butterflies are a common feature of September afternoons.

A new generation of **swallowtails** (family Papilionidae) fly about in September. They have long taillike hind wings. Two broods appear: the first in May and June and the second in August and September. The giant swallowtail (*Papilio cresphontes*) holds the distinction of being the largest butterfly seen in the Northeast. A large one may have a wingspan of five and a half inches. Giant swallowtails are brown and yellow, but their size alone gives them away. Very closely related to them is the tiger swallowtail (*Papilio glaucus*), whose broods appear at the same time. Tiger swallowtails can be at times as large as the giant swallowtails. They vary in color, some females being dark purple, others yellow, and the males yellow. Both have some blue and red spots on the edges of the hind wings.

Harvester, or **wanderer, butterflies** (*Feniseca tarquinius*) have widely separated broods: the first appear in April and May; the second, in July through September. These butterflies spend their time in damp places, such as swamps, and forest trails, often near alders and witch hazels. Harvesters are orange and brown, and their fore wings have a distinct pattern which, when tilted, looks something like the shape of a bird's skull.

These butterflies belong to an Old World tropical group of butterflies, which happens to be carnivorous. Adult harvesters feed on the honeydew of aphids and harvester caterpillars (which are brown-and-yellow-striped) feed on the aphids themselves. Their carnivorous habits set them apart from all other American butterflies.

Warblers

Warblers (family Parulidae) have the distinction of being probably the most difficult of all American birds to identify. Not only are there a great many species, but many look almost identical to one another, only the most subtle differences separating them. Even worse, their plumage changes during the year. In the springtime a bird may have colorful markings; in the autumn it may lack them and be a drab-colored creature that bears little resemblance to its former self. Worst of all, immature warblers look quite different from the adults. For the serious bird-watcher they present the ultimate challenge. Only experts manage to keep them straight.

In September, warblers that spent the summer in New England and Canada and other points north are returning back through more southern parts of the Northeast, en route to their wintering grounds in the south. In the autumn, warblers have become drab-colored, usually with some yellow or greenish tints on their bodies.

Warblers hunt for insects in trees and shrubs or in the leaves on the ground under them. To find warblers, look in trees, especially in parks.

Those warblers that migrate through the Northeast in September are the Nashville, parula, magnolia, Cape May, black-throated blue, Blackburnian, bay-breasted, blackpoll, Connecticut, mourning, and Wilson's warblers.

Some can be readily identified. Parula warblers are the only ones in the Northeast with blue backs and yellow chins. They also have wide white wing bars. Magnolia warblers can be identified because they are the only ones with yellow throats and a white tail band.

White-Throated Sparrows

White-throated sparrows (*Zonotrichia albicollis*) are delightful birds that summer in New England and cool mountain areas of the Northeast. During the cooler months of the year from September to April they stay in the more southerly regions. They stay in thickets, often in shrubs near water. Their song is exceptionally pleasant and well known, often heard coming from deep within some shadowy thicket. The song sounds as if the bird is musically saying "Old Sam Peabody, Peabody, Peabody." Because the "Peabody" is so distinct, the bird is often called the Peabody bird. The call, is one of the jolliest sounds to echo in the woodlands.

The bird can be identified by its white throat and the white stripes on its head, and by a distinct, but sometimes difficult to see, yellow dot near its eye.

White-throated sparrows stay on the ground, where they scratch up leaves with both feet as they search for food among leaf piles.

Migrating Swallows

Of all the birds that migrate southward in the autumn, probably none assemble themselves in flocks more conspicuously than swallows (family Hirundinidae). Large flocks of hundreds gather together to sit on telephone wires, all lined up as though in military formation.

There are several species of swallow. Those that leave the Northeast in September are the barn swallows, cliff swallows, and purple martins, which, in spite of their name, are also swallows. If you see birds on a telephone wire, you can tell which are swallows by noting their wings. Swallows perch in such a fashion that their wings are slightly separated from their bodies. The long wing tips of the purple martin hang farther down than their tail. The barn swallow has a long forked tail, longer than its wing tips. A cliff swallow is more difficult to identify, for its tail is square. Unfortunately, it can be confused with other birds.

Their colors do make their identification much easier. **Barn**

swallows (*Hirundo rustica*) are two-toned, with a dark blue back and russet underparts. Those colors and their deeply forked tail positively identify them. **Cliff swallows** (*Petrochelidon pyrrhonota*) have orange rumps and buffy foreheads. Male **purple martins** (*Progne subis*) are the only swallows that are dark all over.

More than anything, their flight gives them away, for no other bird matches their aerial acrobatics. Their long, pointed wings allow them any motion through the air to suit their impulses. Dipping, swooping, darting their way through the air, they show a breath-taking elegance.

Swallows have a long way to go after departing from the Northeast in September. Barn swallows migrate into central South America; cliff swallows head for southern Brazil and northern Argentina; purple martins head for Venezuela and northern Brazil.

White-Tailed Deer

During the summer, white-tailed deer (*Odocoileus virginianus*) spend most of their time near lakes, ponds, and watercourses, where they have a reliable supply of food, such as the succulent plants that grow near water.

In September, however, deer move into the depths of the forests. By then fruits and many berries will have ripened, luring deer to them and no doubt providing them with better nutrition. Moreover, deep forests provide deer with much better shelter. Not only will trees hide deer, but when much colder weather sets in, trees will also protect them from the wind, cutting down the wind-chill factor. In the dead of winter, that will become an important survival factor.

Deer undergo physical changes in September. The fawns, which have been spotted since birth, will begin to lose their camouflage spots, and their coats will become a uniform brown color. As they become older, fawns will be protected instead by their keen senses and speedy legs.

Male deer, which have been sporting antlers since early summer, will begin to rub off the velvet that covers them. Although the soft brown velvet looks like fur, it is not a fur but a vascular skin filled with a network of blood vessels that nourish the growing antlers. But in September the antlers are fully grown and need no more nourishment, so the deer rub off the velvet.

It is also in September that male deer begin to feel sexual urges.

Though the mating season is still two months away, they get fidgety and nervous.

FIELDS AND MEADOWS

It is in the fields and meadows that you see September at its best. Flowers of the composite family, such as goldenrods, thistles, autumn dandelions, and most especially asters dominate the fields.

In September countless birds flutter everywhere in and near fields, on fence lines, on telephone wires, on roadside trees. The urge to migrate appears to confuse many, forcing them to flock prematurely, separate, and gather together again. Several species of butterflies and moths, which have not been seen since early summer, appear once more, flying over fields. They are of the second brood, the late summer generation. Insect sounds of grasshoppers and crickets incessantly rise from the grass in all directions early in this month. Before it is out, however, the cool weather will silence them.

Balloon Spiders

During September and October many young spiderlings, of several different species, go ballooning; that is, they drift off into the air on "balloons," which in reality are long trailing filaments of spiderweb that can be lifted high above the ground by the lightest of breezes. By ballooning away, spiders scatter and move to new territories. This dispersion permits spider populations to find new sites to colonize.

Spiderlings usually go ballooning on warm, sunny days, when a gentle breeze is blowing. In preparation for their journeys, the spiderlings seek out high places, such as the tops of fence posts, mounds of earth, or weed stalks. The spiderlings face into the breeze and spin long filaments of silk from their posteriors. The wind will catch the silk, called gossamer, and gently blow it away from the spiderling. As more and more silk is spun and the pull becomes greater, the spiderling will brace itself against the tug of the wind. When the pull of the wind is strong enough, the spider will release itself. Sometimes spiders drift for miles.

Gossamer and spiderlings have landed on ships over one hundred miles from land. There are records of airplanes encountering them 14,000 feet above the ground. Most journeys that spiderlings take with their balloons are not, of course, so dramatic. Many spiderlings manage to travel only to the next field.

These balloons are best seen in fields and meadows, where they drift by, glinting delicately, and are almost invisible except for the shine of light on tiny strands of silk, many times finer than a strand of hair. Not infrequently a gossamer will cling to one's clothing.

Eighty percent of all ballooning spiders are of the family Linyphiidae. One member of the family, *Erigone autumnalis*, is an extremely common spider, but it is rarely noticed by most people because it is only 1/20 of an inch long. It has a bright yellow head, which can be seen with a magnifying glass. These spiders are so common that hundreds of thousands of them may live on an acre of land.

Flying Ants

It is also in September that you might see swarms of flying ants (family Formicidae), which at times form large and extremely impressive clouds.

Ants fly only when queens get ready to mate, then queens and males grow wings. As the winged ants exit from the colony, nervous workers follow them. Chaotic masses of moving ants circulate around the queens as they take to the air, surrounded by a great many winged males, which will soon try to mate with them. The ants fly into the air together, often rising out of sight. The males grasp the queens and mate with them, then fall to the ground. After mating, the queens usually start a new ant colony. Queens that start new colonies will lay eggs that will develop into workers. A considerable number of queens, however, are captured by workers and forced to return to old colonies.

The males face a different fate: all die after the nuptial flights. They cannot reenter colonies, as the worker ants force them away. Unable to fend for themselves, they will either be eaten by birds or some other animal, or starve to death.

The two most commonly seen flying ants in the Northeast are the small yellow ants and the big black carpenter ants. The smaller **yellow ant** (*Acanthomyops claviger*) is rather common. These ants build their colonies in the soil or under rotting wood. They never sting a human. You can identify them, in part, by their smell: if disturbed, they release a gas that smells like citronella.

The large black **carpenter ant** (*Camponotus herculeanus pennsylvanicus*) is so named because these ants eat away the interiors of wooden objects. As they do, they make remarkable structures consisting of the most intricate chambers, tunnels, and branching passageways. So well made are these that it would be difficult for anyone to duplicate them.

The ants have their colonies deep within these wooden structures. A queen stays inside her chambers all her life except for the one time when she leaves on the September mating flight. Hordes of female but sterile workers do all the work of building the structures. They also obtain food, fight off enemies, and raise the young. Large black carpenter ants can be identified by their large size and color. The workers, the only members of this species one is likely to see, are among the largest ants found in the Northeast.

Jewelweed Seeds

In September many jewelweed (*Impatiens capensis*) seeds have ripened, and these seeds are quite remarkable. They are encased within seedpods, yet if one lightly touches a mature seedpod it will explode violently, seeds shooting this way and that like tiny shrapnel. The effect can be startling. Because of their ability to shoot seeds about with such vigor, the plants are often called spotted touch-me-nots.

Woodchucks

Driving in the September countryside in the Northeast, you will often see a woodchuck (*Marmota monax*) in a field. The large rodents spend hours on their haunches looking here and there for danger as well as for opportunities for getting food. They might even climb to the top of fence posts and stare at the world. Estimates show that in typical farm country every six acres of land has at least one woodchuck. No other mammal of its size—about two feet in length and about fourteen pounds in weight—can top that figure.

Woodchucks always stay near their burrows. Their summer burrows can be rather complicated structures, usually made in open fields, most often on a hillside or slope. Many burrows have underground networks of connecting passageways, which in turn open to the surface by way of several exits. Chambers inside the burrows branch from passageways. Nesting chambers are raised above passageways so that a sleeping woodchuck will not be drowned in a heavy rainfall, which might fill the lower passageways with water. Woodchucks pad the sleeping chamber and other parts of the burrow with leaves. Meticulously clean animals, they build separate chambers for their feces, so their sleeping chambers always remain clean and sanitary. An elaborate burrow may extend over fifty feet underground.

Oddly enough, not much is known about the winter burrows that woodchucks build for hibernating, except that they build them in concealed places under the tangled roots of trees. The roots probably form a barrier against any animal that would try to dig up a sleeping and very defenseless woodchuck. When a woodchuck is ready to hibernate, it seals itself inside its hibernating burrow for the winter. As it places earth in, and around, the entrance to the burrow, it sees that the earth is carefully placed to look natural and escape detection. Woodchucks do a good job of this. The only burrows that have been found and seen so far have been accidentally opened by bulldozers engaged in construction work.

In September, woodchucks prepare for winter, mostly by stuffing themselves. They eat a wide variety of foods in preparation for their long winter's fast: dandelion, clover, goldenrods, asters, plantains, a few insects, and even a bird or two, if a woodchuck can catch one. They do not mind farm-grown food either, such as corn, turnips, and melons.

Woodchucks start preparing for hibernation especially early in the year. Their preparations are triggered by a change in the length of the days or night. They become stupefied in late September, and to all appearance they have difficulty staying awake. Before the month ends, a large number have succumbed to the urgency of sleep. They have crawled into their hibernating burrows, sealed themselves in, tucked their heads down between their hind legs, and gone to sleep for the winter.

When woodchucks begin to hibernate, they are fat. During their hibernation, which will last until April, woodchucks will lose about one-third to one-half their weight. In the spring they will reappear as skin, bones, and not much more. For more about their hibernation, see November.

Few mammals fall into such a deep sleep as woodchucks. Even so, records show that some occasionally appear for brief periods in January and February, but quickly go back to sleep. A woodchuck spends about half its life—it lives up to about six years—in hibernation.

September Grasses

Many common grasses ripen in September, such as the foxtails, old witchgrass, and redtop.

Foxtail grass (genus *Setaria*) can be told by its spike, which has a shape resembling the bushy tail of a fox, being distinctly cylindrical and hairy-looking. Actually, the sharp and dangerous "hairs" pose a serious threat to cattle and sheep, which may choke to death on them if they eat them. Because of this danger and the grass's rapid growth, foxtail grass is considered a weed, and an especially obnoxious one. Nevertheless, a field of two-foot-high foxtail grass in September is a pleasant sight to see, indicating that summer is on the decline and autumn near at hand.

Redtop grass (genus *Agrostis*), a taller grass, reaches some four feet in height when fully grown. The name implies that the top of the grass is reddish, but it may just as often be purplish or rusty in color. The grass gives an enigmatic coloration to countless fields and roadsides in September. The extremely variable top color changes with every mood, every breeze. From a distance it often looks like the shadow of a cloud on a field.

Unfortunately, redtop grass lacks beneficial uses. Livestock refuse to eat it, finding it ill-smelling and unpalatable. Since they leave it untouched, they allow it an opportunity to spread, which it does, forcing out more useful grasses.

Old witchgrass (*Panicum capillare*), also called tickle grass, has a distinct top. On its spike, thin wiry branches cluster together to form a brushlike top, which may be as much as a foot in diameter. In spite of its large top, the grass itself is not very high at maturity, only about two feet high. Later, in the winter, the tops will blow off the grass and roll across the snow like tumbleweeds.

Short-Eared Owls

In September, short-eared owls (*Asio flammeus*) move into the Northeast from the northlands. Being gregarious, a hundred or more birds may flock together as they migrate southward, most of them heading for marshes and open country, and they will stay in the region until April.

Short-eared owls barely exceed the size of blue jays. As one would guess from their name, their exterior ear tufts do not protrude very far, in fact, it is difficult to see them. If you are watching a short-eared owl in flight, you should look for a black patch at the bend of the wings, as seen from below. The top of the wings have buffy patches. These small owls are covered with numerous brown streaks, which also serve to identify them.

Unlike most owls, short-eared owls often hunt during the day, especially when the sky is overcast and the light is dull, when they can be seen flying erratically over marshes or open fields. Although erratic, their wavering flights take them effortlessly through the air as though they weighed nothing at all. Only phantoms could move so silently and so easily.

In spite of their name, short-eared owls possess very large and convoluted ears, located under their feathers. Their sensitivity to sounds allows them to pick up the slightest noise made by an animal moving below them.

So marvelous is their hearing that the little owls hunt much more by sound than by sight. As they fly on silent wings over areas covered with grass, they carefully and attentively listen for mice, their favorite food. Anytime one scampers about below a flying owl, if finds itself in extreme danger. A voracious short-eared owl can easily devour three mice in a short time. Before the first is digested it will have eaten the third. The owls keep down the mouse populations with a vengeance.

Short-eared owls evidently lack much sense of fear. When roosting, they will allow you to walk up to them. If you get near a short-eared owl, you'll see that the face is encircled with a black line. The eyes, surrounded by black, shine with a reddish bronze glow. In fact, the little owls have an unnerving and penetrating stare.

Houseflies

Though houseflies annoy us because of their dirty habits and persistent attention, they can be interesting to observe, especially in September.

The term *housefly* may actually be applied to several closely related species. All resemble one another in the sense that all have two transparent wings. Their bodies are dark and covered with bristles. All have large eyes.

One type of housefly, *Musca autumnalis*, is more commonly called the **face fly.** It received its odd name because these flies, imported by accident into the United States in 1952, are peculiarly attracted to the faces of cattle, where they eat the secretions that ooze from their eyes and nostrils. In summer they lay their eggs in sun-warmed cow dung.

During the months when the weather stays warm, face flies almost never go indoors. At night they will stay outdoors; they do not even follow cattle into their barns. Because of this reluctance, it is very unlikely that any fly seen indoors during the warmer months is a face fly.

In the autumn, things change. In September, when the weather cools down, one can see face flies clinging to the south sides of buildings and walls, sunning themselves. When the weather turns colder, they will enter buildings or work their way up under the bark of trees. Thus it is in September that most people see them inside their houses for the first time. For several months thereafter they will disappear from view. In late winter or early spring, when the weather warms up, these flies after spending the winter inside a house, will be seen in small groups crawling and buzzing on windows, especially cellar and attic windows, trying to get outdoors again. This later behavior is a good key to their identity.

Another housefly that virtually everyone has seen at one time or another is the **common housefly** (*Musca domestica*)—and common it is. It is a large fly, about ⅜ inch long, with reddish-brown eyes and a grayish body. It can most often be seen in kitchens. If watched closely, you will see these flies go through characteristic behavior patterns. Frequently they land on table or counter tops, stop, pull their legs up, and wipe them off against one another. When a female fly approaches a male—that is, gets within an inch of him—he will jump up on her and mate. The mating follows an easily observed ritual. The mating male buzzes his wings rapidly; at the same time, the female hooks her second pair of legs over her wings, which are held out to the side. The male next takes her front legs with his front legs and pumps them up and down. He positions himself on her back and copulates with her. Occasionally males mistake other males for females; when one jumps on another, they will wrestle but quickly separate.

There are other species of housefly as well, but the above are the easiest to observe. All houseflies closely follow the same egg-laying patterns. After a male fertilizes a female, she lays her eggs, usually about 600, in groups of about 125, in rotting vegetable material or preferably the dung of herbivores, but garbage or compost serves just as well. This habit may result in some danger to humans, but proven cases of human disease contracted from flies are rare.

Eggs hatch with great rapidity: if the weather is hot, the maggots may hatch within twelve hours. These are the larvae. Within a week or so they will be fully mature. After a short pupation of only five or at the most about seven days, they will turn into adult winged flies. The adults will not mate until they are about two days old, when the whole process will begin again. Flies breed at a prolific rate, and during the warm months of the year they can produce a dozen broods. In theory, one female can have 5.5 trillion descendants between April and September!

During the cold months of the year, houseflies winter over as adults. Many—too many—stay inside houses, hiding in cracks and in out-of-the-way places.

Grasshoppers and Crickets

Grasshoppers and crickets (families Tettigoniidae and Gryllidae) are closely related to each other and possess similar wing structures. Tough, leathery, but thin, fore wings cover the hind legs, which the insects use for flying. Both grasshoppers and crickets have long rear legs useful for jumping.

If one listens carefully to the various sounds that crickets and grasshoppers make, it soon becomes apparent that their so-called songs can be divided into two categories. Some are musical; someone with a good musical ear could hum tunes based on them. Others are not musical at all; indeed, they sound like rough materials scraping together. Crickets produce the musical sounds, whereas grasshoppers produce the scraping sounds.

Further subdivisions within the two categories can also be made, in terms of loudness, rhythm, the timing of the songs, and so on. Each species of cricket and grasshopper has its own particular

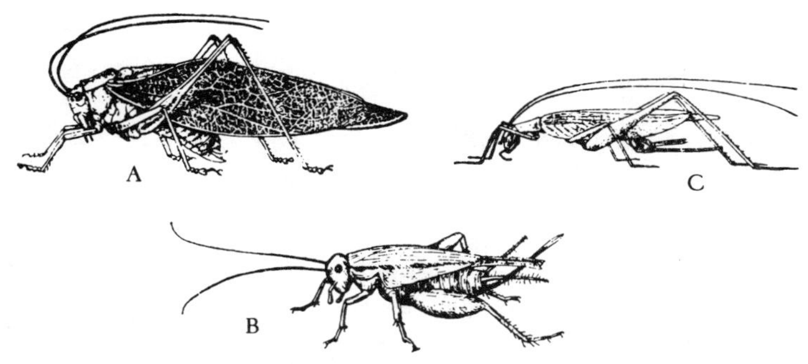

Katydid (A: genus *Microcentrum*); field and house cricket (B: genus *Gryllus*); and tree cricket (C: genus *Oecanthus*)

song. Some species, however, have two different songs. Once your ear is adjusted to them and you know what to listen for, you can tell various species apart by their songs. It would take time to learn them all, for there are dozens of various cricket and grasshopper species living in the Northeast.

The term *song,* in a way, misleads one. Neither crickets nor grasshoppers make their sounds with vocal cords, which in fact they lack. Instead, the grasshoppers drag their wings over a filelike arrangement, forcing the wings to vibrate. Crickets make their sounds by rubbing their wings together.

Most cricket and grasshopper songs are produced by males, for their songs serve the purpose of luring females to them so that they can mate with them. In the case of crickets, the songs also warn other males to stay away, out of their territory. If another male cricket enters into the territory claimed by a prior male, they will fight, usually to the death. They are so fierce that residents of Asia often raise fighting crickets as a sport.

Not all songs are made by male grasshoppers or crickets. Some are made by females who alternate songs with the males as they approach them. Once the female is close, the male she is approaching will sing a soft song, which evidently induces her to mate with him. Once they mate, they become silent.

One can often tell which member of the grasshopper or cricket tribe is making which song, by comparing the following songs:

True katydids (genus *Pterophylla*) go "katy did—she did—katy did."

Meadow grasshoppers (genus *Orchelimum*) go "tsip-tsip-tsip-tsip."
Black field crickets (*Acheta assimilis*) go "treat-treat-treat-treat."
Small ground crickets (genus *Nemobius*) go "ti-ti-ti-ti."

If you count the number of chirps a black field cricket makes per minute, you can determine the temperature in degrees Fahrenheit by means of the following formula:

$$T = 50 + \frac{n - 50}{4}$$

T=temperature; n=number of chirps per minute.

WILD, ROCKY PLACES

Near high rocky summits of mountains, the short growing season that begins so late in the summer and ends so early in the autumn declines rapidly in September. Trees already flame in red leaves among gray rocks, and summits may be touched with frost before the month is out. Snow squalls may temporarily whiten peaks, but the sun will follow.

Below, in the lowlands, grouse, pheasant, and deer move into wild, rocky places to eat the ripened berries and fruits. During many years, wild, rocky places become dried out. Dust coats rocks and plants and colors fade.

Wild Grapes

In spite of the fact that America's first European name was Vinland, apparently meaning "grape land," most of us rarely take note of the wild grapes (genus *Vitis*) that grow here, probably because their flowers are inconspicuous. Moreover, grapes tend to grow in out-of-the-way places and until September could easily be overlooked.

As the first days of autumn arrive, ripe wild grapes become noticeable. Bunches of ripe blue grapes hang from vines, which wrap themselves around trees. They are often found in wild, rocky places, especially on slopes where there is sandy soil, exposed at least part of the time to the sunlight.

It takes an expert to tell one native American wild grape from another. About twenty different species grow within the Northeast section of the country, and they frequently crossbreed with one another, forming numerous new varieties. Even though the average person cannot tell them apart, he can, at least tell which plants are wild grapes. But in general the leaves, more than anything, show them to be grapes, for wild grapes have leaves like those of the ordinary cultivated plants. The grapes grow in bunches, but they are not nearly so luxuriant and large as bunches taken from commercial vines. Wild grapes are bluish black and acid-tasting, but they are nevertheless juicy.

Thistles

Thistledown (of several genera such as *Cirsium*, *Sonchus*, and *Carduus*) can be the prettiest, most unexpected sight of September. Nothing shimmers so jewellike as sunlight moving and glancing through it. A thousand tiny rainbows of iridescent light come to life, glinting along what appear to be the tiniest possible silver-electrum-colored wires. The down, growing high from the tops of seeds, carries them away in the wind.

Thistles are magnificent plants and reach their best in early September. Tall, bold, a composition of abrupt, angular shapes, topped with either royal purple or lemon-yellow flowers or fluffy seed down, they stand strong and challenging.

Many species of thistles grow in the Northeast, often in fields or rocky, waste places. The two most imposing are the big bull thistles (*Cirsium vulgare*) and tall, field thistles (*Cirsium discolor*), which can reach nine feet in height. Even taller are the tall thistles (*Cirsium altissimum*) of rocky banks and woodlands, which may top twelve feet in height.

Yellow-Bellied Sapsuckers

Even though yellow-bellied sapsuckers (*Sphyrapicus varius*) are woodpeckers, they vary in several respects from most other woodpeckers. As their name indicates, they eat the sap of trees.

Yellow-bellied sapsuckers often stay in rather remote areas. Trees located in wild, rocky areas offer them a quiet retiring place. They are never the easiest of birds to find, for their coloration makes them blend right into the bark of trees. Their backs are mottled with black, white, and dirty browns. The males do have a touch of red on their heads, but the immature and females have brown and white heads. Both males and females have a distinct white wing bar. They also have dirty-colored yellow bellies.

Yellow-bellied sapsuckers migrate from Canada and New England into other parts of the Northeast in September, the males preceding the females, which arrive several weeks later. They are the most migratory of all woodpeckers.

Other woodpeckers peck into the bark of trees to obtain insects and insect eggs. Their tongues are quite long, and with them they pull out their food. Yellow-bellied sapsuckers, on the other hand, peck not only into the bark, but right through it to the tree's vascular system, where the sap flows. Their tongues are not as long as those of other woodpeckers, but are tipped with a brushlike apparatus. With it a bird dabs up the sugary sap (all sap has some sugar in it, even the most bitter-tasting). Sapsuckers will often carve out square patches of bark and make rows of them around trees. Sap alone, does not, however, make up the bird's diet: they also devour many insects and insect eggs. Ants, in particular, make up a large part of their diet.

There is a controversy over whether or not yellow-bellied sapsuckers kill trees. In theory, they could if they made enough holes in a tree to drain it of its life-giving sap. At one time it was thought that they did kill trees and cause considerable damage. The more current view is that they do very little if any damage.

Whatever the case may be, these birds enliven the forests by their tapping noises, which are done rhythmically but slowly—only two or three taps a minute. The sounds of their tapping are often heard long before the shy little birds themselves are seen.

Woolly Bears

One could call September the caterpillar month, but of all the many caterpillars seen during the month, the woolly bears (*Isia isabella*) rate as the best known, certainly to children. These are, of course, the hairy black caterpillars that have brown bands around their middles. (The word *caterpillar* comes from an old French word meaning "hairy cat.") The woolly bears can be found just about anyplace: sidewalks, fences, walls, trees, and shrubs. Children often tease them. If disturbed, they will curl up into tight little balls; this position guards their soft, bare underparts. Curled up, they present nothing but bristles to the world. For most enemies this works splendidly—few predators want a mouthful of bristles. Yet skunks relish them. Unlike many other animals, they have discovered that they can carefully pick off the hairs with their paws and gobble up the naked caterpillars. Apparently other animals that could handle woolly bears, such as raccoons, never discovered the trick or were too repulsed to care.

There is a common myth about woolly bears that one can tell how severe the coming winter might be by noting the width of the band. Unfortunately, there is no truth to this saying: as the caterpillar grows older, the band becomes wider.

Though we all know woolly bears, not many of us can say what sort of adult moth they become. Woolly bears, after a pupation, turn into Isabella moths, most unglamorous moths with fore wings that have a span of about two inches, colored a pale, dull orange-brown. Few moths have such a wide range. They can be found all over Mexico and the United States and in parts of Canada.

LAKES, PONDS, AND WATERCOURSES

Summer dies slowly at ponds. Still, often stagnant, waters, thick with weeds and algae, reflect fading trees. Dragonfly populations show a decline. Turtles escape the cooling waters and sun themselves with a stoic stillness.

Yet along the edges of ponds and watercourses the last flowers of summer still bloom and teals and other ducks are arriving from the northlands. Ring-billed gulls circle overhead. Swallows on their way south dip and sway over the waters, and redwing blackbirds nervously dart here and there as the urge to migrate stirs them.

Green-Winged Teals

Each autumn, many species of ducks migrate through the Northeast on their way from Canada and the Arctic to their wintering grounds in the south. These transient ducks begin arriving in September and will continue to pass through the region into December. Among the first to arrive in September are the green-winged teals (*Anas carolinensis*), which are the smallest of all surface-feeding ducks. The males have green and brown heads and are the only ducks with a green ear band.

Teal usually fly in small, tight flocks. At times they travel at very high speeds; in fact, no duck can ascend into the air from the water faster than these small ducks. They move upward so fast that the air moving through the wing feathers makes a sharp whistling sound.

When they are on the wing, one can see why they are called green-winged teal, for a prominent band of green is located along the back edges of the wings. Because of their colorful wing patterns and the streamlined shape of their body, they are often portrayed in paintings and prints. In flight, flocks of teal commonly wheel about and suddenly change direction.

Fortunately for observers, teal lack wiliness and can easily be approached. One place to see them is on mud flats. Unlike most other ducks, they often wade about in shallow water or in the mud. If you can come upon some wading, clap your hands and watch them shoot straight up into the air on whirring, whistling wings.

Muskrats

In September, muskrats (*Ondatra zibethicus*) begin to build new lodges for the coming winter. During the long season from spring to early autumn, many vicissitudes may have taken their toll of old lodges. Some get swept away in floods, human activities destroy others, and ponds frequently just dry out. Muskrats may have eaten all the edible and desirable plants surrounding their old lodges, so that they have become too isolated from food supplies. Canals that muskrats built through cattails may have filled in. Aggressive muskrats may have shoved weaker muskrats out of good areas, so that they are forced to build new homes. Whatever the case, muskrats must face the task of building new lodges in September so that by October the new lodges are ready for occupation.

Muskrats must, first of all, search for a good location for their lodge. If a pond dried out or neighbors are too fierce, a muskrat will go overland and search for a better pond. These journeys rarely take a muskrat farther than eight miles or so from its old haunts. Even so, the muskrat faces many dangers along the way. Though fierce when cornered, muskrats are no match for most land predators.

Once a pond has been chosen, a muskrat must find a decent bulding site. Preferred sites are located near edible plants as well as those used as building materials. The shorter the trip to food and building materials, the less effort and fewer dangers the muskrat faces. Muskrats seem to prefer building sites that have rather deep water nearby; a good site will thus be in fairly shallow water on a shelf next to a deeper pool. Since muskrats build canals from the sites into cattail growths, the soil must be soft enough to dig into so that good canals can be quickly and easily constructed. Of course, a muskrat will accomplish all of this by instinct—it does not deliberately plan or engineer its lodge any more than a bird plans its nest.

Once a site is chosen, it will constitute the middle of the muskrat's territory (usually about sixty-seven yards in diameter). Two muskrats will rarely build their lodges closer than that. Ponds have an average population density of about three to thirty-five muskrats per acre, depending on the supply of cattails.

A muskrat will build its lodge upon a log or willow clump, starting with a solid foundation and then constructing on top of it a dome of cattails and bulrushes, plastered and mortared with mud and waterweeds. Muskrats use only herbaceous plants for their lodges, never woody plants. Once the dome is complete, the muskrat allows it to settle for a few days. Then it will gnaw an underwater entrance into the dome and also gnaw out interior chambers.

A muskrat will also construct radiating canals from the lodge into the cattails so that it can haul building materials back and forth to the building site. If you wish to see a muskrat at work on its lodge, try to find the canals and watch them on a cloudy, dark day. Muskrats rarely work on bright, sunny days, because in bright light they and their wakes on water are easily seen by predators.

Muskrats actually make another type of home as well. If a pond or river has steep banks of firm soil, a muskrat may build its home in the bank. The animal digs an underwater tunnel, which is not visible from the shore, into the bank. The tunnel may extend for five feet or more and end in a chamber located well above the surface of the water. This sort of home is far more permanent than the lodges. Several generations of muskrats may enlarge it, pushing tunnels thirty feet back into the ground with additional tunnels leading into the water. Muskrat lodges and bank homes help the nonhibernating muskrats survive the winters. Holed up in them, they remain protected from most dangers—from the attacks of most predators and from cold and, especially, icy winds.

In September, you may also get a chance to see muskrats searching for food. They mainly feed on cattails, bulrushes, reeds, sedges, sweet flags, water lilies, and various pond weeds. It is possible to find a muskrat munching on any of these plants, especially on gray days.

Beavers store food underwater in ponds for winter use, but evidently muskrats store very little or none at all. During the winter they depend on plants that grow underwater or on roots, which they can easily dig up from mud at the bottom of ponds. Their winter diet consists primarily of pondweeds, coontails, water lily tubers, water milfoil, bladderworts, and burweeds.

During the time a pond is iced over, muskrats will make breathing holes in the ice by breaking the ice with their teeth. As they swim about under the ice, they can come up for air at these holes. Muskrats can easily swim underwater, beneath the ice, going from one hole to another. A muskrat can stay submerged for seventeen minutes, though they rarely stay underwater for more than about three minutes. However, a muskrat has enough time to gather food.

Two-Lined Salamanders

It is in September that the two-lined salamanders (*Eurycea bislineata*) mate. These pale, straw-colored salamanders rarely reach more than four inches in length. As their name implies, they display two black lines, more or less made up of dots, on their backs.

Their mating behavior is much like that of the spotted salamanders (see April). After the female two-lined salamander lays her eggs, she places them carefully under rocks in streams where there is a constant flow of water. The eggs, which measure 1/5 inch, take about ten weeks to hatch. The small larvae, which have gills, will appear. It will take them about two years to become adults. They will be no larger when they begin their adult life—only about two inches long.

Two-lined salamanders usually inhabit brooks and streams where there is a good flow of water. They cannot live in anything but clean, cold, constantly aerated fresh water. These requirements limit them to untouched watercourses, usually far from cities or towns. During the winter, two-lined salamanders may live either on land under piles of leaves or decaying vegetation or in deep water.

Unlike most salamanders, which prefer to hunt in the dark of the night, two-lined salamanders will sally forth in the middle of the day, especially if it is damp, and go hunting for worms, insects, and spiders. Those that stay in deep water will hunt mostly for tiny crustacea.

CELESTIAL EVENTS

Autumn and Fall

On or about September 23 the autumn equinox occurs. Many calendars have written on the appropriate date "Fall begins." Actually, this is a common mistake. Many calendar makers believe, as most of us do, that the words *autumn* and *fall* are exactly synonymous and interchangeable, but they are not. *Autumn* is an astronomical word, defined as the period of time between the autumn equinox, when the sun crosses the equator, and the winter solstice, when the sun touches the Tropic of Capricorn. Fall is not a season per se. Strictly speaking, it refers only to the time when leaves fall off trees, in the Northeast from mid-October to late November. The word *fall* refers to the tangible world around us; the word *autumn*, to an abstract astronomical event.

The Harvest Moon

The harvest moon will appear in September. It is the full moon that occurs within two weeks of the first day of autumn. The term *harvest moon* goes back almost three hundred years, and is first recorded in writing in 1706, when Isaac Watts, in his *Horae Lyricae: Poems Chiefly of the Lyric Kind*, wrote: "Seventy harvest-moons Fill'd his wide gran'ries with autumnal joy." It probably was in the language much longer, carried along as an oral tradition.

The harvest moon should be carefully observed. Each night the full, or near-full, moon rises at almost the same time, within about fifteen minutes. As the moon rises, it moves at a very low angle, about twenty-seven degrees in relationship to the horizon, as seen from most places in the Northeast. It moves more or less sideways, close to the horizon, moving behind the shapes of trees, hills, and buildings, and compared to these familiar objects it appears enormous. Because of the pollen in the air, the harvest moon also often takes on startling shades of oranges and reds. Once the moon is high in the sky a few hours later, it becomes lost in the vastness of space and appears to be small and pale yellow in color. If you take the time to watch the harvest moon rise on several nights, you will note that each night it rises farther to the north.

Moonrises at other times of the year are quite different. Then the moon rises at a much steeper angle and clears the horizon more quickly. Near the spring equinox, for example, the moon will rise in the Northeast at about an angle of seventy-three degrees, so its upward motion appears quite fast. In spite of this extra speed, the moon will arrive back at the eastern horizon to rise on the next night about fifty minutes later because the moon is also moving eastward in its orbit. The following night at the same time the moon will be still farther eastward, in other words, below the horizon.

Only near the time of the autumn equinox do the Earth, sun, and moon line up so that the plane of the moon's orbit is at a low angle to the eastern horizon. The basic reason for this is that during the year the Earth's axis sometimes points away from the sun and sometimes toward it. Likewise the plane of the moon's orbit changes in relation to the Earth's axis. Only around the autumn equinox does everything line up so that we see the harvest moon.

October

Red October signals the end of the green months. After the long sameness of verdant growth, a dramatic change comes to the Northeast. New colors appear everywhere and race from tree to tree like flames out of control. Not one deciduous tree will escape.

October is not just an end but a harvest, a culmination of months of hidden preparations that took place inside fruits, nuts, and developing berries. Seeds thicken on weeds; tree limbs droop with heavy fruit; nuts fall, bounce, and plop on the ground; and shiny berries bulge against each other. As fruit ripen, the air will smell tangy, sweet, and winy.

It is just as well that the harvest will be completed, because before the month is over, a killing frost will reach below the ground and harden it.

WOODLANDS

The Colorful Leaves and How They Change

The Northeast flares with its display of colorful autumn leaves in October, when hillsides turn crimson and red, and rivers become edged with yellow. No other section of the country compares, and actually no other place on earth matches it.

This changeover in colors is the most striking seasonal milestone of all. Ever since people have witnessed it, they must have wondered how it occurred. Until recently not much was known, but discoveries have revealed new information about this process.

The first step for the turning leaf occurs when chlorophyll, which is bound to proteins in green leaves, separates from these proteins. Not only do the proteins separate from the chlorophyll, but they themselves come apart and separate into simpler substances: amino acids. As this happens, the leaves lose their green, assuming other colors, such as reds, yellows, and browns.

The reason that the leaves turn from green to autumn colors is mainly that when light hits chlorophyll, all the light rays are absorbed except green, which is reflected. When we look at chlorophyll, we see only reflected green light, and an intense one at that, so of course it looks green to us. Once chlorophyll no longer reflects green and absorbs all colors, as it does in a decaying autumn leaf, the chlorophyll is invisible. We then see the remaining inner structure of the leaf, which is predominantly red or brown in color.

But other important factors influence the colors. All leaves contain sugar. In fact, the main function of chlorophyll is to manufacture sugar from carbon dioxide in the air and water. Sugar, in turn, can combine with other chemicals to produce *anthocyanin*, a glycoside, which is a red pigment. This turns the leaves of oaks, sumacs, Virginia creepers, and some other trees and vines into reds and crimsons. Anthocyanin is also responsible for other colors: it paints ashes with purples and some oaks with shades of brown. The colors of anthocyanin depend on its acidity or its alkalinity.

Another important chemical for changing the color of leaves is *carotene*, which is a red crystalline hydrocarbon that can be converted into Vitamin A. It colors the leaves of hickories, tulip trees, birches, and sycamores yellow.

As proteins degrade into amino acids, they are retained by the plants. These protein building blocks contain a very valuable element for plant growth: nitrogen. All amino acids contain the amino group NH_2, which is a substance containing nitrogen chemically combined with hydrogen. Although the atmosphere contains some 80 percent nitrogen, most plants cannot absorb nitrogen from the air for their own use. A very few plants containing some bacteria can *fix* nitrogen, that is, force it to combine chemically with other elements. These plants are rarely forest trees, but are instead legumes, members of the bean and pea family. Because most trees cannot obtain nitrogen from the air, they must save whatever they can. They reabsorb the valuable nitrogen-containing amino acids from their dying leaves and store them in their roots for further use. When spring comes, the trees will carry the amino acids up in their sap to their leaves.

No one knows exactly what triggers the breakdown of the proteins in the leaves in autumn. It may be cooler weather, some as yet unknown biologic clock, desiccation, or, far more likely, changes in the duration of sunlight.

The Parade of Colorful Trees

Each year, trees, shrubs, and vines turn color one after another in a predictable progression. Among the first to turn are the sumacs and Virginia creepers. In many parts of the Northeast their colors darken to rich reds, magentas, or purples. The next plants to turn color are the shadblow, a bush that becomes either a red or a bright bronze color; then willows, ashes, and locusts will take on a lovely yellow-green. Black gum will be among the most colorful of trees, afire with a powerful scarlet hue, followed by red and sugar maples, which turn crimson, bronze, red, or orange. For a while their colors will dominate the northeastern landscapes. Sassafras displays either scarlet or orange a little later, and cherries take on a reddish color. Sour gum, another spectacular tree, turns brilliant red, and finally birches and hickories will pale to a buttery yellow.

Among the last trees to turn color will be the oaks, which vary a great deal in color, depending on the species. Their colors range from dark reds to dull paper-bag browns. Late-changing white ashes become yellow. The last trees to turn, beeches, take on various colors from bronze to pale yellow.

From year to year the dates when the trees will turn vary somewhat, about two weeks or so. Moreover, the fall foliage moves southward from the northernmost regions of the Northeast at a rate of approximately thirty-three miles per day. The peak of the autumn colors in northern Maine is around October 7 most years; Connecticut, October 12; and northern Pennsylvania, October 21. Even so the progression of color change among the plants remains the same.

Ruby-Crowned Kinglets

No song is so plaintive and moody as that of the ruby-crowned kinglet (*Regulus calendula*), heard at dusk in autumn; the notes sound "tzee, tzee, tzee, ti, ti, ti, tear, tititi." Because this song can carry well over a hundred yards, on hearing it for the first time you might imagine that it was produced by some large bird. Quite the contrary. Aside from the tiny ruby-throated hummingbirds, the singer is one of the smallest birds in the Northeast.

Ruby-crowned kinglets move into the region from the north in October. When they do, they mainly inhabit conifer forests. These tiny mites are often seen hovering like dots high up among pines and pointed spruces. At other times they accompany chickadees along branches where both hunt for insects and insect eggs in the bark.

Ruby-crowned kinglets, so named because of the male's red crown, can also be identified by their tiny size, greenish upper parts, prominent white eye rings, and rather short tails. Do not expect, however, always to see the ruby crowns. These appear only on males, and they show them at will by uncovering the red crown patch.

When males meet, they often show their crowns to each other, in apparent macho display. Though there appears to be something aggressive in these competitions, the males never fight. However, they may become quite agitated about it all, hopping here and there nervously, flashing their crowns.

These birds may be very small, but they are extraordinarily hardy. Their ability to withstand blizzards and icy winds, considering their size, is remarkable. At the first hint of cool weather, hummingbirds are off and away to the south. The smaller an animal is, the more difficulty it has keeping warm, because for its size it has a large surface area that radiates away body heat. A small animal can compensate with thick fur or feathers, but ruby-crowned kinglets do not possess thick feathers. The only way they can keep so warm is through sheer metabolism and constant activity. And active they are—always on the go.

Jelly Fungi

Someone walking about in October forests may very well come upon an odd jellylike substance. Though artificial-looking, it is a living organism, a fungus called jelly fungus (order Tremellales). In damp weather, especially in rainy weather, these fungi become gelatinous. In dry weather, however, they become much harder and not at all jellylike; during a dry spell their texture becomes horny.

There are several types of jelly fungi, including the **ear fungi** (*Auricularia auricula-judae*). These appear during cool weather and are found on decaying wood, such as old fence posts and dead trees. In growth they do resemble brown human ears to some extent. They thrive on raw, miserable weather. A brisk wind out of the north driving rain before it, with temperatures just above the freezing point, is just right. Ear fungi will appear by the dozens.

Trembling fungus (*Tremella frondosa*)

Orange tremellas (*Tremella mesenterica*) are even more jellylike. Indeed, they look just like globs of lemon jelly. They, too, have a shape vaguely resembling a human ear and grow on decaying wood. *Tremella frondosa* fungi are often called witches'-butter. They quiver and shake if touched and have an unpleasant sticky feeling. No one knows whether or not they are poisonous, probably because no human or animal has ever had the inclination or nerve to eat something quite so disgusting-looking. Yet, for all that, they are brilliant yellow, and certainly weird enough to fascinate anyone.

Coral Fungus

Ashy coral fungus (*Clavaria stricta*) is also a most unusual plant. As its name implies, it looks like miniature coral stems. Even for a fungus, it is colored in a remarkable way, varying from white to black, being mostly an ash gray. Since it does not possess a hint of true color, the fungus can look startling: because of its shape and color, one would be hard put to believe that it is actually truly alive.

Wood Turtles

In October, wood turtles (*Clemmys insculpta*) hatch from their eggs, which were laid in warm sand by their mothers during the month of June.

Newly hatched wood turtles have round shells, long tails, and gray bodies. As they grow older, their appearance will change a great deal. Their shells will be marked by distinct but odd-looking pyramidal lumps with numerous laminations. The bodies of adult turtles are reddish or orange-colored, and their tails become shortened with age.

Wood turtles spend more of their time on land than do most turtles, rarely taking to the water although they swim very well. As their name implies, they inhabit woodlands, often deep forests. They are so at home among trees that, unlike other turtles, they will occasionally climb one.

Like painted turtles (see May), they easily learn mazes, probably because they need such skills in deep forests.

Though they once held wolves and pumas, today's deep forests are not inhabited by fierce animals. Most predators, such as coyotes and foxes, prefer to hunt in open or broken country where they can run their prey down. Only bobcats may hunt in dense woods. Wood turtles therefore find more safety in deep forests than they would in lakes or ponds filled with swift fish, snapping turtles, and other dangerous predators, even though they are not really designed for a forest life.

Wood turtles eat a wide variety of food: insects, earthworms, slugs, and snails. In hunting for food they may at times waddle out of their woodland haunts and browse in meadows and fields. But after feeding, they will return to the seclusion and safety of the woodlands.

FIELDS AND MEADOWS

Compared to the glorious woodlands, fields and meadows seem less noticeable, more reticent. Yet the tufts of milkweed seeds drift out of the shiny silver interiors of pods and drift in Indian summer breezes across fields. Smartweeds still add dots of pinks to the grasses, and a few goldenrods still bloom. Though all is on the decline, a few faded colors cling to the fields and meadows.

Flowers of the October Fields

October is the month when the composite family of flowers (Compositae), which includes sunflowers, daisies, thistles, and dandelions, now puts on its best show of the year. (See June, "Dandelions," for the composites.)

Many autumn flowers of the composite family are big and spectacular, such as the sunflowers that are commercially grown. Chrysanthemums furnish bright fall colors to many gardens and are considered by people around the world to be one of the most beautiful of all flowers.

One can find large, colorful **Jerusalem artichokes** (*Helianthus tuberosus*), which resemble sunflowers, growing wild in October, along roads and fences. These bright-yellow-flowered plants may top out at over ten feet tall, so one can hardly miss them. The Italian name for them is *girasole*, which is close to an Italian phrase meaning "turning to the sun." The flowers, in actuality, do turn their faces toward the sun. At one time, native Americans cultivated the plants for their edible tubers, and in time the plants escaped their gardens and went feral.

Sweet everlastings, also members of the composite family, grow in dry clearings and in fields. Their perfume hovers in the air, giving fragrance to mid-autumn days. Their white flowers, barely tinged with pale yellows, cling to cottony stems, which branch off in many directions. The scientific name of the plant, *Gnaphalium obtusifo-*

lium, comes from the Greek word *gnaphallon*, which means "a tuft of wool." The name refers to the cottony appearance of the flower heads.

Boneset (genus *Eupatorium*) commonly grows in wet meadows. Its small fluffy white flowers offset the damp green shady places of their environment. It can be identified by the manner in which the stem appears to grow directly through the leaves of the plant. Long ago, when herbalists tried to detect signs within plants of their curative powers, they decided that bonesets would heal broken bones, because the stalks (the "bones" of the plant) went right through the leaf. Consequently they believed that adding leaves to casts for broken bones would knit bones together. This quaint but incorrect idea long ago fell by the wayside, but the name stuck.

Teasels (genus *Dipsacus*) may look somewhat like composite flowers, for many small flowers do grow together on a flowering head, but in fact, the arrangement of the flowers is different and the flowering heads lack ray flowers. Instead, teasels belong to the Dipsacaceae family. Teasels are an Old World flower, which fullers, who washed, stretched, and treated woven cloth, brought with them from Europe to America. They utilized teasel flower heads to treat woolens by placing them on spindles to lift the nap from fabrics to make them softer. To meet the demands of fullers, farmers grew teasels as a cash crop. Teasels escaped, went wild, and are now a very common wild plant. Teasels could be mistaken for thistles, for they have purple flowers and similar-looking burs, but of course they are not related. If you watch the small flowers bloom on a teasel's flowering spike over a period of time, you will notice something quite odd: the flowers first bloom in a band around the middle of the spike, then two groups bloom, one above the band and one below it. The two separate bands of flowers continue to bloom around the flowering spike as one band moves up and the other down. No other flowers on spikes move in two directions at once, except on closely related plants. Among common flowers this arrangement is unique to teasels.

Jimsonweeds (*Datura stramonium*), which have large tubular flowers and prickly fruit, grow profligately as large, rank plants in waste places. These plants are saturated with poisonous hallucinogens. They received their name from the Jamestown colony, Virginia, where some British soldiers in 1676 ate the plants and became violently sick. They also suffered from hallucinations. Though the plants can produce exotic, soul-shaking visions and have become known to a wide audience through the writings of Carlos Castañeda and others, they can as easily kill one. Moreover, one can never tell just how lethal a particular plant may be. Large amounts eaten from one plant may produce visions, usually of the nightmarish sort, whereas a far smaller amount from a plant next to it might be deadly.

Jimsonweed (*Datura stramonium*)

In spite of their strange and adverse effects, their startling size and especially the beautiful trumpet-shaped, creamy-white flowers make these plants attractive—but these are truly plants to be seen but not touched.

Velvetleaves (*Abutilon theophrasti*) came to America from India. Few if any other common wild flowers in the Northeast come from such a distant country; though they have come halfway around the world, they thrive here and are spreading. Velvetleaves can be identified because they are large plants, up to six feet high, full and leafy. They grow large, eight-inch-long leaves, which, as one would guess, are soft, attractive, and velvety. Their five-petaled, plain-looking yellow flowers add to their appearance. Most curious of all are their seedpods, which look like pies divided into sections. Because of them, some people call the plant the pie maker. The odd seedpods help identify the plant.

Exceptionally beautiful flowers decorate **musk mallow** (*Malva moschata*) plants: their pink petals are lined with fine red stripes. They smell, richly, of heavy musk. European settlers brought the plants to America and grew them in gardens. Like so many other plants that were once cultivated, they have become over the years part of our wild flower population.

Other wild flowers also bloom in October, but as anyone in the fields during the month will note, they appear fewer and farther apart. As the growing season draws to a close, the dead spaces between them grow ever larger and death and dormancy gain the upper hand.

Slate-Colored Juncos

Beginning sometime in October, slate-colored juncos (*Junco hyemalis*) appear everywhere, in country fields, in suburbia, and on city streets. Most have moved out of the northern, and higher, parts of the Northeast region, migrating toward the south and lower elevations, while others have flown in from more northern parts of Canada.

Few winter birds surpass the slate-colored juncos in sheer numbers. Although rock doves, often called pigeons, and English sparrows outnumber them, it may be that no other birds do. Virtually everyone has seen slate-colored juncos, but in spite of that, not everyone could identify one. They look like sparrows in terms of size and shape of bill—because they are sparrows. But unlike other sparrows, slate-colored juncos are predominantly gray, lacking the brown colors seen on other sparrows. Their backs and heads are gray, and there is a clearly marked boundary between the dark head and chest and the white underparts. They have pink bills and gray tails prominently edged with white.

Slate-colored juncos often come to feeders and frequently join up with English sparrows to form mixed flocks. At other times, in fields, large flocks of hundreds of these juncos gather together. All through the cold months of the year they eat grains and seeds, wherever they might find them, and so can be seen wherever such food is available.

Slate-colored juncos utter the most puzzling collection of twitters, chirps, and odd smacking sounds, yet odder, in a way, is the manner in which a flock will suddenly, for no apparent reason, become absolutely silent. For almost all of us their nervous little voices make up part of the background sounds of our daily lives during the cold months of the year, whether or not we are aware of them.

Ermines

In the wintertime, the fur of ermines (*Mustela erminea*) turns pure white, except for the tip of the tail, which remains pitch black. The fur of European ermines once decorated the lavish ceremonial robes of kings. In terms of clothing, they were the ultimate status symbol. Aside from such exotic uses, the fur was scorned. Since it does not wear well, it can be used only for decoration.

In the summer, ermines, which grow to a length of about twenty inches, can be identified because they have long, thin bodies, the upper parts brown and the lower parts white. All year round their tails are tipped with black. More than anything, one can identify them by their alert expressions, which are greatly enhanced by their triangular faces and pert ears.

In October these weasels go through a transitional period as their brown fur turns white, changing so that they can be camouflaged against the snows of winter.

The ermines can be found in a wide variety of places in the countryside: fields, woodlands, and wild, rocky places. Though they roam far and wide, they usually stay close to some sort of cover. Those seen in fields, for example, will often run along the side of a stone wall, where they can quickly hide by dashing in between the stones if they are disturbed.

On occasion, ermines enter henhouses, but in spite of occasional domestic attacks such as that, they should be considered very valuable animals. Not only are their killing skills exceptional, but they focus most of them upon rodents. If allowed to, ermines will wipe them out of barns. Their beneficial services in that direction far outweigh their destruction of poultry. But most do not hunt near buildings, living far from habitation and hunting in the deep countryside.

Most ermines make their home in rocky crevices or in old tree stumps, located near some open country, such as fields. The animals are frequently heard before they are seen. They often hiss and sometimes make a purring sound or occasionally let loose with a hideous scream, an eerie sound to hear on an otherwise still, silent October afternoon.

If you ever happen to get close enough to an ermine, you might get a whiff of a most disagreeable odor. It comes from musk glands. The scent attracts a mate.

WILD, ROCKY PLACES

Bleak gray walls of rock are offset by the brilliant foliage of October. Reds against grays, yellows against purple shadows, oranges against green mosses, gold against charcoal-colored basalts counterpoint each other and vie for our attention. Gay, sun-filled yellow birches stand out against brooding shadows, while Virginia creepers rise like flames up rock crevices, and fans of burgundy sumac wave in the wind. Thanks to bright leaves, magenta shadows lie on pale granites.

Land Snails

Land snails (family Polygyridae) frequent wild, rocky places. They are, in spite of appearances, well adapted to a life among rocks. Though they lack feet, the underpart of their body is a marvelous tool that can take a snail anywhere, even up the sides of perpendicu-

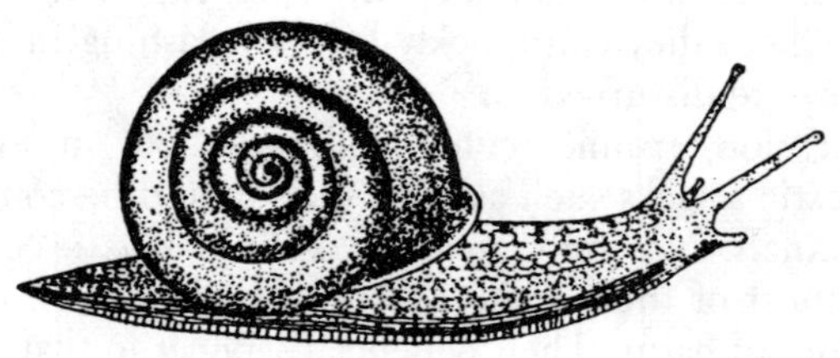

White-lipped land snail (*Triodopsis albolabris*)

lar cliffs—but slowly, of course. A snail can even make its way up a pane of window glass with no difficulty because the underpart of its foot exudes a sticky film on the glass and the muscles of the foot operate hundreds of tiny edges that push the snail along. Obviously, compared to a pane of glass, a rock cliff is a snap. Snails also thrive in rocky places because they feed on mosses that grow there.

Land snails can be distinguished from freshwater snails because aquatic snails have two tentacles, called horns, whereas land snails have four horns. The two longest horns of the land snail are tipped with eyes. The snail can move its horns this way and that, so that the eyes can move independently of each other. The shorter two horns are used for feeling for food and other things. Snails are nearsighted, but they can see things clearly if they are twenty inches away or closer.

Snails mate in an unusual manner. Snails are hermaphroditic; that is each individual possesses both male and female organs. When two snails mate, they can, and often do, mate in such a way that one individual's male organ is penetrating the female organ of the other and at the same time its partner's male organ penetrates its own female organ. At times, rows of snails may mate in chains containing a dozen or so snails all mating at once, male to female organ.

In October, temperatures drop quickly in rocky places, especially those high outcrops near or at the summits of mountains. Late in the month, insects and other cold-blooded creatures have either hibernated in some protected spot or died, yet the snails can still be out and about in cold temperatures, even below the freezing point. They cannot, however, hold out forever. When a really hard frost occurs, they will work their way under leaves or logs and pull their bodies up into their shells. They will then coat themselves with a mucus that dries into a waterproof coating. This conserves their internal moisture, so that as they remain hidden for the winter, they will not dry out and die.

Not only do snails survive cold winters in the Northeast, as a group they have survived through enormous lengths of time. In fact, as far as land creatures go, they are the oldest one could find in the Northeast. Snails developed about 400 million years ago. Though ocean-dwelling, they were not much different in appearance from today's land snails. The little slimy amber-colored beast with its odd tentacles is as close to living tangible history as one can get.

Bumblebee and Wasp Queens

Whatever bees and wasps (order Hymenoptera) are seen in October, buzzing here and there in wild, rocky places, will be queens. Behind them lie ruined societies that were once exquisitely adapted and that functioned with clockwork precision. By October all is over. Genetic codes, not the weather, destroyed those insect cities. With the onset of autumn, many changes take place within insect colonies. Genes within workers instruct them to change eggs slated to be future workers' eggs into drone eggs. When the drones hatch, they are ready to mate with the queens. After the drones and queens fly off on nuptial flights, workers left behind become disorganized. Chemical signals send out new communications, which, in effect, will tell the workers to fail at their tasks. Chaos reigns. Workers scurry helplessly here and there, others languish, and within a short time most die.

The drones that have gone off on their nuptial flights will fare no better. After mating with a queen, it will be a drone's fate to die. Those that did not find a mate will be excluded from their home colonies by workers, which will chase them away. The cast-out drones, unable to fend for themselves, will soon die.

Only the fertilized queens will live. Some can be seen darting here and there near wild, rocky places as they seek deep rock crevices where they will curl up and hibernate for the winter. Others will either find or make holes in the ground and hibernate in them. In the spring they will wake up, start new colonies, lay their fertilized eggs, and produce workers.

By October the bumblebee (genus *Bombus*) populations of the Northeast are many hundreds of times smaller than they had been in the summer. Mortality among drones and workers will have been total. Not one will survive until spring.

Black Rat Snakes

The largest snakes one is likely to see in the Northeast are the black rat snakes (*Elaphe obsoleta obsoleta*), and it can be an awesome sight. They often inhabit wild, rocky places, for they can find not only protection among the rocks but also rodents. Broken rocky areas provide them with many places where they can alternatively sun themselves and retreat into holes or get behind rocks where they can cool off. Since the snakes are cold-blooded, the easiest way for them to keep their blood temperature within a normal range is to warm up and cool off at regular intervals.

Black snake (*Coluber constrictor*)

Many people are a little afraid of snakes. Nevertheless, one should keep on the lookout for a black rat snake. In spite of its size (large ones may reach seven feet in length and there are reports that some have reached nine feet), it is harmless to humans. It can be identified quite easily, because it is the only snake that has shiny scales and also a black back and is mostly white underneath.

As they move, these snakes display an extreme agility. Unlike most snakes, a black rat snake can easily climb up and over rocky cliffs and get about in places that would stop or slow most creatures, even those that are fleet of foot. It is most often seen sunning itself on top of walls or large boulders, but it also drapes itself over tree branches.

Black rat snakes are in a group of snakes called constrictors. These snakes do not strike out at their prey and kill them by biting them, as many snakes do. Instead, the swift-moving, agile black rat snakes coil around their prey with lightning speed and smother it, preventing inhalation of air. The prey is not crushed. Black rat snakes attack only warm-blooded animals—birds and mammals—responding to the heat that radiates from their bodies. Rat snakes ignore the cold-blooded animals such as frogs and other snakes. As their name implies, these snakes are marvelous hunters of rodents.

Black rat snakes hatch from late summer through October. In June and July, females lay from six to twenty eggs in the ground, sometimes in old stump punk. The eggs hatch on their own without benefit of any parental help. The young do not look at all like adult snakes. In fact, they are brown in color, and black blotches cover their backs. They grow rather rapidly for reptiles, maybe reaching a length of thirty inches in their second year. If they do not meet with calamity, they will live to be at least sixteen years of age. Like all cold-blooded animals of the Northeast, they will be forced to hibernate in a den throughout the winter, but they will appear earlier in the spring than most other snakes.

Sumac and Poison Ivy Colors

In many rocky places, sumacs (genus *Rhus*) with their colors at their height, look like flames leaping upward around boulders and cliffs. In the shade their colors turn purple and quiet, but in sunlight their leaves shimmer brilliantly. Some of the finest colors of autumn are seen within sumac groves. Magenta-colored leaves appear scattered on many sumacs, their pure color so powerful that they almost seem dyed with synthetic dyes.

Vying with the sumacs in terms of bright colors are the poison ivy vines (*Rhus radicans*), sometimes also found growing as bushes. The leaves—for looking only, not touching!—look redder and more tinselly than those of the sumacs. It is difficult to believe that such stark, raw, bright colors are not metallic. They glisten so because of the poisonous oil on their surface.

For most people, sumacs and poison ivy fall into the category of weeds and dangerous plants. Yet, from the point of view of wildlife, the plants are lifesavers. The fruits and berries of both are ripe and ready for animals to eat in October. Though the berries of the poison ivy plants would be most harmful to us, they do not harm the wild animals that eat them. Deer in particular seem to relish this delicacy.

LAKES, PONDS, AND WATERCOURSES

The most notable activity near ponds in October takes place in the air as migrating ducks and geese wheel about suspiciously searching for landing spots. With splashes and calls they take off on flights that will take them far southward.

Most of the frog choruses have become silent, though a few spring peepers may be heard on bright sunny days, and a couple of turtles can still be found basking in the sun. Leopard frogs might be spotted as they return to ponds after spending the summer in meadows and woods.

Brook Trout

Of all the trout, the brook trout (*Salvelinus fontinalis*) are the wiliest, the gamest. Their world consists of shadowy places in plunging streams and beneath overhanging branches and even waterfalls, where they leap like salmon. These trout are found only in swift-running water.

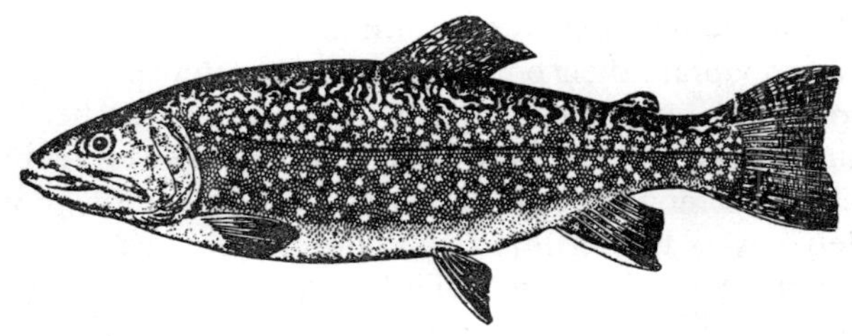

Brook trout (*Salvelinus fontinalis*)

Brook trout, which closely resemble other trout, do have a few distinguishing features. Their tails, which are not forked, are partly covered with numerous black spots, and their bodies have red spots encircled by blue borders.

In October or early November they spawn. When their instincts tell them that the time has almost arrived for them to mate, males and females make their way upstream toward headwaters. Nothing will stop them, not even cascades or waterfalls. This magnificent fish can leap far out of the water and successfully fight its way up and over roaring waters. Once at the headwaters, where the stream's water temperature is very close to 49° F, the males and females will pair off.

The female makes a nest at the bottom of the stream, a small circular depression about two feet across in a gravelly place; the stones can be no larger than three or four inches. The completed nest will be about ten inches deep. Constructed below springs, the nests are built either at the foot of a pool, just where the water current starts moving rapidly again, or in riffles. Walking along a shore, you should look in such places for the nests.

The female makes her nest by moving upstream over the circular depression chosen for the nest and, as she does, tossing stones and gravel out of it with a vigorous twisting motion of her body. A sweeping thrust of her tail will flick away pebbles. It usually takes a day or two for a female to build her nest. While the female works, the male, which takes no active role in building the nest, stays close by, attacking any other fish coming near the nest.

When the nest is finished, the fish spawn. As they begin, the male forces the female over on her side. The eggs and milt are ejected from the female and male simultaneously. While this happens, the fish vibrate their bodies vigorously. After spawning, the female moves just upstream from her nest. She sweeps her tail back and forth, loosening gravel from the streambed. The current will roll the loose gravel downstream and over the nest, until gravel soon completely covers the fertilized eggs and fills the nest to the brim. The spawning activities of no other fish are as easily observable.

The eggs will not hatch until the next spring. When they do, the new brook trout will wiggle their way up out of the gravel on top of them. Once free and in the stream, they will immediately begin feeding. They grow slowly: it will take them a whole year just to grow to a length of about two or three inches.

Newts

Newts (genus *Notophthalmus*) are a type of salamander, though different from others. Unlike other salamanders, they have teeth in the roof of their mouth behind their nostrils, or nares. As adults, they have lungs but lack gills. Unlike some other salamanders, they have eyelids. More than anything, though, it is their habits and coloration that really set newts apart from other salamanders. The most common newt of the Northeast is the red-spotted newt (*Notophthalmus viridescens*).

Like all newts, red-spotted newts have a complex life history unlike that of any other animals. They go through three distinct changes. After their eggs hatch in water, the larvae appear. They have four legs and conspicuous external gills, which resemble feathers sticking out of the sides of their necks. Later on in life, the newts will lose their gills and develop lungs; then, since they will now have

Red-spotted newt (*Notophthalmus viridescens*)

to breathe air, they leave the water for the land. At about the same time, they change color, becoming an orange-red, and are now called efts. Red efts are quite common in the Northeast; they often scamper about on woodland floors, mostly in or on top of damp debris. The small but brightly colored efts reach a length of only about three to four inches. After spending two or three years as land dwellers, they do a turnabout and head back to ponds, to spend the rest of their lives in the water. They do not grow gills back, but must make do with lungs until they die. To breathe, they must come to the surface and inhale air from the atmosphere. In this last stage they make only one anatomical adjustment: the shape of their tail changes. It becomes a vertically flattened tail. With their newly formed tail, they swim about with ease. The adult water-dwelling animal is now called a red-spotted newt.

In the fall, usually in October, the newts change into red efts and leave ponds or slow-moving streams to take up their new life in the woodlands. October is thus a good time for seeing them, when they are on the move.

In the wintertime, some newts and red efts hibernate, but newts will sometimes swim about under the ice of frozen ponds.

Migrating Geese

In October, geese (subfamily Anserinae) reappear in the skies over the Northeast as they make their way south. This is the quintessential sight of autumn.

As geese move along, the birds work out their ever-changing flight patterns. At one moment they form Vs; at another, straight lines; at yet another; offset lines. Aeronautical engineers have calculated that, in a V formation, each bird, with the exception of the leader, benefits from the downdraft of wind from the wings of the bird ahead. The extra current of air, moving over a bird's wings, gives the wings more lift, and so the bird uses less energy in flight. Every now and then a lead bird will shift about in a formation so that it, too, can benefit from the V formation for a while.

Many species of geese can easily maintain a thirty-mile-an-hour pace for several hours on end. If they fly only five hours a day, they can cover a thousand miles in less than a week. They truly have the whole range of the North American continent at their disposal.

Larches

Almost all trees that possess cones and needlelike leaves—pine trees, for example—are evergreens. There exist, however, some exceptions to the rule. Larches (*Larix laricina*) possess cones and have needlelike leaves, yet are not evergreens. In October their rather delicate leaves will begin to turn to a brownish bronze color and fall off.

Most larches, also called tamaracks, grow in the northern parts of the Northeast in moist soil, often at the margins of ponds or in swamps. They also thrive in wild, rocky places where there is constant moisture.

Larches, when seen from a distance, can usually be distinguished from other conifers because they grow straighter and have a lovely feathery, delicate look to their foliage. If you look at the needles up close, you will see that they protrude from little wooden knobs in clusters of about eighteen needles. Unlike most needles found on conifers, they feel soft and flexible to the touch.

Though larches may appear delicate, they possess great strength. Even the strongest winds cannot warp or twist them. Though pines and other conifers often become misshapen by storms and can become permanently wind-warped, larches ignore the elements and have erect trunks. Because larches often grow in damp areas, where the soil is mucky and loose, they require very long, strong roots, which may penetrate twenty feet of muck in search of a firm hold below. Because of their enormous strength and the water-resistant qualities of the roots, native Americans employed them for sewing birchbark canoes together.

After losing their leaves in the autumn, larches lack their dignified, serene qualities and appear unkempt and forlorn, but all in the interests of survival. Bare, they will suffer less of a lashing by the blasts of wintry winds, nor will their branches bend or break under the weight of snow. They therefore get through the winter in far better shape than most conifers. In the spring they can safely afford the luxury of appearing delicate and feathery again.

CELESTIAL EVENT

The Great Nebula in Andromeda

You may have wondered at times which object that you can see with your naked eye is a farthest away. It happens to be the great nebula found in the constellation Andromeda.

The great nebula is a galaxy, very much like our own in shape—a flat spiral galaxy, which slowly rotates in the sky. It has a diameter of about 150,000 light-years. It is located about 2 million light-years away. The light you see at night left the great nebula just about the time that our hominid ancestors the australopithecines were roaming the African plains.

October is about the best month of all for seeing the Andromeda Nebula. To find it, look at the sky at 12:00 P.M. on October 15. Look north, and you will see a group of stars in the shape of a wide M; they form the constellation Cassiopeia. Just to the south of the zenith, you will see a large square formed by stars of the constellation Pegasus. To the east of Pegasus lies the constellation Andromeda. In it are three stars noticeably close together. Next to the northernmost you will see a fuzzy "star," which is not a star but the great nebula. If you have good eyesight and the air is clear, you should just be able to make it out. With a pair of binoculars, it is not at all difficult to see. Even with binoculars of a power of about 7, you can just make out its elliptical shape.

If you do not get to see it at 12:00 P.M. October 15, try 1:00 A.M. October 1, 11:00 P.M. October 31, or 10:00 P.M. November 15. It will be at the same location all those nights. It is visible someplace in the night sky from late summer until early spring, but on the above dates it is seen high in the sky.

How slow the decline of the year really is. Since some indefinite moment in September the long autumn has worn away at the look of the landscape. It takes a fourth of a year, and then some, to complete the job. The coming of spring is incredibly swift in comparison.

November, with its scudding leaves and bare branches, is restless, wild, even witchlike. Its nights are noisy, with November's own haunting sound as gusts push racing, clattering leaves back and forth—leaves scurrying across pavements, pouring over walls, tapping on windows, and then disappearing into the night.

WOODLANDS

In forests, the newly fallen leaves carpet the ground in mosaics of colors. Thin whispers play among those leaves that still cling to trees. The sun, casting its long, slating rays on tree trunks, is brighter, starker than it has been for months. Exposed to the glare of a more horizontal light, woodlands take on a complex of chiaroscuro effects.

In November the leafless woodlands open up. Forest vistas are longer and the sky, peeking above the sticklike limbs, is cold and blue. The air is crisp, filled with a sharp chill hinting at winter.

Mast and the Smell of November

November has its own unique perfume. A tangy, slightly pungent odor hovers in the air, especially noticeable when the ground is damp. Unmistakable, it is the bitter odor of leaves. As they rot, they break down from complex organic compounds into simpler ones. Large molecules of proteins (the largest molecules of all), starches, alkaloids, and sugars will eventually decompose into water, simple gases, minerals, nitrates, and a few other compounds. Next year's plants will use this natural and beneficial compost. Plants for years to come will too, especially using the valuable nitrates utilized for the production of proteins.

Not only do we smell the rotting leaves, but we also smell nuts and acorns and their tannins. In America, early settlers used to let their swine roam loose in the forests in the autumn to allow them to eat nuts and acorns. Such food found on forest floors is called mast. Though mast is rarely used today for swine food, many wild animals, such as squirrels and mice, benefit from this rich nutriment. The woodlands have a mood of their own in November: a time of both harvest and decay, fullness and loss.

Witch Hazel Flowers

Witch hazel trees (*Hamamelis virginiana*) have the distinction of bearing the last flowers of any plants of the year. These yellow flowers are striking: their long, ribbonlike petals dangle raggedly from the flowers. The bright yellow color bears a touch of ocher and a tint of green. Curiously, the flowers on this tree appear on the branches as they are losing their leaves. As the yellow leaves drop, the yellow flowers bloom.

Witch hazel flowers linger for many weeks. Eventually seedpods form. These pods have a unique adaptation for scattering the seeds, as they can pop them a great distance. A springlike arrangement in the seedpod can shoot a seed fifteen feet through the air with ease. The force is so great that should a seed hit you on the skin, you would feel a real sting.

Pinesaps

A stroller in November pine forests might come across a curious-looking plant, the pinesap (*Monotropa hypopithys*). Autumn-blooming pinesaps are highly colored plants of various yellow, orange, and red hues, both bell-shaped flowers and stems having the same color. Moreover, the plant appears to lack leaves, though, it does have leaflike scales. Again, pinesaps, like Indian pipes (see July), lack chlorophyll and cannot utilize solar energy to produce their own food. This plant is a parasite, its roots feeding off beech and pine roots. All the food the plant needs is produced by trees; the pinesap steals only enough for its own needs.

Hop Hornbeams

Hop hornbeams (*Ostrya virginiana*), also called ironwood trees, are rarely trees, most being the size of shrubs and only a few attaining tree size. Because of their size and lack of distinguishing characteristics, they are usually unnoticed. They are humble members of the forests.

In November, however, the trees become noticeable because they retain their leaves longer than other trees—well into winter. If you are in a woodland filled with bare-branched trees, you may be surprised to see in their midst a hop hornbeam still shaking its leaves in the wind. If you come across one, take a look at the odd fruit. Hanging down are dry conelike fruit resembling the fruit seen on hop plants (used to give a bitter flavor to beer). The conelike fruit of a hop hornbeam does not have hard scales but papery ones.

The tree also has an exceptionally rough, scaly bark—it is not called ironwood for nothing. The very hard wood is used for mallets and tool handles.

Hibernation

Before November ends, most animals that are going to hibernate have already become dormant, and many have already been hibernating for weeks before November begins. The woodchucks (see September), the chipmunks, the snakes, the jumping mice, and others are asleep for the winter.

Animals choose a wide variety of places in which to hibernate.

Amphibians and some reptiles often dig themselves into the mud at the bottom of ponds and spend the winter there in deep sleep. Some snakes—garter snakes, for instance—coil together in rock dens. In fact, many snakes will travel miles to reach their winter dens.

Insects that survive the winter usually hibernate under rocks, under bark, or under the leaves of plants. Mulleins, for example, harbor numerous insects under their large woolly leaves all winter long. Ants simply retreat into deeper parts of their colonies to hibernate.

Mammals usually hibernate in dens, although bears may be satisfied with a pile of leaves in a hollow next to a log. Some dens, however, such as those used by chipmunks and woodchucks, can be rather elaborate with various chambers and connecting tunnels and several exits.

Hibernating animals try to find a *hibernaculum* (a shelter in which to hibernate) where the temperature does not go below freezing. Most animals must not freeze, for if their blood turns to ice, they will die; very few species can withstand a frozen state.

Some animals that appear to be hibernating are merely asleep. Their apparent hibernation does not differ from their ordinary sleep. Some animals, such as woodchucks, actually hibernate, and are not merely asleep. Their bodies have undergone many profound changes. When a woodchuck is active, its heart beats approximately eighty times per minute. Its body temperature is close to 98.6° F. When it hibernates, its heart rate falls, perhaps beating only four times a minute. Its body temperature is maintained at only a few degrees above freezing. A woodchuck will not wake up even if it is handled. It hovers close to death. If its body temperature falls below the freezing point, it will die. It survives by a narrow margin.

When an animal hibernates, it lowers the setting on what might be called an internal thermostat, controlled by an internal biological "clock." This clock in turn, is influenced by the weather and by the number of hours of daylight. This is known because of the way animals in captivity hibernate. Though held under conditions of constant lighting and warmth, they still hibernate on a yearly basis. However, after a few years in captivity their internal biological clocks often get out of phase. The animals may begin to hibernate in the spring or even in the summertime. This indicates that they need the sun and changing seasons to keep their hibernation correctly timed and in step with winter.

Many animals will start shivering as it gets cold and will start hibernating when they stop shivering, for once an animal's shivering ceases, its body temperature falls. At the same time, the blood will flow at a reduced rate to certain body areas, such as the muscles. The animal's metabolism will slow down, as will its heartbeat and respiration rate.

Most mammals have a normal body temperature of about 100° F, about the same as humans. During lengthy hibernation periods, when the body temperature is low, animals will be aroused whenever their body temperature rises to normal. Most hibernating animals wake up for brief periods to urinate. It is believed that they are also aroused so that chemicals needed for the brain can be produced. Evidently these chemicals are produced only while the animal has a normal body temperature.

In spring, when an animal finally wakes up, it rouses very quickly. An almost instantaneous liberation of heat is produced by the brown fat and muscles. The anterior parts of its body heat up first. Of course, this is where the lungs and heart and brain are located. It is thought that this localized warm-up facilitates the blood flow to the brain. After the anterior section is thoroughly warmed, the posterior section warms, and soon the animal is ready for its springtime activities.

White-Tailed Deer

White-tailed deer (*Odocoileus virginianus*) mate in November, and almost everything that happens in a buck's life leads up to this month.

Deer are mostly solitary animals, especially in the summer. Some bucks may gather in groups of two, three, or four and stay together, but in the autumn they separate. Changes take place in their bodies. To begin with, their antlers, which have been developing since May, are fully grown in August. In September the bucks have scraped off the velvet, which is a vascular skin filled with a network of blood vessels that cover and nourish the antlers, and their necks swell with muscles as they prepare themselves for display to females and the battles of October and November.

By the way, you cannot tell exactly how old a deer is by looking at its antlers. Though in general older bucks have larger, more splendid antlers than younger bucks, a few young ones also have such antlers. Even does occasionally sprout antlers.

The rutting season begins in October. The bucks become extraordinarily nervous and hypersensitive. To try to relieve their tension, they make muddy hollows in trails with their hooves and attack bushes with their antlers, thrashing them about in a wild manner. If two bucks meet, the odds are they will fight. Most fights end with neither hurt. Usually the weaker buck will eventually retreat, but occasionally one buck will kill another. On rare occasions two bucks will get their antlers locked together in such a way they cannot get free, and they will die miserably of thirst or starvation.

In November the does come into heat. Each doe is receptive for only twenty-four hours; if she has not mated during that period, then a second estrus will occur about twenty-eight days later.

Bucks waiting for does to come into heat will follow them around night and day. Some does may be constantly followed for days, even weeks, by one or more bucks. If several bucks follow a doe, then the strongest will lead and the weakest and youngest will take up the rear. If a doe in estrus rejects a buck, he will quickly seek another mate.

After mating, a doe will drop twin fawns (occasionally one might be born or sometimes three), usually in June. After the mating season ends and the snow comes, deer will form a group. Under the leadership of an old doe, they will trample down the snow in what are called yards, so that they can all move about more easily. Several deer will stay together in a yard until conditions improve.

Deer have keen senses, including excellent eyesight. As with many animals, their sight is such that they can quickly see and recognize moving objects. On the other hand, they have trouble making out an object if it is perfectly still, so if you stand still and silent, a deer may walk over to you to investigate. When the deer does that, it will stamp its feet, snort loudly, and flick its tail back and forth. It is thought that deer do this to frighten the object so that it will move and the deer can see it better.

This problem should not be incomprehensible to us, since we also find it easier to separate a moving object than a nonmoving object from a stationary background. As an example of this, consider fish in water. If is often difficult, if not impossible, to make out a still fish in a pond, but when the fish moves, we can see it very easily. Moreover, the very type of motion typical of a fish as it wiggles tells us that we are seeing a fish.

In spite of their keen sight and hearing, deer, like many mammals, actually rely much more on their sense of smell to understand the world. They never cease sniffing the air.

A deer's body is a masterpiece, perfectly proportioned. When a deer walks, it has a lively, springy, but cautious gait; its tail is in constant motion, switching back and forth. If a deer is startled, it grunts, then bounds away in graceful leaps. If chased, a deer is able to run at 45 miles per hour. Because they are excellent swimmers, deer are not afraid of water. They have been known to cross channels six miles wide and certainly can swim farther.

Deer range within strict boundaries. Most live within a territory from 40 to 300 acres in extent, depending on the food supply and cover. Deer survive because they know their territories so well. A deer knows every bush, brook, boulder, and trail within its territory by sight and smell. If chased, it always stays within its own territory, bounding along paths and through brush it has studied. If a chased deer reaches the edge of its territory, it will circle back in.

Deer are constant browsers, and each day, usually at dawn and dusk, they eat five pounds of food for every hundred pounds of weight. During their twilight feedings, they eat a wide variety of buds, twigs, and saplings. Among their favorites are white cedar, red maple, red osier dogwood, sumac, and basswood. In autumn their fondness for apples lures them into orchards. One of the easiest ways to see deer is to wait in a country apple orchard when the light is dull and crepuscular, at dawn and sunset. There are many more deer now than there were in A.D. 1492. During pre-Columbian times, wolves, pumas, and other large predators thinned their ranks. Native Americans also killed them, because they had to have the deer in order to survive. When settlers arrived, the deer population declined even farther and reached a low point at about the end of the nineteenth century. Since that time their numbers have soared. Today, on average, there are about thirty-four deer per square mile in eastern woodlands. Actually this number represents too many deer for the food supply. Their numbers are now so great that each year a large percentage of yearlings die of starvation.

FIELDS AND MEADOWS

In spite of the pale, drying look of the meadows, there is something invigorating about a walk through fields and meadows in November, especially on a cool, crisp, slightly windy day. Pheasants may be flushed up on whirring wings. Rabbits may hop out of tall yellow grass. Circling flocks of birds—vesper sparrows, horned larks, crows, starlings, and others—are about. Most are attracted to the seeds, the bonanzas of the late autumn fields.

The Last Flowers of Fields and Meadows

Though no species of flower, aside from the witch hazels of the woodlands, bloom exclusively in November, some species which began blooming during earlier months will continue to bloom this month, even at times showing new flowers. They appear few and far between, a scattering of color in a sea of grays and yellows.

Horseweed (*Erigeron canadensis*)

Many of the flowers are mummified. They are so desiccated that if a petal is touched, it will shatter into tiny pieces. They stand, on stiff, dry stems, which do not bend supplely in the wind.

The largest flowering plant seen in November fields is the **horseweed** (*Erigeron canadensis*). Growing up to seven feet in height, it is a tall, rank weed with a hairy stem; countless branches, tipped with many small greenish white flowers, angle upward from the stem. This extremely common weed grows in dry, bare ground in meadows.

Wavy-leaved asters (*Aster undulatus*) add color to the fields. The flowers are typical of asters, with lavender ray petals surrounding a golden orange center, an unusual and attractive color combination.

Fringed gentians (*Gentiana crinita*) are the brightest, most colorful flowers of November. True to their name, the fringed petals of the flower, a shiny, very intense blue, are their most noticeable attribute. In the middle of the flower is a bright yellow pistil. These rare flowers, which must not be picked, are found in wet areas of meadows.

Henbits (*Lamium amplexicaule*) are a pleasing and unmistakable plant. The reddish, tube-shaped flowers cluster together around the square stem. Clusters of scalloped-shaped leaves clasp the stem, which seems to pierce them. The flowers and leaves meet in a tight cluster.

Crows

A November field would not be a November field without flocks of crows (genus *Corvus*) circling about. Of all birds, none has become so embedded in mythology. J. E. Cirlot states in his *Dictionary of Symbols* that crows, symbolically speaking, stand for the beginning, the fertilized earth, the maternal night. These attributes have to do with the fact that they are black. Native Americans, the Celts, and Germanic tribes all considered crows to be the creators of the world. The caw of a crow has often been associated with divination. When it comes to crows, it is difficult to disentangle myth from reality.

Crows have always been considered to be smart, and numerous reports confirm this. But just how clever are they? Studies on the Corvidae, the family of birds to which crows belong, along with jays, have shown that all the birds of the family possess high intelligence. Crows hide objects, seeming to prefer shiny articles—spoons, broken glass, pieces of aluminum foil, and the like—and can relocate their hidden treasure without any difficulty at all, even weeks later.

It is in the fields that the intelligence of crows really pays off in terms of survival. To begin with, scarecrows rarely work. Crows quickly catch on that they are harmless fakes, and it's not unusual to see a crow perched on the arm of a scarecrow. Even more impressive, flocks of crows organize themselves, almost in a military fashion. Flocks often have sentinels that warn their companions of danger. Because of the effectiveness of these sentinels, it is very difficult for a human to get close to a flock of crows: a slight mistake, and the flock is off.

The naturalist John Burroughs wrote of a most peculiar experience with crows. He described how he sneaked up on a flock in which all were cawing. Suddenly they became silent, and one crow, which Burroughs called the master, was heard. Immediately the flock turned on one crow and executed it by pecking out its eyes.

Although crows shift about during the fall and winter, they are not considered migratory. They move about, not according to season, but according to weather. During mild November spells and even during mild days in the middle of winter, crows usually stay in hilly backcountry. If the weather becomes cold and stormy, they usually head for the lowlands. They may even fly south and wait out the cold weather. When it warms up, they will move north again.

Almost everyone is familiar with the caw of crows, but few realize that on rare occasions undisturbed crows in isolated places will sing, for not many people have heard that unusual song. But in fact Shakespeare remarks upon it in *The Merchant of Venice*: "The crow doth sing as sweetly as the lark / When neither is attended."

There are two species of crow in the Northeast: the common crow (*Corvus brachyrhynchos*) and the fish crow (*Corvus ossifragus*). The common crow is the larger of the two, but it is almost impossible to gauge that unless they happen to be seen side by side. The common crow has a good clear, no-nonsense "caw." The fish crow has a "yar" sound. Often fish crows call out "yar-yar." Fish crows are found only south of the Cape Cod near the coast and about a dozen miles inland, whereas the common crow is found almost everywhere in the Northeast.

Shrews

By November many animals have disappeared from fields and meadows, but some carry on as though autumn had never occurred.

One of these is the shrew (family Soricidae). Several species inhabit the Northeast, and they are one of the most numerous mammals.

Shrews are the smallest animals of all. Most species weigh only about 1/5 ounce. Newborn shrews arrive in the world weighing only about 1/100 ounce. Some insects are larger than shrews.

Common or masked shrew (*Sorex cinereus*)

The shrew's small size is both a benefit and a problem, especially as the weather becomes colder. Its small size pays off because shrews usually eat insects, worms, mice, and other small prey, as well as berries and soft vegetation, which are abundant. It is far easier for a shrew to find a meal than for a bobcat or fox to find a rabbit. On the other hand, the shrew's size works against it in this way: the smaller an object, the larger its surface area in relation to its volume. A cube 3 inches high has a surface area of 54 inches and a volume of 27 cubic inches, whereas a cube 2 inches high has a surface area of 24 square inches and a volume of 8 cubic inches. For the 3-inch-high cube the surface area proportional to the volume is 2:1, whereas for the 2-inch-high cube it is 3:1. Proportionally, the smaller cube has a surface area 1.5 times as large as that of the larger cube.

What has all this got to do with shrews? Since they are so small, they have a very large surface area for the weight of their bodies. Since heat leaves an animal by radiation and convection from its skin area, the larger the area, the more heat the animal loses. In short, shrews cool off more rapidly in the autumn and winter than any other mammals, even though they are protected with fur. This is a great disadvantage to a shrew, for it must eat more for its size than any other mammal, to produce the fuel to keep warm. Just to stay alive, a shrew must eat its own weight in food every twenty-four hours.

Because of this pressing need for food, shrews hunt during every single moment of their waking hours. They can never relax, but search constantly for prey.

Fortunately for them, they are aided by a most singular weapon: they have sharp, red teeth. The bite of one is poisonous. The short-tailed shrew (*Blarina brevicauda*) is the only mammal in North America to have a poisonous bite. The poison is a nerve poison. When a shrew bites an animal such as a mouse, it paralyzes it instantly. The mouse collapses, but is not dead. In fact, the poison is short-lived. The shrew must kill the paralyzed mouse as quickly as it can—and it does, dispatching it with its teeth.

It is remarkable that a shrew would dare attack a mouse, even though it is so well armed, as a mouse may be more than twenty times its weight. But shrews are fearless and voracious and do not hesitate to take on mice or other animals of that size.

True to their name, shrews are pugnacious and probably ill-tempered as well. As one might expect, they lead solitary lives. Except to mate, they avoid other shrews if possible. Studies of European shrews have revealed what happens when two males meet: they engage in a curious territorial struggle. First they touch each other's whiskers, possibly to make sure that they are not meeting possible prey. (On occasion, though, shrews are not above cannibalism.) Once satisfied that they are indeed encountering another shrew, they then begin an odd "singing contest." Each begins a squeaky, high-pitched song, which is a warning. One should back away, and usually does. If not, the shrews rear up on their hind legs and continue frantically singing. If neither gives in, they will do something quite unexpected. Both will roll over on their backs. Eventually one will grab the tail of the other and throw him, judo style. Finally one gives up and leaves. In spite of their poison, neither will bite the other. Once the loser retreats, the winner takes over, or keeps, his territory.

The shrew's song is interesting for another reason. In fields and meadows, shrews get about by running back and forth in tunnels in the grass. These tunnels doubtless seem like endless mazes to the tiny animals. There is evidence to show that shrews use their high-pitched squeaks as an echolocation device, very much as bats use their very high-pitched squeaks to find their way about in the dark. Shrews, however, have not developed the art of echolocation to the point that bats have.

Shrews have musk glands, which give off a foul odor, so that few animals will eat a shrew. A cat might catch one, but when it comes to eating its victim, it hesitates and walks away. Owls, however, which evidently cannot detect odors, kill and eat many shrews.

November is a difficult month for shrews, since they are exposed to cold winds but lack snow cover, which protects them in the winter. Many shrews die off in the late autumn. They do not die directly from the cold weather, but because they have gone hungry for a few hours. Once they cannot keep up their metabolism, they die from what is called cold starvation.

Most people think shrews are rodents, but they are not. They are classified as insectivores.

WILD, ROCKY PLACES

There is a sterile look to wild, rocky places in November. Aside from a few lingering red leaves and brightly colored berries, they tend to be gray and monotonous. Yet mammals and birds are attracted to these places to find and eat those berries and buds and twigs, particularly those of the mountain ash, and poison ivy.

Bayberries and Myrtle Warblers

In the damp recesses of thickets in wild, rocky places, you will find bayberries (genus *Myrica*), noted for their waxy berries, which are still used for making candles. In November they are at their best, though they will last deep into winter. The berries, which grow on a large shrub, are whitish, tinged with blue, and easy to identify. All one has to do is rub them and feel the wax, which also has a strong odor.

Many birds feed on bayberries, which have a high fat content. Of all the birds that eat the berries, none likes them more than the myrtle warblers (*Dendroica coronata*): wherever there are bayberries, there are myrtle warblers gobbling them up. Actually the warblers are named after the berries, for the bayberry plant is also called wax myrtle. Bayberry is the more common name, however.

A myrtle warbler is a strikingly colored bird, with a yellow cap, white throat, black chest, and body decorated with yellows, blacks, and whites. The bird can be positively identified by the fact that no other warbler has a yellow rump and white throat.

Surprisingly for a warbler, it is a poor singer, but it has a peppy little call, which sounds like "sweet." The call may be heard not only in wooded areas in wild, rocky places but along thickets bordering roads. This is a very common bird, sure to be found in November. In December they leave the northern part of the Northeast. A November stroll can become delightful when one comes upon bayberry bushes filled with myrtle warblers.

Great Horned Owls

Perhaps it is the influence of Halloween, but for most people no bird symbolizes November better than the great horned owl (*Bubo virginianus*), the largest owl in the Northeast. It is unmistakable, in part because of its great size but also because of its two "horns." They are neither horns nor ears, but feathery tufts that stick out of the side of its head. The ears are hidden under the feathers, just behind the owl's eyes. This owl's ability to hear is exceptional, especially in the high frequencies of the audible range. In fact, it mostly hunts by sound. As it flies through a forest at night, it listens for the sounds of mice in leaves.

Great horned owls have enormous yellow eyes set in front of the head. As with other nocturnal animals, because the lenses of their eyes are so large, far more light can enter them, than can enter most eyes.

Though able to hear and see very well, the owls evidently cannot smell very well, if at all. Many naturalists have mentioned that it is next to impossible to find a great horned owl that does not smell of skunk. They are one of the few predators that eats skunks. Still, when an owl attacks a skunk, it must protect its eyes. The great horned owls have an inner nictitating membrane on their eye, which can cover the eyeball to protect it against the skunk's spray.

The primary feathers in the owl's wings are soft and pliable, allowing the owl to fly soundlessly through the air while it hunts. But because they are soft, not hard like those of a hawk, owls cannot fly very swiftly. Even so, the advantages of moving about soundlessly outweigh those of speed for an owl. Its body is enclosed in soft, thick inner feathers, which in cold weather it can fluff out for a thicker, warmer covering.

During the day, owls are difficult to find. They almost always spend the day asleep in conifer trees, for the evergreen needles both protect them from the wind and hide them. To stay out of sight, they often perch right next to the trunk. At sunset they wake up and fly to their exposed perches on the bare branches of deciduous trees, where they can easily see around them and begin to search for prey.

Great horned owls prey on a wide variety of animals, ranging from rats, mice, and rabbits to grouse, pheasants, and crows. They are exceptionally powerful birds of prey and their attacks are fearsome. If their prey is small enough, they carry it back to their perch and swallow it whole. After an owl has digested the soft parts, it regurgitates the fur and bones in a pellet known as a *casting*, which is about two inches by one inch in length. These pellets, seen on the ground, are a sign that owls are around.

Great horned owls have unusual feet: they can move their outer toe so that it points either forward or backward. When they walk on the ground, they have two toes pointing forward and two back, thus leaving distinct X marks on the ground or in the snow.

If annoyed by a person, an owl will usually hiss and snap its beak. This is a warning to retreat, and it is best to heed it. A cornered great horned owl can be dangerous and will not hesitate to drive its talons into one. Great horned owls are fearless, cunning, and fierce.

Honeybees

During those capricious days of November when the temperature rises and the pale sun is still able to warm up the air, a few honeybees (*Apis mellifera*) will still appear outdoors, hunting for flowers to visit. They may be seen visiting flowers in wild, rocky places.

Though wasp, bumblebee, and hornet societies collapse in the autumn, honeybee colonies remain intact all winter. The honeybees stay in their hives, where their stores of honey will see them through until spring. Indeed, that is a major reason why they put in all that time and effort building up their supplies of honey.

Unless weather conditions are most unusual, honeybees will settle down for the winter in late November. An average-size colony of bees inside a hive will require about 480 pounds of honey. Of that they will eat 400 pounds to live on, eat about 10 pounds, which is used by body secretions to make wax, and save the rest for a brood.

As bees are cold-blooded creatures, one might easily wonder how they could keep from freezing to death even in a beehive. After all, winter temperatures in the Northeast may easily dip below the zero degrees Fahrenheit mark. The body temperature of an inactive cold-blooded animal will, of course, drop below the freezing point if the temperature goes below freezing, but honeybees do not remain inactive in their hives. When the temperature drops to 57° F they beat their wings. As they do, they use the sugar in the honey, which is their food, as a fuel, so that heat is produced. Since a windproof hive is well insulated, heat produced from their activities is contained and does not escape very easily. Thanks to their busyness, honeybees within a hive can easily survive a winter, even a severe one.

Honeybees, however, do have a problem: though they eat, they do not drop their fecal matter in the hive but must go outdoors to get rid of it. Because they cannot go out when the temperature is near the freezing point, they must wait until the weather improves. They can wait because they have a special hind gut that stores fecal matter, but often honeybees are forced to take their chances outdoors when the hind gut is full. Many then die by freezing to death. Yet the vast majority survive until spring, when they can freely come and go from their hives again.

LAKES, PONDS, AND WATERCOURSES

By November a drastic change has taken place at ponds. Gone are the blue waters and their colorful reflections of red-leafed trees. Few sights are more subdued than a pond on a somber day in November when lowering clouds ride in the wind over the dead gray cattails, creating the quintessential scene of gloom.

Pond Hibernation

In November many animals of the ponds are preparing for winter. At this point the last frogs, toads, and salamanders are digging down into the loose mud, where they will lie covered until springtime. Very rarely does the mud at the bottom of a pond freeze, killing hibernating animals.

One might wonder, however, why they do not die of suffocation down there in the mud. There is a reason why not. Although the mud is wet, there is water between the tiny grains of sand and clay forming the mud. Oxygen molecules in pond water diffuse into that water and so oxygen reaches the animals. There is not much, but the still, silent sleeping animals need very little because their metabolism rate is so low. Their hearts hardly beat, and their body temperature is almost at the freezing point. In such a state they require much less oxygen than they would if they were active.

Bladderworts

In November one might be surprised to come upon a yellow flowering plant growing in the water. The flower is held on a stalk that rises about two inches above the water. The flower has a *corolla* (a set of petals) that is not symmetrical, the lower lip being longer and broader than the upper.

No flowering plant in the Northeast is more curious than this bladderwort (genus *Utricularia*). Not only is it a carnivorous plant that eats insects and, at times other animals, but its whole way of life is most unusual.

Bladderworts come in various species. The most common has a mass of stalks that float horizontally in the water. They are arranged around the central stem of the plant much like the spokes of a wheel. The leaves always stay underwater and look like green threads. Among the leaves one can see little globular bladders—thus the name of the plant. These innocent-looking bladders are death traps.

Bladderworts are unique. From a mechanical point of view they are remarkably well made and have an elegant, ingenious design. Each bladder is filled with air, and each has a trapdoor, which can swing inward. Attached to the bladder is a set of bristles. If an insect happens to touch a bristle, the trapdoor pops open. A gush of water rushes into the bladder, carrying along the helpless insect. Once the bladder is filled with the water, the trapdoor snaps shut. The trapped insect cannot escape. Soon digestive juices enter the bladder and slowly digest the animal over a period of a day or two. Once the insect is digested its remains, as well as all the water, are absorbed by the walls of the bladder, which becomes empty, ready to trap its next victim.

If you find a bladderwort, lift the roots up out of the water so you can investigate the bladder traps.

Whistling Swans

Swans are the largest waterfowl in North America. Very few birds anywhere on Earth are larger or heavier—only whooping cranes, condors, ostriches, bustards, and some others. A few, like the albatross, have longer wings. By all standards, swans are giant birds.

Swans are so big, so pure white, so graceful, so magnificent, and so noble that at one time in England all the swans in that country were the property of the monarch. There are only two species of swan in the Northeast. One is the **mute swan** (*Cygnus olor*), which is commonly seen in parks. Almost all mute swans are either tame or semitame. Mute swans can be easily identified by the knobs on their bills, which are either red or flesh-colored; while they swim, these swans hold their necks in a curved position, their bill at an angle. **Whistling swans** (*Olor columbianus*) do not have knobs on their bills, which are never red, though they may be flesh-colored. When whistling swans swim, they hold their necks vertical and the bill straight and horizontal.

In October and November whistling swans migrate through some sections of the Northeast. After spending the summer on the islands of the Arctic Ocean, they have finally been frozen out, so they fly south to find open water. The swans fly in a V formation, as do Canada geese, but the swans are far larger. As they move along, their powerful wings take long, deep strokes, which appear leisurely. However, the strokes push the birds through the air at high speed. They often cruise at between forty and sixty miles per hour. At times they may possibly attain eighty miles per hour; some naturalists believe that under exceptional circumstances they may even hit one hundred miles per hour. No goose or duck can begin to match those speeds. Speed has much to do with the size of a bird and a whistling swan has an eighty-inch wingspan.

Though they are called whistling swans, their call, made to each other while flying overhead, is more like the call of Canadian geese. It is a muffled sound, somewhat like a high-pitched horn going "wow-wow-oo." If Canadian geese are on the wing, flying overhead on a clear day, we can both see and hear them, which is not always true of whistling swans. They are among the highest-flying of all birds. They have been known to fly at about ten thousand feet above the ground. At such a height, they are invisible to the naked eye and their muffled call is inaudible. As they travel at such heights, the sky is theirs alone.

Everyone, of course, has heard that swans sing when they die. Is it only a myth? Most swans do not sing when they die, yet there are reliable reports by ornithologists that they have heard the song of a dying swan.

According to Daniel G. Elliott, author of *North American Shore Birds,* the song of a dying swan that is descending through the air, is plaintive. At its last moments it sings as though it were swiftly running over an octave.

CELESTIAL EVENT

Orion

The great constellation Orion announces the arrival of the cold months ahead. Like the summer triangle, which governed the night sky during the warm months, Orion will take over during the cold months.

No constellation has so many bright stars as Orion, nor is any constellation so conspicuous. You can easily identify it by its shape, bright stars, and by the fact that three stars within it are close together and form a straight line. These three stars cannot be mistaken for any other three in all the heavens. They form the belt of Orion, the Hunter. Above and to the left of the belt you can find a bright reddish star, Betelgeuse. Below and to the right of the belt is a bright blue-white star, Rigel. Hanging from the belt is Orion's sword, made up of a group of stars.

On November evenings you can see Orion low on the eastern horizon. Throughout the nights of the cold months until April it will be visible in the night sky. If you watch it at the same time each night, say 9:00 P.M., you will note that Orion, like all the constellations in the sky, slowly moves westward with each passing night. Though we can see it rise in the east in the evening in November, we will see it set in the west in the evening in April.

When you look at Orion, it is difficult not to see the star Sirius in the constellation Canis Major, below and to the left of Orion. It is the brightest star of all, and it too adds drama to November nights.

December is a month of many moods. There can be days of drizzle and gloomy fog, crisp rich blue skies (some of the purest of the year), or glistening ice storms. Yet other days, stolen from autumn, are glorious, hinting of warmth. Few months rival its variety, its changes. None matches its unexpected qualities.

Yet we see winter wherever we look: in the newly barren woodlands and on ponds where ice tightens its grip. Ironically, we may see winter best on sunny days when midday is streaked with late afternoon shadows and twilight drains the world of light before five o'clock.

WOODLANDS

The temperamental moods of December are all heightened in the woodlands. At one moment pale branches, bleached in appearance, stand against intense blue skies; at another, forests are filled with veils of gloom. There are also the moods of the wind. The unfamiliar sound of the wind whistling through the branches, which has not been heard since March, returns like a half-forgotten melody, and with it comes an accompaniment: the knocking and rattling of bare limbs. But there is nothing as December-like as the soft sound of snow blowing off trees, moving through the woodlands.

Winter Tree Identification

During the spring, summer, and fall, deciduous trees are usually identified by their leaves, flowers, or fruits, but how does one identify a deciduous tree in winter when none of those can be seen? In fact, many trees are more easily identifiable in the winter than at any other time of the year.

The outer bark of trees varies enough so that many species can be identified by that alone. For example, canoe birch has a distinct white bark; cherry bark has swollen gashlike horizontal slits; beech bark is smooth and aluminum-colored. The inner bark of many trees varies a great deal, too. Black oak, for example, has a yellow and very bitter-tasting inner bark. The inner bark of the slippery elm is gummy and good to taste. The inner bark of basswood is tough and stringy. The color of the wood beneath the bark varies and can also be used as an aid to identify a tree. Of course, it is a very harmful practice to cut open a tree, as that can kill it. You can identify winter trees without harming them in the following ways:

Identify trees by the texture and color of the bark. Cherry trees have horizontal welts. Hickories have a very shaggy bark. Honey locusts have thorns on their bark. Sycamores have a smooth yellowish bark covered with loose dark patches. Yellow birches have curly yellow-bronze bark that peels off.

Identify trees by their winter seedpods. Ailanthuses have a seed in the middle section of a propeller-shaped wing. Ashes have a seed attached to the end of a propeller-shaped wing, which has no twist to it. Basswood has seedpods attached directly to a bract, which looks like a leaf. The elm seed is encased in the center of a wing. Horse chestnuts have one or two smooth, very shiny brown nuts inside a prickly case. Oaks have acorns. Maples have two seeds attached to each other; their wings are propeller-shaped and whirl if dropped.

Identify trees by leaf scars. There are leaf scars on twigs where leaves fell off. Elms have leaf scars that look curiously like little faces (three holes form two eyes and a mouth) under a "cone hat." The cone is a new bud. Sycamores have no leaf scars, but their leaves fall off pointed projections, which remain. Walnuts have heart-shaped leaf scars.

Identify trees by their buds. Some trees have very distinct buds. Beeches have thin buds that come to a sharp point. Dogwoods have elegant silver-colored buds, which resemble the spires seen on Russian churches. Slippery elm buds are covered with red hairs. Willow buds look more like scales than buds and cling to the stem.

Identify trees by the arrangement of buds. Of all the many trees in the Northeast, only four have buds on their twigs that are opposite each other. These trees are the ashes, buckeyes, dogwoods, and maples. Their twigs are also arranged opposite each other on the branches of the trees.

Identify trees by their pith-filled chambered twigs. The twigs of some trees have hollow pith-filled chambers in the middle of them, such as black gums, black walnuts, and butternut trees.

About 85 percent of all the trees in the Northeast appear on the following list. All are easy to identify.

Maples. They have buds clustered together at the tip of a twig. The buds are never more than ½ inch long. On twigs, the buds are opposite each other; on branches, the twigs are opposite each other.

Buckeyes. Like maples, they also have terminal buds and opposite buds, but the buds are longer than ½ inch long and resemble, to some extent, Russian church steeples.

Oaks. They have four pointed, scaly buds at the terminal end of the twigs. The buds are not opposite but alternate. Also, most oaks retain a few leaves all winter. The tree can also be identified by the leaves, which are deeply lobed.

Sycamores. They have a distinctive yellow bark with dark loose patches on it. Seed balls hang on threadlike stems from the branches.

Beech. They have a distinctive aluminum-colored bark. The buds are long, thin, and sharply pointed.

Birch. Horizontal slits mark the bark of the tree. Catkins hang from upper branches. Sweet and yellow birch twigs taste of wintergreen.

Aspens. They resemble birch. Though their bark is white, it also becomes tinged with green high up in the tree. Birches have catkins that look like foxtails. Aspen lack them and have buds; quaking aspens have dark brown buds; bigtooth aspens, downy buds.

Cherries. They are identified by the bark, which is dark, almost chocolate-colored. The bark has distinct horizontal slits, which are raised near the edges.

Tulip trees. Their seed clusters look like crowns and are unmistakable. They bear many petallike scales.

Hop hornbeams. They are identified by the fact that a group of catkins grows at the ends of twigs. The twigs are zigzag, with sharp-pointed buds. The bark has loose scales that can be peeled off.

Walnuts. They are identified by the leaf scars, which have hairy protrusions above them. The leaf scars are heart-shaped. Some buds are both globular and hairy.

This list should help you identify many trees of parks and woodlands. Once you learn to identify trees by small details, you should then take a good, careful look at the general shape of the tree and learn how to spot it, in the winter, from a distance.

Snowshoe Rabbits

Snowshoe rabbits (*Lepus americanus*) are among those animals—ermine, for example—that change color in the wintertime. In the summer the rabbits are brown, but with the coming of winter they turn white. Their white coats are very effective in camouflaging them on the snow. The ear tips, however, remain black. Experiments have shown that the black tips break up the form of the rabbit so that predators have difficulty seeing the shape. Apparently what they see are two black dots, rather than the rabbit beneath, and they pass it by.

Snowshoe rabbits, which live in the mountainous and northern parts of the Northeast, are technically hares. Hares are long-legged and leap; rabbits are short-legged and run. Also, hares are born with fur and can immediately see, whereas newborn rabbits are naked and blind.

It is usually easy to find evidence of snowshoe rabbits, and other species of rabbits as well, on days when snow covers the ground. Rabbits often reuse trails they have made. These trails are often packed down because rabbits travel over them many times, especially at night. They learn the trails by heart, knowing every single escape route, every shelter, every place where they can get away from an enemy.

During the day snowshoe rabbits sit motionlessly in what are called *forms*. These are generally brushy clumps in clearings, where sunlight can warm the rabbits. A hollow carpeted with grass or leaves keeps them from contact with the cold snow. A motionless snowshoe rabbit in a snowy form is almost invisible.

Snowshoe rabbits have a large number of enemies. At night, owls fly low through the woods looking for them. They are the most sought-after prey of bobcats. Foxes hunt them; so do mink.

Snowshoe rabbit populations fluctuate wildly from year to year. Records in Ontario show that in one area they varied from 1 to 2 per square mile one year, but in a single year only ten years before that they had risen to a population of 3,400 per square mile. Figures from other parts of Canada and the United States are similar.

Biologists studying these fluctuations believe that they are caused because of an interrelation with bobcat populations (in Canada, lynx populations). As the rabbits become more numerous, bobcats, or lynx have a reliable food source. Well-fed bobcats have more offspring, so that the bobcat population soars. Once that happens, there are more bobcats out looking for rabbits. The tide turns as the bobcats kill off the huge numbers of rabbits. Another factor that comes into play is the rabbit density. As more and more rabbits come more and more into contact with each other, diseases among them spread more rapidly and more rabbits die.

Because of these ups and downs, you may have much better luck finding rabbits in some years than in others.

Common Redpolls

Few birds will delight a winter stroller more than the common redpoll (*Acanthis flammea*). In December these hardy little birds often arrive in the Northeast out of Canada in the blasting winds of a snowstorm. Very rarely are they seen alone; mostly they move about in flocks of a hundred or more. These sparrow-sized birds can be positively identified by their red caps and black chins. No other birds of the Northeast are marked that way. Though perfectly capable of living in the wildest regions of Canada, they are not disturbed by the presence of humans. In fact, few birds can be approached as easily.

Red polls eat seeds and the nuts of pines. In pine forests they often set up a relationship with crossbills. Crossbills (genus *Loxia*) are reddish birds, the mandibles of whose bill actually do cross each other but are powerful enough to quickly open stubborn pinecones and release nuts. Crossbills are sloppy feeders, and nearby, redpolls dart about picking up nuts that fall on the ground. Apparently crossbills do not mind the redpolls' obtaining a free meal at their expense.

In open country redpolls often flock with goldfinches (genus *Spinus*). Flocks protect birds in a numerical sense. If a hawk spots a single bird and heads for it, the prey has little chance of escape. If a bird is in a flock of one hundred birds and a hawk attacks, the bird has a 99 percent chance of escaping. So it is probably a flocking instinct that keeps the redpolls with their close cousins the goldfinches.

For the winter stroller, it is fortunate that the two birds do flock. The red of the redpolls and the gold of the goldfinches, as faded as it may be, provide about the most colorful sight one can find on a dreary winter's day.

Redpolls add to that pleasure, for they sing in the middle of the winter. Since very few birds sing except in the mating and nesting season, it can come as a surprise to hear sweet notes rising from a field of slush. The redpoll's song sounds like that of the goldfinch, but the redpoll has more élan and is considerably more melodic.

Gray Squirrels

The gray squirrel (*Sciurus carolinensis*) is one wild mammal that needs no introduction—though perhaps the word *wild* should be explained. Not all gray squirrels are park animals. Some in the Northeast go months without seeing a human. Others, which have been shot at by hunters, are extremely difficult to approach. They are completely different beasts from the half-tame gray squirrels seen eating peanuts in cities.

A hunted squirrel becomes canny. If a hunter approaches, it is able to stay away from him by moving around a tree, so that no matter where the hunter goes, there is always the tree between him and the squirrel. If two hunters approach so that that tactic is impossible, the squirrel climbs up on a branch and lies down with its tail flat against the bark. In such a position, it is almost impossible to see, much less hit with a bullet.

At times great multitudes of squirrels are seen during incredible squirrel migrations, when squirrels will leave a region where the autumn nut and acorn food supplies have dwindled. Hundreds of thousands of squirrels may be on the move together and, like a tidal wave, inundate the countryside. Nothing can stop them, not even large rivers, which they cross in spite of mass drownings. Though great numbers die, some do make it to the other shore.

Several reports describe these unique migrations. W. J. Hamilton, Jr., in his *American Mammals: Their Lives, Habits and Economic Relations*, wrote of a squirrel migration that took place in the fall of 1933. More than a thousand squirrels were observed swimming across the Connecticut River between Hartford and Essex. Many, exhausted, faltered and drowned. In 1969 squirrel bodies littered both sides of the Hudson River. Many, swimming one way, passed others going the other way. E. T. Seton estimated that half a billion squirrels migrated in southeastern Wisconsin in 1842.

At an earlier time, when America was more rural, there were so many squirrels because eastern North America was, essentially, one huge forest. Of course, there were several reasons for this dense forestation, but not the least was the fact that squirrels hid nuts in the autumn. Though they ate most, they forgot others. Some of these sprouted and became trees. In a sense, there were trees because there were squirrels and there were squirrels because there were trees.

Autumn is the busiest season for gray squirrels, when they collect and hide nuts. They scamper away and furiously dig holes to put them in. Their little paws move so fast they become a blur. The posture of a digging squirrel is quite curious. It does not dig a hole as a dog does, with both front paws working at once. Instead, the squirrel stands on three legs, in a humped position, and digs with one paw.

Instead of resting in December and January, though, the squirrels are put into a frenzy because the mating season begins. The males feel the sexual urge before the females do. Once stirred, they are off chasing females. Being reluctant to mate, and probably puzzled by the sudden attention, the females flee. Off the two go at high speed, the female zipping along with a male right behind her. The males rarely catch them. Even if they do, no act is performed.

To make matters worse, males are ready to fight one another on sight. When two males spot each other, each gives the other a piece of his mind, chattering a mile a minute. These arguments build up into an aggressive action: another chase. Down a tree limb they go, their feet barely touching the bark. Around and around a trunk they spiral. Across a lawn they bounce, at high speed.

Since the males and females look alike, it is difficult to tell whether a male or female is being chased. However, a male is doing the chasing, that's for sure.

Of course, the time arrives when females are ready to mate, and they do. After mating, the males and females separate and take no more interest in one another. The young are born forty-four days after mating takes place.

It is also in December that the squirrels must begin to dig up their hidden nuts. Some say that they don't hide them, because, according to the doubters, they never return, but that is not true. Many observers have seen squirrels walk across deep snow, come to an unmarked place in the middle of its uniform white surface, dig down through the snow into the dirt, and come up with some nuts. Unless the squirrel had known where to search, probably by aligning some landmarks, it could not have known where the nuts were, for the snow would have blocked any odors.

Though squirrels live in airy nests made of leaves, they retreat into the hollows of trees during the winter. For emergencies, they keep a large collection of nuts in the hollows. During severe cold snaps, a squirrel will stay in its den and eat. Apparently squirrels do not like to stay cooped up, for they quickly leave the dens whenever the weather permits. This may have something to do with cleanliness. The dens are hardly clean, and worse, they are often heavily infested with lice, mites, and other parasites.

Strangely enough, squirrels become most active on gray, drizzly days. Possibly they are less visible to their enemies then, or the wet trees are so slippery that predators feel reluctant to climb after them.

It is amusing to watch a squirrel eating in a drizzle. It will sit on a branch and use its fluffy tail as an umbrella while it calmly munches away on a nut. Eventually the tail gets soaking wet, then with a quick snap of the tail the squirrel shakes off all the water. The dry fluffy tail then once more serves its purpose as an umbrella.

FIELDS AND MEADOWS

In December, life diminishes the most in the meadow whose most prominent feature is now its barrenness. At best one may find irregular humps of ice sticking up from snow and imprecise forms of stalks under drifts, bales of hay turned into crude igloo shapes, tall wind-bent weeds rattling their seeds while gusts of dark birds land to poke about and become silhouetted against the glare of snow. At worst, puddles stand like broken shards of glass, slush rots buckling stalks, and tall rigid weeds held in sheaths of ice sway in subdued gray mists.

Mice of the Fields

There are many species of mice and their very close relatives the voles (family Cricetidae). In the Northeast neither true mice nor voles hibernate in the winter. (Jumping mice, see August, do hibernate.) Mice are active all winter long and will explore everything and anything. There is no place in the fields they do not visit. They check out holes and nooks in stone walls, pop in and out of bales of hay, climb up to the highest branches of trees. For their size, they are extremely robust. Needless to say, as a group they are successful animals.

Mice know how to utilize the snow for their benefit far better than most animals. In fact, many mammals and birds find the snow an absolute burden; indirectly it kills many, too. But mice thrive when fields are covered. Meadow mice, for example, dig tunnels under the snow. These tunnels, which follow well-established mice pathways, may go for long distances. Not only do they serve to protect the mice from roaming predators, who cannot see them under the snow, but also they shield the mice from the wintry blasts of wind. The temperatures above the snow may be 0° F, with the wind-chill factor making it feel much lower, but thanks to the insulative value of the snow, the temperature in the tunnels may be only a very few degrees below the freezing point.

The tunnels not only are more comfortable than the world outside, but give mice another important advantage: they do not have to eat as much food to keep warm. Many animals, such as deer, must eat a great deal more food in the winter than in the summer because much of it is used, not to help them in terms of nutrition but as a fuel to burn for warmth. A high percentage of the food consumed by animals in the winter is used for just that purpose. Thanks to their tunnels, mice can save on food supplies. Warmth for them, as for any mammal or bird, means less hunger.

A mouse's territory is truly large, considering the size of the animal and the dangers it faces. An average territory is about twenty-five yards across. Often an inquisitive mouse will explore outside its regular territory, making long trails that go far beyond it.

Mice make winter nests connected to their feeding areas by pathways. They usually make their nests out of grass or other soft, pliable material and form a hole inside the materials. Several will share the nest. Most nests are on the ground but not in tunnels. Many are built inside old, abandoned birds' nests, even in nests high up in trees. Because mice are less than clean, their nests quickly become fouled with their own wastes. This forces them out, and they must make new nests. All winter long they abandon old nests and make new ones.

As is well known, mice can, and will, eat almost anything. In the wilds, out in the snowy fields, they devour berries, nuts, hibernating insects, carrion, and, most of all, seeds. Their amazing athletic abilities, seen in their remarkable jumps and climbing skills that allow them to go up seemingly unscalable walls, allow them to search almost any place for food. They peek in haystacks, under rocks, and in tree hollows; climb weed stalks to get seeds; work their way under loose bark to find insects and insect eggs. Mice thoroughly investigate every field. Moreover, they store surplus food to tide them over through the lean days ahead.

Snow Buntings

If any bird is at home in the blowing snow and sweeping blizzard winds, it is the snow bunting (*Plectrophenax nivalis*). They even look as though winter were written on them, for they are whitish in color—the only land birds in North America that are mostly white. No wonder they also go by the name of "snowflakes." They usually appear in the Northeast when the weather worsens, when

Snow bunting (*Plectrophenax nivalis*)

northern Canadian temperatures drop and snow is in the air. They come in with the north wind.

Very rarely are they found anyplace but in the open countryside. Actually, they spend most of their lives on the bleak, treeless tundra of northern Canada. In the Northeast they feed on seeds, especially pigweed and ragweed seeds, which have a very high oil content: their oil-rich diet helps keep the birds warm.

You can identify the birds not only by their color but also by their behavior in a field. When a flock of snow buntings is feeding and moving forward, the birds in the rear of the flock will suddenly take wing and fly over the rest, landing just in front of the leading birds. A few minutes later, this action will be repeated by the trailing birds. In other words, they all cross a field by leapfrogging over one another. Their actions give one the impression that they are both very nervous, but also very orderly: a strange mix. This behavior gives each bird a chance to glean ungathered seeds ahead of the flock.

Like a very few other winter birds, snow buntings sing in December, even in the worst of weather. The song sounds like the tinkling of far-off bells—a melodic "duree, duree, duree, duriwee." The notes, heard through swirls of blowing snow, rise incongruously beautiful but defiant.

WILD, ROCKY PLACES

In December, wild, rocky places become studies in contrasts: hard and soft, permanent and temporary. As if to frame this starkness, icicles drip in wild formations over the lips of rock cliffs. Many look like fantasies of glass, filled with grotesque and jewellike lights. Some ice formations reach to the tops of high cliffs, while waterfalls of pure ice plunge soundlessly over the edges.

Ground Pine

During December many rocky places, seen from a distance, appear to be painted a vivid green color. Most likely these are patches of ground pine. Huge mats of these mosslike plants creep at the base of cliffs, snake their way up crevices, and droop over ledges. The dark green is vivid. Unfortunately, the plant's beauty is its undoing, at least in many areas, for it is used for Christmas decorations.

Though called ground pine, for the plant appears to have pine needles, it is not a pine at all, not even remotely related to any pine or conifer. Ground pine belong to a very primitive group of plants called *club mosses* (family Lycopodiaceae). During the Carboniferous Period, some 345 to 280 million years ago, club mosses grew to great heights, many reaching over one hundred feet tall, and resembled trees. For hundreds of centuries they grew in dense forests. As they fell they decayed, and their remains slowly turned into coal. Though other plants also produced coal, the club mosses were a major contributor to the coal supplies we use today.

As millions of years went by, club mosses survived their more successful competitors by becoming smaller. The smaller plants could find room to grow among the more highly evolved trees. Today club mosses, including ground pine, rarely grow more than a few inches high. That might seem like quite a comedown, until one recalls that they were far more successful at surviving than the dinosaurs and thousands of other extinct plants and animals. It should be added that several other plants and animals that have survived from millions of years ago also did so by becoming smaller in size. The list, which is quite long, would include salamanders, turtles, dragonflies, nautiluses, giant bisons, giant elks, ferns, scouring rushes, and others. Aside from their size, all these plants and animals look very much like their ancestors.

You can identify ground pine because it does look like low-growing pine boughs. It has, however, no flower, no cone, no true roots. Its leaflike appendages are not true leaves but scales and have one and only one central, unbranched vein.

Whatever their origins may have been, they are alive and thriving, and their green colors add needed cheer to the drab gray rocks.

Bobcats

Few animals are as rarely seen as bobcats (*Lynx rufus*). They are the invisible ones. It is a tribute to their skills that these animals, which are around us all the time (many live in suburbs), can remain out of sight while on the prowl.

It is said that one can judge a true nature lover by how many bobcats he or she has seen in the wild. In general, that's quite true, but it is also possible to come upon one by surprise in unlikely places

Bobcat (*Lynx rufus*)

such as golf courses, parks, and backyards. They look like cats, but they are larger and have long legs and bobbed tails.

In wintertime it is not at all unusual to discover bobcat tracks in the snow. They look exactly like those of a house cat, except that they are larger. They differ from the tracks of large dogs, which show claw marks—bobcats, like house cats, retract their claws as they walk.

Bobcats mostly hunt at night. During the day they remain in the hollows of the trees, holes in logs, or small caves in rocky places. Quite often they frequent wild, rocky places, which offer them not only caves, but an area free of humans.

Bobcats are superb hunters: smart, fast, and extraordinary fighters. They are one of the very few animals that have no natural enemies. No predator hunts them; only a few carnivores could hold their own in a fight with one. There is virtually no animal in North America that would purposefully meet up with one. Only humans ever kill them—and bobcats give humans a wide berth.

Winter weather holds no terror for bobcats, for they have thick warm fur. Snow, however, does pose a problem. Though closely related to lynxes, bobcats do not have the same large feet and cannot walk across deep snow as lynxes do. Their feet are so small that bobcats will sink down, so they avoid snow six inches or more deep. If they must go through deep snow, they take a run at it and trust to the momentum of their body to help get them through it. Because of this problem, they stay put after blizzards. They always have a cache of hidden meat to tide them over for several snowy days.

Very few carnivores attack animals larger than themselves, but bobcats do. Though they rarely weigh 40 pounds, and often weigh less, a lone bobcat can kill a hundred-and-fifty-pound deer. To do so, it takes advantage of winter conditions, when deer are having problems getting through the snow. There are two ways in which a bobcat will kill a deer. The most common way is to wait beside the tramped-down trails used by deer. The bobcat waits as still as a rock (only its tail twiches nervously) and must rely on surprise. It usually prefers to attack an old or sick deer. When a deer comes within two quick bounds of a bobcat, it will take its chances and spring toward the deer at high speed. In a split second, if all goes well, the bobcat will land on the back of the deer, just behind the neck. Quick as lightning, the bobcat bites a major vein that runs along the deer's neck. If this is slashed, the deer will quickly bleed to death. When it dies, it will lie on the ground in a characteristic position, with its neck bent back.

Sometimes a bobcat will rush a group of deer in their "yard." When attacking deer in a yard, the bobcat must cautiously sneak up until it is almost in the yard, then must rush into the herd and make an attack on one member.

Deer, even young ones, are so large that a bobcat cannot possibly eat the whole animal. After a kill a bobcat eats, proportionally, very little of the deer. The rest is left in the snow. Yet it does not go to waste, for foxes, weasels, and, in the more southern parts of the region, turkey vultures will eat the rest of the carcass, as will another passing bobcat.

On a day-to-day basis, bobcats must depend on smaller game. They survive mainly on rabbits. As we have already seen, their populations fluctuate with those of rabbit populations. When rabbits are plentiful, bobcats thrive.

LAKES, PONDS, AND WATERCOURSES

As the cold weather of December sets in, ice moves out from the shores of ponds, and even lakes, and closes slowly on shrinking blue areas of water. At the same time, brooks may become almost, but never quite, silent under ice. A few become nearly dry as their sources freeze, though other streams often throb and gurgle under ice bridges that span rocks.

Animals Beneath the Ice

Many animals—toads, frogs, turtles, and others—hibernate in the mud at the bottom of ponds and lakes. But many insects and a few other animals carry on their daily activities in the water below the ice. If you can see through clear ice, or make a hole and look down into the water, you can see various water beetles, especially diving beetles, in action. Many insect larvae also carry on through the winter, crawling about on the bottom of ponds and on plant stems. On occasion you might see odd little freshwater shrimps (see "Life of Spring-Fed Streams," in February).

Mud puppy (*Necturus maculosus*)

One of the most remarkable creatures to be seen in the Northeast, although mainly in the western half, is a mud puppy (*Necturus maculosus*), a primitive salamander. Unlike all other salamanders in the region, the adult mud puppy retains gills. A mud puppy is olive or gray-brown, measures up to seventeen inches in length, and has three pairs of red gills sticking out of its neck.

It is odd that these creatures live in the Northeast and are able to withstand the cold temperature of the water in wintertime, for they are related to some tropical salamanders. But while almost all other amphibians and reptiles are hibernating, the sturdy mud puppies hunt insect larvae beneath the ice.

You might see a mud puppy during the day, but mostly they hunt by night. Then the best way to see them is with the aid of a flashlight.

Many fish stay active all winter. In fact, ice fishing is an important sport in much of the Northeast during the winter. Fish quickly respond to temperature changes. They sense heat and cold with the ampullae of Lorenzini, sense organs in their heads. They may also feel heat and cold with free nerve endings in the skin. Many fish in the Northeast thrive in cold water and in fact do poorly or die when waters warm excessively.

Cattails

In December, beige-colored cattails (genus *Typha*), those tall marsh plants that border countless ponds and lakes, become more noticeable when the woolly seeds come out of their cigar-shaped tops. On a windy day you are more likely to see many seeds floating about in the air. As these seeds ripen and the tops open, they push their way out like stuffing coming out of a pillow and fly away. You are also likely to see birds attacking the tops, pulling out the seeds to eat.

Cattails indicate that a pond is dying. In fact, they accelerate a pond's demise, for as they grow, their roots move forward toward the water and new plants spring up from them. Rotting leaves eventually collect in the roots, and dirt collects in the debris until soil is formed. In time, cattails strangle a pond or lake. In winter, when the ice is strong enough to support a human being, one can walk among the cattails and see this invasion in progress.

As ponds fill in, they become replaced with either bogs, meadows, or later on, woodlands. Plants and animals that live on the land benefit as ponds become replaced. On the other hand, the loss is great, for on an acre-for-acre basis, a pond usually contains more life than land does.

Canvasbacks

In December the canvasbacks (*Aythya valisineria*) fly in from the northern lakes of Canada. As those lakes completely freeze, they finally force the ducks southward in search of open water.

Canvasbacks are among the largest of all ducks. The males have red heads and necks and white bodies; the females are brown and white. They are powerful fliers, famed for their flying speed. There are probably not five species of birds in North America that can fly faster than they can. With the wind behind them, they can at times hit speeds of seventy miles per hour as they go by one, their wings whistling.

Some ducks, such as mallards, will not hesitate to live near humans, but not the canvasbacks. They are wild, wily, and cautious. Before landing on a lake or bay, they circle about, checking everything over very carefully. Quick to distrust anything out of the ordinary, they are off in a whir of wings.

When they do land, they often stay far from any shore. Large rafts of them stay together, in an almost unapproachable group. They prefer large lakes and bays, where they are protected from anything on a distant shore. However, canvasbacks often fly in the mornings and evenings, and before they take off, they often approach shorelines, where they can usually be easily observed. Canvasbacks, like some other ducks and geese, take off by running on the surface of the water. As they do, they flap their wings wildly, slowly ascending into the air.

Unlike most ducks, such as mallards, which are surface feeders, canvasbacks are remarkable divers. They can dive into the water not only from the air but from the surface. They can swim swiftly underwater and can go greater distances than most ducks can underwater. Canvasbacks confuse almost any enemy by diving and unexpectedly popping to the surface faraway.

Beavers

After working tirelessly all autumn to make dams and lodges, beavers (*Castor canadensis*) finally have a chance to rest in December. During the following winter, spring, and summer, for that matter, beavers will not have to work so hard. Though we often use the term "busy as a beaver," their work effort is rather limited, namely, to the autumn.

Contrary to popular belief, not all beavers make dams or lodges. Many dig tunnels in streambeds. The entrance to the tunnel is underwater, and it eventually leads up to an underground chamber above the water level.

Beavers are the largest rodents of North America, and a large beaver may weigh sixty-five pounds. They are extraordinarily well adapted for their semiaquatic life. To begin with, they have a marvelous fur coat, which they keep oiled and waterproofed, thanks to an oil gland, or *castor.* A beaver oils the fur on its body after it has finished with a dip. First it carefully combs its fur with the cleft toes of its hind feet. Once its coat is well combed, the beaver exudes oil from the gland and works it into the fur with its dexterous front paws. Thus oiled, water is repelled from its fur when it plunges into a stream.

A beaver uses its tail to swim, moving it up and down for propulsion and side to side for steering. The back feet, which are partly webbed, also aid the swimming. A beaver can stay underwater a long time, up to fifteen minutes, about five times longer than a human can. Physiologically, a beaver can tolerate a great deal more carbon dioxide in its blood than most mammals. The longer a stay underwater happens to be, the more this waste gas builds up. When the beaver is swimming underwater the internal blood flow shifts. Very little blood goes to its feet and more blood is shifted to its brain. In addition, all the internal bodily functions, except in the brain, slow down markedly, so that oxygen is saved.

Externally, the beaver also has adaptations. Valves in the nose and ears shut when the beaver goes underwater, so that no water enters them. As anyone who has swum underwater knows, it is difficult to see underwater unless one is wearing goggles. Beavers are equipped with special transparent membranes, which are under their eyelids and are like eyelids. They cover the eyes when underwater. By means of them beavers can clearly see objects beneath the surface. On land, the membranes would interfere with vision. The beavers can, however, pull back the membranes and obtain clear vision.

Most people who have observed beavers even for short periods of time have heard them slap their large tail on the surface of the water, making a loud report. After doing it, the beaver almost always dives. Why? No one knows. There are two theories. The slap may be used to signal other beavers that there is danger about. The other theory is that the slap is to startle a predator, such as a bear, coyote, or bobcat, and put it off balance. It must be disconcerting for a stealthy hunter to hear such a loud report just as it is nervously moving forward. It might be that both theories, or neither, are right.

Beavers do not make their lodges the way we build houses. We form rooms by putting up walls, and the rooms appear in the negative space between them. Our rooms, when you think of it, are mental concepts more than anything else. Beavers, perhaps because they lack such a concept, construct their lodges and rooms and tunnels within it in an entirely different manner. They first build their lodge by piling up sticks and mud and patting them down with their forepaws. Contrary to myth, they do not pat the mud down with their tails or trowel it with their tails. Once a mound is made, the beavers gnaw into it and cut rooms and escape tunnels out of the solid mass. The rooms or chambers where the beavers will spend most of the winter are above the water level, so that the animals will be dry.

Before they became rare, some animals such as wolves and wolverines could have ripped open the lodges before the ponds froze, but then they were not hungry enough to bother. In the winter, when they became ravenous, their attempts, apart from a few rare instances, were defeated because the mud of the lodges had frozen solid. By wintertime a lodge can be as solid as concrete. A few air holes exist, however, and air does circulate down into the lodge.

By December beavers have retreated to their lodges. There they live, and they feed from the bark of sticks that are underwater, stuck by the beavers, spearlike, into the mud.

Beaver lodges are inhabited by parents, who stay together for life, their recent offspring, and the two-year-old offspring. In other words, they are nuclear families. Aside from humans, there are very few instances of nuclear families living together. And how do these groups get along? Some experimenters have lowered microphones into lodges and tape-recorded these families. They squeal, they growl, they grunt.

Beavers are quite safe in their lodges. All winter they have little to worry about. On rare occasions, otters may swim under the ice, breathing the air between ice and water, and rush up a tunnel in the hopes of getting a beaver. This usually fails, for the beavers have escape tunnels already built for just such an event. Even if the otter succeeds, it will only dare to grab a small beaver. A healthy, adult beaver is capable of fending off most otter attacks. Aside from such infrequent encounters, the beaver family has it made for the winter.

A Selected Book List

Agricultural Research Services of the United States Department of Agriculture. *Common Weeds of the United States.* New York: Dover Publications, 1971. There are very few books that cover weeds. An excellent guide.

BANFIELD, A. W. F. *The Mammals of Canada.* Toronto: University of Toronto Press, 1974. An excellent and informative guide not only to the mammals of Canada but also to those of the Northeast.

BORROR, DONALD J. and WHITE, RICHARD E. *A Field Guide to Insects.* Boston: Houghton Mifflin, 1970. There are so many insects that no field guide can approach completeness. This book probably covers them as well as can be done.

BROCKMAN, C. FRANK. *A Guide to Field Identification: Trees of North America.* New York: Golden Press, 1979. All in all, probably the handiest and best guide.

COBB, BOUGHTON. *A Field Guide to the Ferns.* Boston: Houghton Mifflin, 1956. A bit difficult to use for someone who knows nothing about ferns, but very good.

COLLINS, HENRY HILL. *Complete Field Guide to American Wildlife.* New York: Harper & Bros., 1959. Condensed information. An excellent book.

FORBUSH, EDWARD, and MAY, JOHN. *A Natural History of American Birds of Eastern and Central North America.* New York: Bramhall House, 1939. On the whole, gives excellent coverage.

HEADSTROM, RICHARD. *Nature in Miniature.* New York: Alfred A. Knopf, 1968. The title says it all: a gem of a book for those who want to see nature through a magnifying glass.

LEVI, HERBERT. *Spiders and Their Kin.* New York: Golden Press, 1968. A very good book on spiders and their kin. The color plates, which are lacking in other easily obtained books on spiders, are extraordinarily helpful.

MARSHALL, ALEXANDRA. *Still Water.* New York: W)illiam Morrow, 1978. Covers the seasons at a New England pond. The well-written text deals with several interesting and informative aspects of pond life. Very good illustrations.

NIERING, WILLIAM. *The Audubon Society Field Guide to North American Wildflowers.* New York: Alfred A. Knopf, 1979. Serves as a guide and is also informative; unlike most books on wild flowers, it includes some grasses and berries.

PALMER, E. LAURENCE. *Fieldbook of Natural History.* New York: McGraw-Hill Book Co., 1949. An excellent one-volume book on natural history. None surpasses it.

PETERSON, ROGER TORY. *A Field Guide to the Birds.* Boston: Houghton Mifflin, 1980. This book and *Birds of North America: A Guide to Field Identification* are the standard field guides for birds.

———, and MCKENNY, MARGARET. *A Field Guide to Wildflowers.* Boston: Houghton Mifflin, 1968. Lacks some of the information in *The Audubon Society Field Guide to North American Wildflowers,* but is considerably better for use in the field.

PYLE, ROBERT MICHAEL, *The Audubon Society Field Guide to North American Butterflies.* New York: Alfred A. Knopf, 1981. Serves as a guide and is also informative.

ROBBINS, C. S., BRUUN, B., and ZIM, H. *Birds of North America: A Guide to Field Identification.* New York: Golden Press, 1983. This book and Peterson's *Field Guide to the Birds* are the standard field guides.

SHUTTLEWORTH, FLOYD S., and ZIM, HERBERT. *Nonflowering Plants.* New York: Golden Press, 1967. Good basic coverage of lichens, mushrooms, ferns, and other nonflowering plants.

SMITH, ALEXANDER. *The Mushroom Hunter's Field Guide.* Ann

Arbor: University of Michigan Press, 1963. Considered to be the standard guide.

STOKES, DONALD, *Stokes Nature Guides* (series). Boston: Little, Brown, 1976–83. These guides are usually excellent, although the scope tends to be narrow; however, the subject matter is so broad that this is necessary.

TEALE, EDWIN WAY. *A Naturalist Buys an Old Farm.* New York: Dodd, Mead, 1974. Teale takes the reader through seasons on an old farm; charming and informative.

Index

APR 1985

Davis Library
6400 Democracy Blvd.
Bethesda, Md. 20817